Names of the Building Elements

Half of the knowledge about something is knowing what to call it. —Don Weiner, MIT

This card lists building elements from the Robotics Invention
The elements listed here are slightly different from those fo

1 x 1 round plate white	2x	
1 x 1 round plate blue	2x	
1 x 1 round plate black	2x	
1 x 1 stud plate gray	8x	
1 x 2 stud plate gray	20x	
1 x 3 stud plate yellow	2x	
1 x 4 stud plate gray	10x	
1 x 6 stud plate gray	10x	
1 x 8 stud plate gray	8x	
1 x 10 stud plate gray	6x	
2 x 2 stud plate green	2x	
2 x 2 stud plate blue	4x	
2 x 2 stud plate gray	8x	
2 x 4 stud plate with holes gray	4x	
2 x 4 stud plate yellow	6x	
2 x 6 stud plate with holes gray	4x	

2 x 8 stud plate with holes gray	
2 x 8 stud plate green	
2 x 10 stud plate gray	6x
6 x 10 stud plate gray	1x
3 x 6 stud corner plate green	2x
2 x 2 brick black	20x
2 x 3 brick with arch green	4x
2 x 4 brick green	1x
2 x 4 brick black	25x
2 x 6 brick black	6x
2 x 8 brick black	8x
1 x 2 brick with cross hole green	8x
1 x 2 brick green	4x

D1405793

brick yellow
brick black
brick black
1 x 2 beam yellow
1 x 2 beam black
1 x 4 beam black
1 x 4 beam green
1 x 6 beam black
1 x 8 beam black
1 x 10 beam black
1 x 12 beam black
1 x 16 beam black
2 x 2 round brick black
2 x 2 skid plate black
2 x 2 turntable gray/blue
2 x 2 round plate blue
2 x 2 round plate white

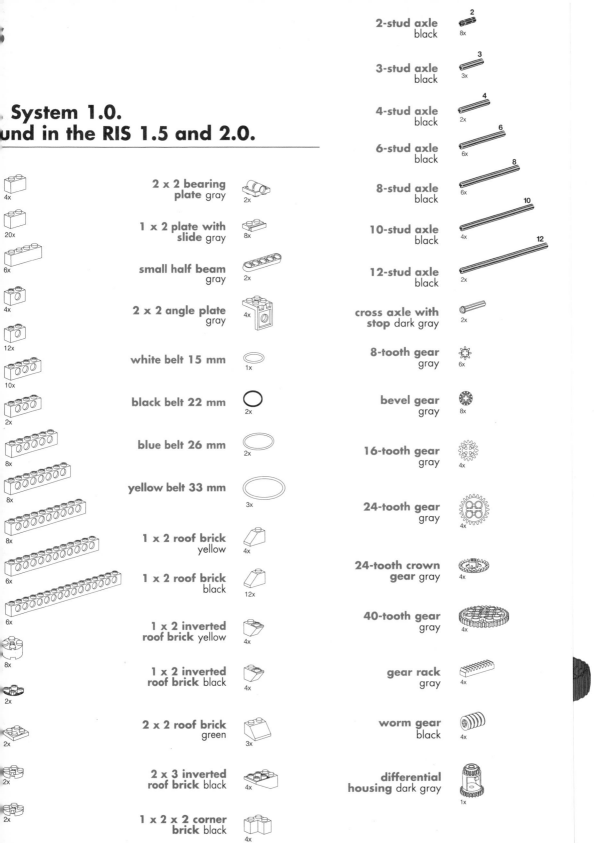

4x

2 x 2 bearing plate gray — 2x

20x

1 x 2 plate with slide gray — 8x

6x

small half beam gray — 2x

4x

2 x 2 angle plate gray — 4x

12x

white belt 15 mm — 1x

10x

black belt 22 mm — 2x

2x

blue belt 26 mm — 2x

8x

yellow belt 33 mm — 3x

8x

1 x 2 roof brick yellow — 4x

8x

1 x 2 roof brick black — 12x

6x

1 x 2 inverted roof brick yellow — 4x

6x

1 x 2 inverted roof brick black — 4x

8x

2 x 2 roof brick green — 3x

2x

2 x 3 inverted roof brick black — 4x

2x

1 x 2 x 2 corner brick black — 4x

2x

2x

2-stud axle black — 8x

3-stud axle black — 3x

4-stud axle black — 2x

6-stud axle black — 6x

8-stud axle black — 6x

10-stud axle black — 4x

12-stud axle black — 2x

cross axle with stop dark gray — 2x

8-tooth gear gray — 6x

bevel gear gray — 8x

16-tooth gear gray — 4x

24-tooth gear gray — 4x

24-tooth crown gear gray — 4x

40-tooth gear gray — 4x

gear rack gray — 4x

worm gear black — 4x

differential housing dark gray — 1x

Creative Projects
with LEGO®
Mindstorms™

Creative Projects
with **LEGO**®
Mindstorms™

Benjamin Erwin

✦Addison-Wesley

Boston • San Francisco • New York • Toronto • Montreal
London • Munich • Paris • Madrid
Capetown • Sydney • Tokyo • Singapore • Mexico City

The publisher offers discounts on this book when ordered in quantity for bulk purchases and special sales. For more information, please contact:

U.S. Corporate and Government Sales
(800) 382-3419
corpsales@pearsontechgroup.com

For sales outside of the U.S., please contact:

International Sales
(317) 581-3793
international@pearsontechgroup.com

Visit Addison-Wesley on the Web: www.awprofessional.com

Library of Congress Cataloging-in-Publication Data
Erwin, Benjamin.
 Creative projects with LEGO Mindstorms / Benjamin Erwin.
  p. cm.
 Includes bibliographical references and index.
 ISBN 0-201-70895-7
 1. Robots—Design and construction. 2. LEGO toys. I. Title.
 TJ211.E79 2001
 629.8′92—dc21   00-067381

Text printed on recycled and acid-free paper.

ISBN 0201708957

4 5 6 7 8 9 QWT 07 06 05

4th Printing   November 2005

For Xuan

Contents

Foreword   xv

Preface   xvii

List of Asides   xxv

Part I. Introduction   1

1. Introduction   3

Welcome   3

The Robotics Invention System Kit   4

The RCX   4

Other Kits   4

Programming   5

The CD-ROM   6

What Is a Robot?   6

Organizing the Kit   8

The Design Process   10

Come up with an Idea for a Robot   *10*

Construct the Mechanics of the Robot   *11*

Create a Program for the Robot on a Desktop Computer   *11*

Download the Program from the Infrared Transmitter to the Robot and Test It   *11*

Modify the Mechanics and Program of the Robot until It Works as Planned   *11*

2. Getting Started   13

Batteries, Built-in Programs, and Firmware   13

Troubleshooting   15

Saving Battery Life 16
Getting out of Guided Mode 18
General Guidelines 18
Important Web Sites 19

3. Smart Acrobot   21

Acrobot 21
The Constructopedia *21*
Building the Acrobot 22
Testing Which Way the Acrobot Will Go 22
Programming and Testing 23
Smart Acrobot 25
Inspiration 25
Designing and Building 27
Programming and Testing 28
A Different Design 31
Advanced Design Considerations 31
Advanced Programming 32
Further Work 34

Part II. At School   35

4. The Giraffe   37

Inspiration 38
Investigation: Deciding on a Goal 38
Invention: Defining the Requirements 39
Coming up with Alternatives 40
Designing and Building 41
Implementation: Testing 52
Programming 55
Further Work 57

5. Walking Mechanisms   59

Dog 59
Inspiration 59
Designing and Building 59
Programming and Testing 61
Further Work 62

Puppy   62
Bug   63
  Designing and Building   64
  Further Work   67

6. FIRST LEGO League   69

Inspiration   69
The Contest   70
  Bumper-Car Robot   71
  Line-Follower Robot   73
The Competition   80
Advanced Programming   81

Part III. At Home   83

7. Tickle Me LEGO Robot   85

Inspiration   85
Research: Taking It Apart   85
Designing and Building   86
Programming and Testing   90
Further Work   94

8. Animal Feeder   95

with John Galinato and young engineers from build-it-yourself.com

Introduction   95
Inspiration   96
Designing and Building   96
Programming and Testing   102
Further Work   102

9. CodeMaster   105

with Paul and Julian Kramer

Inspiration   105
Brainstorming   106
Designing and Building   108
Programming and Testing   109
Further Work   110

10. Painter 113

with Tom and Brendon Kellner

Inspiration   113
Designing and Building   114
Programming and Testing   116
Further Work   118

Part IV. At Work 119

11. Kinetic Sculptures 121

Bubble Machine   121
Inspiration   121
Designing and Building   122
Programming and Testing   131
Further Work   134
Mathematica   134
Twisting and Turning   135
Inspiration   135
Further Work   135
Machine with Minifig   136
Further Work   137

12. Keep On Moving 139

Inspiration   139
Designing and Building   140
Programming and Testing   143
Further Work   144

13. Flashlight Follower 145

Inspiration   145
Designing and Building   146
Programming and Testing   147
Further Work   149
Advanced Programming   150

14. RCX-to-RCX Communication 151

IR Tag   151
Inspiration   151

Designing and Building   152
Programming and Testing   152
Further Work   154
Remote Control   155
Inspiration   155
Designing and Building   155
Programming and Testing   156
Further Work   159

Part V. Advanced Programming 161

15. Visual Basic 163
Introduction   163
Smart Acrobot   166
Line-Follower Robot   171
Spirals   174
Flashlight Follower   176
Further Work   179

16. ROBOLAB 181
Introduction   181
Smart Acrobot   184
Line-Follower Robot   186
Spirals   186
Flashlight Follower   187
Further Work   188

17. NQC 189
Introduction   189
Smart Acrobot   191
Line-Follower Robot   192
Spirals   194
Flashlight Follower   196
Further Work   198

18. Going the Distance 199
Inspiration   199
Designing and Building   199
Programming and Testing   200

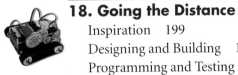

Advanced Programming   202
Visual Basic   203
ROBOLAB   205
NQC   206
Further Work   208

---

19. Elevator
209

Inspiration   209
Designing and Building   209
Programming and Testing   210
Visual Basic   216
NQC   219
Further Work   222

---

20. Data Logging
223

Introduction   223
Refrigerator   224
Designing and Building   224
Programming and Testing   224
Doorway   232
Designing and Building   232
Programming and Testing   232
Motor Speed   234
Motor Power Level   237
Further Work   241

---

21. Advanced Communication
243

Copycat   243
Inspiration   243
Designing and Building   244
Programming and Testing   245
Further Work   250
Infrared Fax Machine   250
Programming and Testing   250
Internet Communication   256
ROBOLAB   257
Internet Copycat   260
Further Work   261

Part VI. Appendixes

263

Appendix A: Further Work

265

Train 265
Intelligent House 265
Submarine 266
  Inspiration 266
  Designing and Building 267
  Programming and Testing 267

Appendix B: Musical Notes

269

Appendix C: Where to Buy

271

Appendix D: Related Internet Sites

273

LEGO Curricula and Ideas 273
ROBOLAB 274
NQC 274
Software Developer's Kit 275

Appendix E: ROBOLAB Commands

277

Appendix F: Resources and Suggested Readings

283

For Teachers 283
Inspirational/All Ages 284
Elementary School/For Kids 284
Middle School/Young Adults 285
High School/College/Adult Hobbyists 285
Psychology 286
Videos 286
Magazine Articles 286
Papers 286

Glossary   291
Index   299

Foreword

This is an important book written for important people. Yes, dear reader, I mean *you*. The people who read this book are pioneers in a movement that will change the way people play and learn. Perhaps it will change the way they think. It will certainly change the way they teach. Perhaps you will say, "Hey, wait a minute. I didn't buy it to be a pioneer or to learn or to teach or any of that stuff. I bought it to have more fun making robots." But that's the point. This book is about how you can have fun and do all these other things at the same time. Working with LEGO Mindstorms materials is a good example of what much more learning will be like in the near future.

I love this book because it is written for many different kinds of people. Kids and parents and teachers can all get something from it. And they can all get different things from it because it is many books rolled into one.

Of course it is an *instruction book*: It tells you how to make things. That's probably why you bought it. But it is also a *storybook*. Ben Erwin describes it as a book of "learning stories." For example, I loved reading the chapter on making a giraffe even though I had no intention of making any such thing. And it is also—now hold your breath and don't be scared off—a *textbook* of philosophy, epistemology, and pedagogy. If you don't know these big words, don't worry. Just do it. Philosophy and epistemology are about the nature of thinking. And as you take in Ben

Erwin's thinking about robots, you will also take in his way of thinking about thinking. You will become an epistemologist.

The people who are most likely to know the word *pedagogy* are teachers, and I want to mention why teachers should read this book. (But if you're not a teacher, stay on the line; we're going to need your help.) This book is obviously required reading for anyone who means to teach robotics. But it also has a lot to offer anyone who wants to teach children . . . in fact, it has a lot to offer anyone who wants to teach anyone. Nobody can read it without gaining a more vivid perception of how to bridge the divide between "content" and "process," between "basics" and "higher-order thinking skills." Teachers of history and literature as well as teachers of science and mathematics will find that this perception will cast light on what to do in their own subjects. They are perfectly capable of doing this on their own, but if you are one of their students, you can help them do it far better. So, I appeal to all the kids who have the lucky chance to work with this new material: Use this opportunity to talk to teachers and to parents about the wonders of what you are doing and how you are thinking. And I appeal to all the grownups that know and care about these kids to use the opportunity to get a better understanding of the richness of their thinking.

For what is most wonderful about Constructionist work for young people is that it opens new possibilities for them to communicate and share—with adults and with each other— their thinking about thinking and learning.

—*Seymour Papert*

Preface

The greatest thing about LEGO is that when you are building something and have a problem, you can take some of it apart, change things, and then keep building.

—Cale Putnam, eighth grader

When the way comes to an end, then change; having changed, you pass through.

—I Ching

The LEGO Mindstorms product line is a breakthrough in the world of technological toys. With plastic gears, pulleys, beams, bricks, axles, connector pegs, and other building elements, you can create mechanical contraptions that would make Leonardo da Vinci jealous. Combine these mechanisms with motors, sensors, and a programmable LEGO brick, the Robotic Command Explorer (RCX), and your creation can run on its own, interacting with and responding to you and its environment, including other robots. There are limitless possibilities to building and programming with LEGO Mindstorms. Mobile robots, kinetic works of art, toys, robotic animals, and robots that gather data are just some of the types of projects that you will see in this book.

It's unfair to simply refer to LEGO Mindstorms as a "toy," however. The robotic devices that you can create can serve very real, practical, and serious purposes. More importantly, building and programming a robot is a rich learning experience. Your creation will never work right the first time you test it, and the process that you go through to figure out what went wrong is when the learning takes place. This book is about that process.

At the Massachusetts Institute of Technology (MIT), Gene DiSalvatore has this saying on a piece of paper in his office: "*Good* judgment comes from experience, and experience comes from *bad* judgment." Applied to LEGO robots, this statement means that building a robot that works involves building a robot that doesn't work and then figuring out what is wrong with it. The more robots you build, the better your mechanical and programming skills will become.

Figure 0.1
The LEGO Dacta serial interface box

The LEGO Group has been designing educational products for many years. LEGO Dacta is the educational division of the LEGO Group, in the same way that LEGO Mindstorms is the new "robotic" division of the LEGO Group. In the early days, LEGO Dacta models that were connected to a serial interface box could be programmed from a computer with a language called LEGO LOGO (see Figure 0.1).

LEGO LOGO was an extension of the kids' programming language LOGO, developed by Dr. Seymour Papert and others at the MIT Media Laboratory. After the serial interface box came a prototype for a programmable brick, which later became the RCX. More work has been done since the development of that first programmable brick, too. Smaller programmable bricks called *crickets* are less bulky than the Mindstorms RCX (see Figure 0.2).

Figure 0.2
The RCX, the brain of the LEGO Mindstorms Robotics Invention System, next to a third-generation programmable brick prototype, the cricket

But Dr. Papert and his colleagues aren't just developing hardware and software; they're developing ideas, philosophies, and theories about the nature of learning and learning environments. Dr. Papert has coined the phrase *constructionism* to describe his philosophy of learning. The earlier theory of *constructivism* states that knowledge has to be constructed—put together into coherent understandable pieces—inside of the head, and that knowledge cannot be forced into your head or passively absorbed. Constructionism adds to these ideas the notion that by constructing something of personal interest *outside* of your head—a robot, a work of art, or a computer program, for example—you're better equipped to construct knowledge inside of your head, using the experience that you've gained from the physical world. Those experiences give you "objects to think with" and become the tools with which you can construct knowledge. Building and programming a LEGO robot is such an experience.

For the past four years, my life has revolved around LEGO in one way or another. In 1996 I graduated from MIT and went to Tufts University to work on a project with Professor Chris Rogers to create an engineering curriculum for young students using LEGO. Dr. Rogers and his graduate students had already created a graphical programming environment for the LEGO Dacta serial interface box. Borrowing some ideas from LEGO LOGO, I made modifications to this graphical programming environment and gave it a name—"LEGO Engineer." We showed LEGO Engineer to LEGO Dacta, and they liked the concept. We were then asked to create the educational version of the software for the RCX, which is now called "ROBOLAB." Our philosophy for ROBOLAB was to create software that could be used by anyone from preschool to graduate school. ROBOLAB has easy-to-use programming interfaces that very young students are using in elementary schools, and a high-level programming environment, which includes data analysis capabilities, that is being used in middle schools, high schools, and colleges around the world.

Being involved with LEGO spread to the people around me as well. Around the same time that we were working on ROBOLAB, we were asked to recommend people who could design robots that would push the boundaries of what the RCX could do. Among other things, LEGO wanted some "cool" examples of complex mechanical creations on the cover of the upcoming Robotics Invention System box. Dr. Rogers and I recommended my housemate Anthony Fudd, who had designed a LEGO airplane complete with hot-wire airplane wing cutter. Now Anthony is employed by LEGO Mindstorms as a master builder. He is the designer of the LEGO copy machine, ATM Machine, Refrigerator Fred, Card Dealer, a robot that can clean up LEGO bricks from the floor, an elephant that squirts water, and numerous other creations.

Because of the popularity of the RCX and the growing on-line community surrounding it, the LEGO influence spread even further than among my housemates. When looking for beta testers for ROBOLAB, I thought of Dave Baum, a fellow MIT Phi Kappa Theta alumnus[1] like Anthony Fudd and someone I had met on the LEGO User Group Network at www.lugnet.com. Dave beta-tested ROBOLAB and became one of the first users of the RCX. Although Dave loved ROBOLAB, his first love was C. After learning ROBOLAB inside and out, Dave went on to create NQC, which stands for Not Quite C. It's a C-like programming environment for the RCX.

While at Tufts, I also worked toward a master's degree in education. One of my favorite classes was "Technological Tools for Thinking and Learning" with Professor Uri Wilensky. One of the first assignments in this class was to read a little book called *Mindstorms: Children, Computers, and Powerful Ideas*, written in 1980 by Seymour Papert. It was a powerful experience to read about ideas that were coming into their full fruition with the preparation of the launch of the LEGO Mindstorms product line. It was inspiring to be a part of it.

In Dr. Papert's books and papers, he writes about his and others' experiences as educators working with students on various LEGO design projects. In this book, I wanted to do the same, to convey what it's like to design and build a LEGO robot. I didn't want to write a book full of instructions that show you how to build my robots. I wanted to write a book that would help you build *your* robots. To accomplish this, I've filled this book with descriptions of problems that were encountered when trying to design various LEGO robots, and how those problems were solved. Dr. Papert calls his stories "learning stories." The following chapters are my "learning stories" for you.

There are several reasons why I chose to write a book about LEGO robotics that would be accessible to young adults as well as full-grown ones. In my experience with LEGO robots, I have seen lots of examples of wonderful creations that have been built by adults and kids alike. By looking on the Internet

---

1. Ironically, at least three other MIT Phi Kappa Theta alums have also been involved with LEGO in some form or another: Dylan Glas, who worked on LEGO Engineer and the pilot year of FIRST LEGO League in my after-school Robotics Club in Weston, Massachusetts (see Chapter 6); Brian Silverman, who worked at the Media Lab in its early days; and Bill Silver, who was a parent volunteer for the pilot of FIRST LEGO League.

or attending a robotics festival such as Mindfest at the MIT Media Lab (www.media.mit.edu/mindfest/), it's tempting to think that everyone who has used a Mindstorms kit has had success in creating wonderfully creative projects. In my experience of teaching hundreds of students and educators how to build LEGO robots, and talking to hundreds of parents and educators in person and online, however, I've seen that this isn't the case.

Students and novice adults usually encounter two problems when they make a LEGO robot. I have seen many of these same problems, frustrations, and mistakes repeated over and over again. First, the largest frustration is when the robot "falls apart." Some people blame the robot's "falling apart" on the robot, without thinking about how they can use the LEGO building elements to make their robot stronger. Parents have told me stories of kids in the home setting who have given up completely on their Mindstorms kit out of frustration because they cannot get their robots to be crash-proof, or even stay together at all. I chose, therefore, to concentrate on construction techniques throughout the book. Second, I have heard from a lot of students and their parents about the lack of inspiration for ideas about what to build with their LEGO Mindstorms kit at home. After building the obligatory bumper car, a lot of Mindstorms kit owners that I have met cannot decide what to do next, and the kit goes unused. I consider this to be a great travesty because the Mindstorms Robotics Invention System kit isn't merely a bumper car kit, but a kit that enables anything out of your wildest imagination to be built. I have tried in this book, therefore, to include example robots that span a wide range of projects from artistic kinetic sculptures to scientific laboratories. One section called "Inspiration" in most chapters is devoted to recognizing the source of the inspiration for the robot. In addition, I have included a concluding section called "Further Work" that suggests improvements or modifications to the design found in the book. My hope is that this book as a whole will serve as an inspiration for you, and that you will take these ideas even further.

Acknowledgments

Throughout this book, I have tried wherever possible to mention where the inspiration for a LEGO creation has come from. I feel that inspiration for a project idea is a large part of the project. However, inspiration comes in many forms. I received inspiration not only for particular LEGO models, but also for my ideas, thoughts, and theories about designing, programming, and learning with LEGO.

In the world of learning, I'd like to thank my parents for teaching me the importance of education, Chris Rogers for bringing me into the world of LEGO, David Hammer for his insights about physics education, Uri Wilensky for his insights about technology and education, and Seymour Papert, Mitch Resnick, Fred Martin, and others from the MIT Media Lab for their insights about learning with LEGO.

I'd also like to thank Robert Rassmussen, Cathy Fett, Mike Guiggio, and Tracy Dagon from LEGO Dacta for their support and assistance with the ROBOLAB Demo (on the CD-ROM) and borrowed LEGO Dacta images. John Galinato from www.build-it-yourself.com/, whose work with kids is featured in Chapter 8, deserves many thanks for his amazing sense of tinkering, good design, and pleasant demeanor. Paul and Julian Kramer and Tom and Brandon Kellner, two father-and-son teams whose robots are featured in this book, serve as an inspiration for all parent-child teams.

I'd like to thank the reviewers of the manuscript: Jeff Canar, Scott Gettman, Scott Holdren, Tom Kowalczyk, Gary Lorensen, Bahram Shahian, Lon Shapiro, and Cliff Young. I'd also like to thank the staff at Addison-Wesley for their help during the development and production of this book: Karen Gettman, Mary Hart, Emily Frey, Jason Jones, Kim Dawley, and Tyrrell Albaugh.

Thanks also go to sculptor/mechanical engineer Arthur Ganson, who introduced me to kinetic art, and LEGO Mindstorms Master Builder Anthony Fudd, for his friendship and mechanical genius. Although his job at LEGO Mindstorms kept him too busy to coauthor this book, Fudd's building and programming advice and his inspiration can be felt throughout. Finally, I have to thank Xuan for her help with the design and creative aspects of the book, and for her inspiration, support, and vision.

Ben Erwin
Roxbury, Massachusetts
June 2000

List of Asides

Programming Aside: Looping   24

Engineering Aside: Feedback   26

Programming Aside: Decision Making   28

LEGO Aside: The View Button   29

Programming Aside: Variables   33

Engineering Aside: Top-down and Bottom-up Design   38

Engineering Aside: Break It Down   40

LEGO Aside: Searching the LEGO Mindstorms Web Site   41

Mathematical Aside: Gaining Speed with Gears   42

Scientific Aside: Gaining Strength with Gears   44

Mathematical Aside: Beam Geometry   49

Mathematical Aside: More Beam and Plate Geometry   51

Scientific Aside: Friction   56

Engineering Aside: Statically Stable versus Dynamically Stable   63

Engineering Aside: Gear Ratios and Idlers   65

Engineering Aside: Trade-Offs   73

Programming Aside: Multitasking   75

LEGO Aside: The Inside of the Gear Motor   86

Mathematical and Scientific Aside: Making Music   91

Programming Aside: My Commands   117

Engineering Aside: Form Follows Function   123

Mathematical Aside: Compound Gear Trains   124

Engineering Aside: Pulse Width Modulation   128

LEGO Aside: Plastruct   129

Mathematical Aside: Major Gear Ratios   136

Scientific Aside: Torque   141

Programming Aside: The Repeat While Loop   148

Programming Aside: Comments   165

Programming Aside: Constants   169
LEGO Aside: Four Touch Sensors on Only Three Ports   210
Programming Aside: Creating SubVIs in ROBOLAB   211
LEGO Aside: A Light Sensor and a Touch Sensor on the
Same Port   213
Programming Aside: Using Microsoft Excel to Graph
RCX Data   230
Scientific Aside: Momentum and Inertia   239
LEGO Aside: The Inside of the Angle Sensor   244
Programming Aside: Encoding and Decoding   245

PART I

Introduction

These first three chapters introduce the LEGO Mindstorms product line, give you an overview of robotics, get you started with the Mindstorms software, and take you through your first project—building and modifying a robot from the Mindstorms *Constructopedia*.

Introduction

This chapter introduces you to the LEGO Mindstorms product line and provides an overview of robotics.

Welcome

Welcome to *Creative Projects with LEGO® Mindstorms™*! Whether you're a first-time user or a seasoned expert, you'll find a variety of different projects in this book to inspire your own creations or to adapt and make your own. Whether you're a teacher, student, or the parent of a student, this book has been written to be accessible to you.

This book is a series of "learning stories," which means that every chapter is a story about the learning process involved in designing a particular LEGO robot. You might have seen a LEGO robot on the Internet, on television, or on the cover of the Robotics Invention System box and wondered, "How did they come up with that?" or "How did they *do* that?" This book will answer those types of questions. Although you can skip around to different chapters if you want to, some scientific, mathematical, engineering, and programming concepts that are presented in earlier chapters are needed to understand discussions in later chapters. When a concept is mentioned, which has been described in more detail in an earlier chapter, I refer you to that chapter.

Figure 1.1
The Robotics Invention System versions 1.0 and 1.5

Figure 1.2
The RCX, the programmable LEGO brick

The Robotics Invention System Kit

Most of the robots in this book are compatible with the Robotics Invention System (RIS) kit, version 1.0, 1.5, or 2.0 (see Figure 1.1).[1] When additional building elements not found in the RIS kit have been used to create a robot in a particular chapter, that information is provided in a note. Some building elements used in the book can be found only in RIS version 1.5 and not in RIS 1.0. An upgrade kit to 1.5 is available for owners of RIS 1.0.

The RCX

The "brains" of these RIS kits is the Robotic Command Explorer (RCX), the programmable LEGO brick (see Figure 1.2). The RCX brain is a microprocessor inside of a plastic LEGO casing. Three input ports and three output ports allow sensors (light, touch, temperature, and angle,)[2] and outputs (motors and lamps) to be attached to the RCX. LEGO studs on the RCX enable LEGO beams and bricks to attach easily to your robot. Two holes on each side of the RCX exist for attaching connector pegs.

Other Kits

In addition to RIS, the LEGO Mindstorms product line includes other kits such as the Robotics Discovery Set and Droid Devel-

---

1. The building elements in RIS 1.0 differ slightly from the elements in versions 1.5 and 2.0. RIS 1.5 and 2.0 are identical kits. A note to educators: The building elements in RIS 1.0 are identical to those in the LEGO Dacta Team Challenge kit.

2. PITSCO-LEGO Dacta sells a sensor adapter that enables you to use other sensors such as pH, voltage, sound level, humidity, air pressure, and higher quality temperature and angle sensors. See www.pldstore.com/. PITSCO-LEGO Dacta sells only to customers in the United States. For other countries, visit www.lego.com/dacta/addresses/wheretobuy.asp.

oper Kit, which feature simpler programmable bricks called the Scout and the Micro Scout (see Figure 1.3).

The LEGO Mindstorms product line also includes "expansion sets" such as Robosports, Extreme Creatures, and Exploration Mars. These sets contain additional building elements that enable you to build more complex robotic creations and CD-ROMs that install additional programming challenges into your RIS software. The LEGO Mindstorms Ultimate Accessory Set includes a rotation sensor, remote control, lamp, extra touch sensor, and other building elements (see Figure 1.4).

Figure 1.3
The Robotics Discovery Set (left) and the Droid Developer Kit (middle). The RCX, Scout, and Micro Scout are shown side by side (right).

Programming

Most of the software code examples used in this book were created with RCX Code, the graphical programming environment on the Robotics Invention System 1.5 CD-ROM. Code examples for all programs using LEGO Dacta ROBOLAB,[3] the educational software for the RCX; NQC (Not Quite C), the C-like programming environment for the RCX; and Visual Basic code[4] can be found on the CD-ROM that accompanies this book. These three alternative programming environments are also presented at the end of the book in Part V (see Figure 1.5).

Figure 1.4
The rotation sensor and remote control are two of the accessories found in the Ultimate Accessory Set. They can also be purchased separately from www.pldstore.com/.

---

3. ROBOLAB and NQC are both compatible with Macintosh computers.

4. The LEGO Mindstorms Software Developer's Kit (SDK) provides an example of how you can create your own Windows-based programming environment in Visual Basic or other Windows programming environments. Although the examples in this book and on the CD-ROM use Visual Basic code, you don't need to own Visual Basic to use them. You need to have only a Microsoft software package such as Microsoft Word or Access. The SDK can be downloaded from mindstorms.lego.com/.

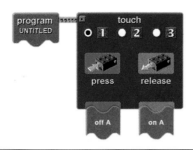

```
Task main()
{
    SetSensor(SENSOR_1, SENSOR_TOUCH);

    while(true)
    {
    if (SENSOR_1 == 1)
        Off(OUT_A);
    else
        On(OUT_A);
    }
}
```

```
With PBrickCtrl
  .BeginOfTask 0
   .Loop CON, 0
    .If SENVAL, SENSOR_1, EQ, CON, 0
      .On OUTPUT_A
    .Else
      .Off OUTPUT_A
    .EndIf
   .EndLoop
  .EndOfTask
End With
```

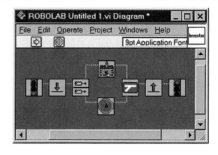

Figure 1.5

A program to stop the motor when the touch sensor is pressed, shown in RCX Code (upper left), NQC (upper right), Visual Basic (lower left), and ROBOLAB (lower right)

The CD-ROM

The CD-ROM that accompanies this book contains

- Programs in RCX Code (when possible), Visual Basic, NQC, and ROBOLAB

- Step-by-step building instructions in Hypertext Markup Language (HTML)

- Movies of robots in action in multiple movie formats[5]

- The latest version of NQC and RCX Command Center (RCXcc), the GUI (graphical user interface) for NQC

- A demonstration version of ROBOLAB 2.0

What Is a Robot?

Just what exactly is a robot? Besides LEGO robots, think about robots that you've seen in museums, in schools, on television, or

---

5. Before reading each chapter, it might be useful to first watch the movie of the robot to get a good sense of what it can do.

in the movies. What do all of these robots have in common? Although different people have different answers to that question, most robots have five basic things in common:

- They have some kind of digital computer or electronic circuit that acts like the "brain" of the robot. This computer can usually be programmed to make calculations and decisions, receive information from sensors, and send power to actuators such as motors.[6]

- They move somehow, such as with motors. Besides actuators (something that causes an action), robots might have other outputs such as sounds and lights.

- They're made out of mechanical parts. Gears, pulleys, and other mechanisms transmit force and motion throughout the robot, while other materials provide the robot with its basic structure.

- They have some kind of power source: the wall outlet, batteries, solar power, and so on, and a means for electricity to be carried to outputs and back from inputs.

- They have sensors that allow them to receive information from and react to their environment.

One of the most important features of a robot is its sensors. When a rover or probe goes to Mars or the moon, for example, the sensors gather important information about those faraway places. Designing and programming a robot that doesn't use sensors can be dangerous, just as walking around with a blindfold on and your hands tied behind your back is dangerous. Sensors tell a LEGO robot when it's about to hit something, when it's about to fall off of the table, when it's stuck, or when another robot is nearby. Not only is not using sensors dangerous, but it's also considered poor engineering practice. More will be said about the importance of using sensors in Chapter 6.

---

6. An area of robotics called "artificial life," as opposed to "artificial intelligence" (AI), uses only transistors and other analog devices to construct a robot without a digital computer.

In a way, robots are a lot like humans. As humans:

- We have a brain that we use to process information and make decisions.

- We have muscles and tendons that we use to move.

- We're made up of bones, joints, and cartilage that enable us to make complicated movements.

- We eat food to gain energy, and we have a nervous system that carries signals to make our muscles move and carries signals back from our senses.

- We have senses such as sight, touch, hearing, taste, and smell.

Organizing the Kit

To start making robots with your LEGO Mindstorms Robotics Invention System Kit, you first need to learn about which materials are available. If you're like me, you keep your RIS kit neatly put away on the shelf when you're not using it. When you use the kit, you pull out small piles of LEGO elements to find a specific one. If you're like my friend LEGO Mindstorms Master Builder Anthony Fudd, on the other hand, your bedroom looks like a LEGO factory that was hit by a tornado. In either case, organizing your kit into different types of building elements in the beginning will help you find specific elements while you're building, instead of having to dig through a pile every time. Organizing the materials will also help you learn the names of each LEGO element.

It's important to know the names of the elements so that you will be able to communicate with other people about your designs. When you set up your own LEGO Mindstorms home page at mindstorms.lego.com/, knowing the names of the elements that you used in your robot will enable you to tell other members how you designed it. See the registration card that came with your kit to become a member of this online LEGO community.

A picture on the back page of your *Constructopedia* book lists the different elements in the RIS kit. A number next to each element identifies how many of each element are in the kit. The insert at the beginning of this book provides a look at a similar list that includes the name of each element. Refer to this list if you come across element names in this book that you're not familiar with.

Although RIS contains over 700 pieces, most fall into one of several main categories. If you've ever been to a hardware store or home improvement store like Home Depot, you will recognize the names of the categories that I've chosen for LEGO pieces (see Table 1.1).

Table 1.1
Similarities of Categories of Materials at Home Depot and in the Robotics Invention System Kit

	Home Depot	LEGO Mindstorms Robotics Invention System
Building materials	2x4s, bricks, plywood	Beams, bricks, plates
Fasteners	Screws, nails, bolts, nuts, washers	Connector pegs, bushings, axles, axle extenders
Electrical	Lights, wires, switches, batteries	Motors, wires, sensors, batteries

Home Depot is arranged into sections: Building materials such as lumber, bricks, and plywood are in one area (LEGO structural elements such as beams, bricks, and plates); screws, nails, bolts, nuts, washers, and threaded rod are in another aisle called "fasteners" (LEGO connector pegs, bushings, axles, and other specialty connectors); and lights, wires, switches, and batteries are in the "electrical" section (LEGO motors, wires, sensors, and batteries). By organizing the kit into these main categories, you end up with a kit that looks similar to the one shown in Figure 1.6.

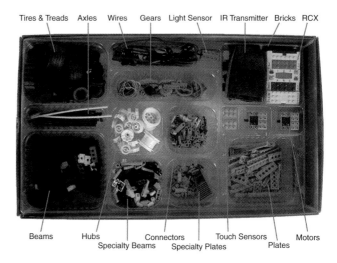

Tires & Treads Axles Wires Gears Light Sensor IR Transmitter Bricks RCX

Beams Hubs Connectors Touch Sensors Motors
Specialty Beams Specialty Plates Plates

Figure 1.6
An organized Robotics Invention System kit

The Design Process

Being familiar with the names of the LEGO elements and what they do is part of learning to design robots. Another important part is learning about the process of designing a robot, from beginning with an idea to creating a working design. The process of designing a robot with the RCX involves several steps. They are

1. Come up with an idea for a robot.

2. Construct the mechanics of the robot.

3. Create a program for the robot on a desktop computer.

4. Download the program from the Infrared (IR) Transmitter to the robot and test it.

5. Modify the mechanics and program of the robot until it works as planned.

Come up with an Idea for a Robot

The hardest part about creating a robot often can be coming up with the idea for it. This is why the first part of every chapter in this book is a discussion of where the inspiration for the robot came from. In addition, a list of Web sites in Appendix D and a list of books and videos in Appendix F offer further resources for inspiration.

Construct the Mechanics of the Robot

Constructing the mechanics of a robot is a difficult and frustrating process. Although it gets easier with time and experience, the mechanical design of a robot often is a long process of trial and error. The content of this book largely deals with that process. Along the way, many Scientific, Mathematical, Engineering, and LEGO Asides go into detail about a particular robotic concept.

Create a Program for the Robot on a Desktop Computer

Programming a LEGO robot can be simple or complex, depending on what the robot must do. Most of the programming examples in this book use RCX Code, the software found on the LEGO Mindstorms CD-ROM. When necessary, more sophisticated programming environments have been used. Programming examples in ROBOLAB, NQC, and Visual Basic for all of the programs in the book can be found on the CD-ROM that accompanies this book. Programming Asides that discuss various programming topics can also be found throughout the book.

Download the Program from the Infrared Transmitter to the Robot and Test It

Downloading the program (see Figure 1.7) from a desktop or laptop computer is usually a quick process, but there are several potential problems. Some tips for troubleshooting these problems can be found in the next chapter.

Figure 1.7
Programs are downloaded from the Infrared Transmitter to the RCX.

Modify the Mechanics and Program of the Robot until It Works as Planned

There is no better way to learn about the building and programming process than to experience it directly, so let's get started.

2
Getting Started

This chapter serves as a setup and troubleshooting guide for getting started with the Robotics Invention System (RIS). Although much of the information in this chapter will be useful to all users of the RIS, only the Mindstorms RIS software is covered. If you are starting out with ROBOLAB, NQC, or another software environment, refer also to the Teacher's Guide *or tutorial that came with your software.*

Batteries, Built-in Programs, and Firmware

The easiest way to get started with your RIS is to install the software and follow the setup movies from your computer. The *User Guide* also contains more detailed setup information and other useful notes on the basics of RCX operation. After installing the software, log in by clicking New User and creating a username (see Figure 2.1). You can create multiple users if more than one person will be using the software. Once a username is created, you can simply select the name and press Enter to start using the software on subsequent visits. Users created by mistake can be deleted with the Delete User button.

Figure 2.1
Create a username to log in to LEGO Mindstorms.

Figure 2.2
The Tour and Set Up portions of Getting Started

Figure 2.3
The Set Up options

Figure 2.4
The Advanced Set Up options

After creating a username, click on Getting Started. You are in Guided mode at this point, so you cannot click anything else yet. Watch the "Tour" video for some exciting examples of LEGO robots in action (see Figure 2.2).

The "Set Up: Part 1" video guides you through installing six AA batteries into the RCX and running each of the five built-in programs. (Rechargeable batteries will work too, but just remember that they don't come charged out of the package.) The *User Guide* explains the purpose and function of each program in more detail. "Set Up: Part 2" guides you through installing a nine-volt battery in the Infrared (IR) Transmitter and downloading the firmware into the RCX. The firmware is the operating system of the RCX. It must be downloaded into the RCX before it can be programmed from your computer.

Note: The LEGO Mindstorms remote control, not included in the RIS, won't be able to control the RCX until the firmware has been downloaded.

If everything has worked properly up until this point, you shouldn't have to edit anything in the Set Up options section of the RIS software. However, you might want to take a look at the list of available options in case you need to make changes later (see Figure 2.3).

The Set Up options include changing the COM port that the IR transmitter is connected to, downloading the firmware and built-in programs, changing the RCX system time (the clock that appears on the display), setting the RCX power downtime, and checking the battery level of the RCX. The Advanced Set Up options (see Figure 2.4) include locking, unlocking, and deleting programs, unlocking the ability to use the temperature and rotation sensors, and selecting Celsius or Fahrenheit for the temperature sensor. Having the ability to lock and unlock programs can be useful at times. If you ever need to present your robot at a show or a science fair, locking the programs that you've downloaded into the RCX ensures that nobody will accidentally download a new program into the RCX and erase them.

Troubleshooting

Several things can go wrong when trying to communicate between the IR Transmitter and the RCX. Although the "Set Up: Part 2" video includes troubleshooting hints, the following general tips can be helpful in troubleshooting communication problems that may arise:

- Make sure the RCX is turned on. The RCX needs to be on for communication to occur. There is no on-off switch for the IR Transmitter.

- Check to make sure that the six AA batteries and the nine-volt battery were placed in the RCX and IR Transmitter in the proper orientation.

- Check that the nine-volt battery is pressed firmly into the IR Transmitter until it clicks into place.

- Check the battery levels of the six AA batteries and the nine-volt battery. The battery level of the RCX can be checked in the Set Up options screen.

- Check to see if the AA batteries fall out easily if you shake the RCX. Some cheaply made AA batteries are actually slightly smaller than a standard AA, and you may need to buy replacement batteries.

- Try changing the transmitter range of the IR Transmitter or RCX (read the section "Saving Battery Life," later in this chapter) from low to high or vice versa.

- Make sure that the serial cable is securely connected to the back of the desktop computer and to the IR Transmitter.

- Try blocking out ambient light in the room from interfering with the infrared transmission. Folding a piece of paper in half and covering the RCX and IR Transmitter or blocking the light with your hand will help.

- Try connecting the IR Transmitter to a different communications port on your desktop computer, if one is available.

- Make sure that a second RCX isn't turned on and within range of the IR Transmitter.

■ Make sure that the IR receiver on the RCX—the end of the RCX near the gray sensor ports—is facing the IR Transmitter and that it isn't blocked by too many building elements.

■ Make sure that no other RCX programming environment or other application that uses the serial port, such as an application for a portable hand-held device, is running on your computer. Don't run ROBOLAB and RCX Code at the same time, for example.

■ Make sure that no other infrared devices are interfering with transmission, such as a television remote control.

■ If you are using a Macintosh computer and the black LEGO Dacta serial cable, try replacing the cable with the gray LEGO PC cable and a nine pin to Macintosh serial adapter, such as the dark gray adapter made for Palm Pilots. (The LEGO Mindstorms software won't run on a Macintosh computer. This bullet and the one that follows are for ROBOLAB and MacNQC users.)

■ If you are using a Macintosh computer that has USB ports, such as an iMac or G3 or G4 computer, check the compatibility with your serial-to-USB adapter and software drivers at the LEGO Dacta Web site (www.lego. com/dacta/).

For additional assistance, read the troubleshooting help in the RIS software or online at mindstorms.lego.com/ and www. lego.com/dacta/robolab/.

Saving Battery Life

Soon you will be writing programs and downloading them into the RCX, but first, read these considerations for saving battery life, the firmware, and your stored programs in the RCX:

■ **Replace the batteries quickly.**
Once the RCX has its firmware, it won't be lost after you've shut off the RCX. The firmware *will* be lost, however, if the batteries fall out and remain outside of the

RCX for more than a minute or so. If the batteries do fall out, replace the batteries as quickly as possible so that the firmware and your programs that are in the RCX aren't lost. If you aren't able to replace the batteries quickly enough and the firmware and programs are lost—don't worry. You can redownload the firmware in a few minutes' time, and you can redownload your programs into the RCX if you've saved them on your computer. If the batteries start to die on their own, a battery symbol with an "X" on it will show up in the RCX display, and you'll notice that your robot runs slower than usual. The battery level can also be checked from the Set Up options in the software. If the batteries start to die and you need to replace them, here is a tip to keep the firmware: Plug the RCX into the wall with a LEGO AC adapter while replacing the batteries[1] or replace the batteries *one by one* with new ones.

■ **Shut off the RCX when it isn't in use.**
To save battery life, it's a good idea to shut off your RCX whenever it isn't in use. The RCX does have an auto-shutoff feature as well, the time of which can be altered from the Set Up options.

■ **Consider using rechargeable batteries.**
If you plan on using your RCX often, it might be a good idea to invest in rechargeable batteries. They are more expensive than regular alkaline batteries but are worth the cost. For a battery recharger, try to find one that will recharge all six AA batteries at one time (some recharge only four at a time). Remember that rechargeable batteries don't come charged out of the package.

---

1. Beginning with the RIS 1.5, the commercial version of the RCX no longer has an AC adapter port, but PITSCO-LEGO Dacta still sells a version of the RCX that has this port. Visit www.pldstore.com/ or call 1-800-362-4308. Outside of the United States, visit www.lego.com/dacta/addresses/wheretobuy.asp.

- **Never let a motor stall.**
  Never hold on to a gear or wheel on a spinning motor to try and make the robot stop moving. Along the same lines, if a robot is stuck on something and the motors are still trying to move, rescue the robot quickly. In both of these situations, a humming noise resulting from the motors trying to spin will be audible. This stalling of the motors will drain the batteries quickly. Instead, pick up the robot and press the Run button to stop the current program or press the On-Off button to shut it off.

- **Keep the IR Transmitter and RCX on low power.**
  To lengthen the life of the batteries, keep both the IR Transmitter and the RCX infrared on low power. For the IR Transmitter, this is accomplished by moving the switch on the front of the base to the left (next to the little arrow). For the RCX, it's accomplished by setting the RCX range within the Set Up options in the RIS software.

Getting out of Guided Mode

Figure 2.5
Holding down the Ctrl key and clicking on the About button takes you out of Guided mode.

At this point in the setup process, the only option available is to click on Program RCX and then Training Center. The Training Center is a series of training missions to get you accustomed to creating, editing, and downloading programs within the RCX Code environment. Although this training process is worthwhile, you might prefer to enter the RCX Code environment yourself and learn by poking around. If that is the case, go to the main menu and click on the About button while holding down the Ctrl key on the keyboard (see Figure 2.5). This will take you out of Guided mode. Whether you've graduated from Guided mode or simply opted out of it, you are now ready to program your own LEGO robot.

General Guidelines

When reading the chapters in this book, be aware that each chapter describes the engineering process that was undertaken to design and develop each robot. Oftentimes the beginning of each chapter shows some designs of the robot that didn't work and then discusses why. If you read the chapter and try to build the robots from every picture you see, you will get easily frustrated at all of the "wrong turns" that the designers of the robots have made. If you only want to build a copy of a particular robot for yourself, refer to the building instructions on the CD-ROM for that particular robot. I also recommend watching the movie of each robot from the CD-ROM to get a sense of what the robot can do before reading the corresponding chapter.

A special warning should also be given about light sensors. Light sensors detect the ambient light in the room in addition to the reflected light from a red light emitting diode (LED) on the light sensor. Because every room has a different level of lighting, the numbers that I've chosen for the light sensor in my programs won't always match the numbers that work for you. When writing a program that involves a light sensor, always use the View button first to check the light levels of the objects that you'll be sensing. More information about the View button is given in Chapter 3.

If you are using the LEGO Mindstorms 1.0 software, your programs will look slightly different than the ones presented in this book. In RCX Code 1.0, for example, wait times are entered in tenths of seconds. In RCX Code 1.5, the wait times are in seconds. Therefore, the numbers for the program examples that you see in this book contain decimal places that don't exist for RCX Code 1.0 programs.

Important Web Sites

You may find the following Web sites helpful:

- **mindstorms.lego.com/**
  The online community where you can learn about new products, read about new challenges, get building and programming tips, search through creations that others have built, and post your own designs. See the registration card that came with your kit for information on creating your own Mindstorms Web page.

- shop.lego.com/
  If the nearest toy store that sells Mindstorms products is too far away, LEGO World Shop is the place to purchase LEGO Mindstorms products. Or call 1-800-453-4652 for this shop-at-home service.

- www.lego.com/dacta/robolab/
  This site provides information about ROBOLAB, the educational version of the Mindstorms software that is more powerful than RCX Code. ROBOLAB runs on Macintosh computers, and version 2.0 includes a data collection and graphing feature for science projects. ROBOLAB examples of the programs in this book and a demonstration copy of ROBOLAB 2.0 can be found on the CD-ROM that accompanies this book.

- www.pitsco-legodacta.com/
  PITSCO-LEGO Dacta is the U.S. distributor of Dacta products such as ROBOLAB. See www.lego.com/dacta/addresses/wheretobuy.asp to find out about distributors in other countries.

- www.lugnet.com/
  The LEGO User Group Network is the most important Web site for LEGO enthusiasts to ask questions, exchange information, and discuss all sorts of LEGO-related topics.

- www.enteract.com/~dbaum/lego/nqc/
  This is Dave Baum's NQC site. NQC stands for "Not Quite C." It's a C-like programming environment for the RCX and can be downloaded for free. A Macintosh version is also available. Like ROBOLAB, NQC allows full access to the capabilities of the RCX. NQC examples of the programs in this book and NQC itself can be found on the accompanying CD-ROM.

3
Smart Acrobot

In this chapter, a sensor is added to the Constructo-pedia *Acrobot, turning it into a "Smart" Acrobot. Two different methods of building a Smart Acrobot are presented.*

Acrobot

The *Constructopedia*

Flipping through the *Constructopedia* that came with your Robotics Invention System (RIS) will give you an idea of the kinds of robots you can build (see Figure 3.1). In addition, selecting the Challenges section in the RIS software accesses examples of the kinds of programs that you can write to give the *Constructopedia* robots different behaviors (see Figure 3.2).

   If this is your first time building a LEGO robot, constructing one of the robots from instructions in the *Constructopedia* is a good place to start. After building only one robot, you can write many different programs for that robot to make it perform increasingly complex maneuvers. In addition, you can change the mechanics of the robot a little yourself and cause the robot to perform functions that the original robot designer might not have even thought of.

Figure 3.1
The Constructopedia *versions 1.0 and 1.5*

Figure 3.2
Programming challenges come with the RIS CD-ROM and with each expansion set.

Figure 3.3
The Acrobot from the Constructopedia *1.5. The Acrobot can be modified in many interesting ways.*

Figure 3.4
*A test program that turns on the
motors for one second in the same
direction. It's easy to remember that
two arrows pointing to the right
mean "drive forward."*

Building the Acrobot

To begin, build the Acrobot from the instructions that begin on page 38 in the *Constructopedia* 1.5 (see Figure 3.3). If you have the *Constructopedia* 1.0, building the Acrobot 2 from the instructions that begin on page 20 results in an Acrobot that differs only slightly from the one used in this chapter.

Testing Which Way the Acrobot Will Go

A good first task to do with any robot is to test which way the robot will move when the motors are programmed to spin in a certain direction. Looking at the Acrobot's motors, the right motor will have to spin clockwise, and the left motor will have to spin counterclockwise for the Acrobot to drive forward. The motors therefore actually have to spin in opposite directions for the Acrobot to move forward or backward. When programming the Acrobot, however, it's easier to represent "forward" by two arrows pointing to the right and "backward" by two arrows pointing to the left than it is to remember that the motors actually have to spin in different directions (see Figure 3.4).

When this test program is executed, for example, it will turn on both motors in the same direction (both clockwise or both counterclockwise) for one second. After running the program, you will see what the Acrobot's motors do when the direction arrows are both pointing to the right. If the Acrobot doesn't go forward, the orientation of the wires on the motors and the output ports can be changed until it drives forward.

To change the direction that the motors turn, change the orientation of the wire on the output port or on the motor itself (see Figure 3.5). When the wire is pointing up or to the right, the motor spins in one direction, and when it's pointing down or to the left, the motor spins in the opposite direction.

Instead of writing your own test program, you can use built-in program 1 to test motor direction (see Figure 3.6). Program 1 turns both motors indefinitely, with arrows to the right. The arrows that represent motor direction show up on the display when the program is running. Alternatively, the LEGO

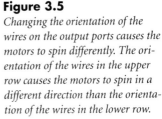

Figure 3.5
Changing the orientation of the wires on the output ports causes the motors to spin differently. The orientation of the wires in the upper row causes the motors to spin in a different direction than the orientation of the wires in the lower row.

Mindstorms remote control can be used for testing motor direction as well (see Figure 3.7). The top row of buttons for outputs A, B, and C corresponds to the arrows that point to the right on the display and in RCX Code.

Programming and Testing

An interesting feature in the Acrobot model is that it can completely flip over and keep on driving. In order to flip over, the Acrobot has to drive backward and then forward. It either does a wheelie or completely flips over, depending on how much speed it has picked up. The Acrobot also flips over if it drives straight into something, lifting the front wheels off of the ground.

The program in Figure 3.8 will make the Acrobot drive backward and forward three times for three seconds at a time. If the motor direction isn't specified, the default motor direction is indicated by the arrows that point to the right on the RCX display. If the Acrobot doesn't run into something, the Acrobot flips only after traveling backward and then switching abruptly to go forward. When traveling forward and then backward, the Acrobot merely switches directions without flipping over. When

Figure 3.6
Arrows above outputs A and C indicate the direction that the motors are programmed to turn in built-in program 1.

Figure 3.7
The LEGO Mindstorms remote control can also be used to test motor direction. The remote control comes in the Ultimate Accessory Set and is also sold separately.

Figure 3.8

First program for the Acrobot

you're testing the program in Figure 3.8, the Acrobot should travel on a flat, smooth surface, such as a linoleum or hardwood floor. A carpet might prevent the Acrobot from being able to flip.

Programming Aside: Looping

A loop in a program causes a certain set of commands to repeat a certain number of times. RCX Code includes three different kinds of loops: *repeat, repeat forever,* and *repeat while.* In the first Acrobot program example in Figure 3.8, a *repeat* loop is used. The *repeat* loop repeats the commands that are placed inside of the red **repeat** and **end repeat** commands a certain number of times. The number entered into the **repeat** command specifies the number of times the loop repeats. Clicking on the graphic of the dice makes the loop repeat a random number of times. That random number is picked between a range of two numbers that you specify. A **repeat forever** command loops forever, and a **repeat while** command loops while a certain condition is true, such as while the touch sensor is pressed in. A regular *repeat* is called a *for loop* in other programming languages because the loop is repeated *for* a certain number of times. A **repeat forever** is often called an *infinite loop*, and a **repeat while** is often called a *while loop.*

Figure 3.9

Holding the Acrobot by the back wheels

To understand how the Acrobot can flip over, it's helpful to perform an experiment. If the Acrobot is held by its back wheels and the motors are turned on, it spins around in the air (see Figure 3.9). When you are holding the wheels in place and the motors try to spin the wheels forward, the body of the Acrobot flips upward, or toward you. When the motors try to spin backward, the body of the Acrobot flips forward, or away from you. The first motion, the upward flipping motion, is the same motion seen when the Acrobot drives backward and then forward. The Acrobot flips upward until the top of the RCX is toward the ground.

When the Acrobot is driving and suddenly changes direction, the conditions are similar to when you are holding the wheels in place momentarily. For a brief moment, when the Acrobot is changing from one direction to another, it's as if the wheels have been held still for a split second. This is why holding the Acrobot in midair by the back wheels produces the same kind of flipping motions. When transitioning from backward to forward, the Acrobot has the ability to flip upward. The weight of the RCX and the motors at the back of the Acrobot, combined with the speed that it picks up when traveling backward, give the Acrobot the necessary momentum to perform the flip.

Smart Acrobot

The really fun part of building and programming a robot is adding special features and programming new behaviors. One such special feature for the Acrobot is the ability to know when it's upside down and when it's right side up. If the Acrobot could know whether it was right side up or upside down, it could determine the best direction to drive to avoid a wall, for example.

For a robot to "know" anything, it must have at least one sensor. For the Acrobot to turn into a Smart Acrobot, and know when it's upside down or right side up, a sensor must be added and a program written for it to dictate its behavior. This idea of making a Smart Acrobot came from two different sources.

Inspiration

When I was helping run a LEGO robot workshop for teachers in Texas, an engineering professor brought in a motorized toy car to illustrate some principles of feedback and control.

■■■■■■■■■■■■■■■■■■■■■■■■■■■■■■■■

Engineering Aside: Feedback

Feedback is when a robot gathers information from its environment that can help control its own operation. A thermostat and heater use feedback, for example, when monitoring and controlling the temperature of a room. The thermostat and heater are linked by a common electrical circuit. When the thermostat senses that the temperature is too low, the heater is turned on, and when the thermostat senses that the temperature is too high, the heater is turned off. A LEGO robot can also use feedback from its sensors to control its outputs, the motors. For example, it might turn its motors in different directions depending on the value of a sensor reading.

■■■■■■■■■■■■■■■■■■■■■■■■■■■■■■■■

Like the Acrobot, this toy car had the unique feature of being able to flip over and keep going. This toy car, however, not only could flip over, but was also able to hit a wall, flip over, and then drive in the opposite direction away from the wall. The Acrobot, as it's built from the *Constructopedia*, isn't smart enough to do that. The toy car accomplishes this feat using feedback, which the Acrobot cannot do because it doesn't have any sensors.

The other source of inspiration for the Smart Acrobot came from the videos "Extreme Machines III: Incredible Robots" and "Robots Rising" (see Appendix F for more information). These videos depict a robot crab named Ariel that can walk underwater at the ocean shore. When the waves tip Ariel over, it detects that it's upside down, folds its legs backward, and keeps on walking.

To prove that feedback is involved in being able to detect when you are flipped over, try repeating the behavior of the toy car with your Acrobot:

1. Try running program 1, the built-in program that just turns on motors A and C.

2. Flip the direction of the wires on the ports of the RCX until both motors are making the Acrobot drive forward.

3. Try making the Acrobot run into something hard, like a wall, so that it starts to climb and then flips upside down.

You will notice that after flipping upside down, the Acrobot still tries to drive forward into the obstacle that it hit. It doesn't know any better. The motors are still turning in the same direction. The toy car that I saw in Texas turned on its motors in a certain direction when the car was right side up and turned on the motors in the opposite direction when the car sensed that it was upside down. A sensor must be added to the Acrobot to make it as smart as the toy car.

Designing and Building

One way to make the Acrobot detect when it's upside down is to use the light sensor and a spinning wheel (see A in Figure 3.10). The wheel can be a 40-tooth gear with a piece of paper taped to

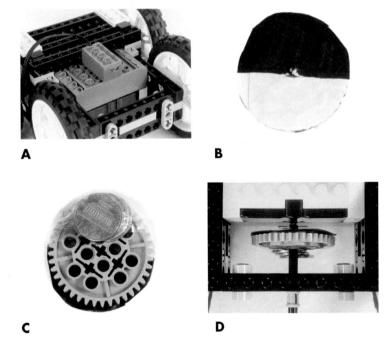

A

B

C

D

Figure 3.10
A. The light sensor mounted to the bottom of the Acrobot. B. A piece of black-and-white paper taped to a 40-tooth gear. C. Pennies add weight to the 40-tooth gear. D. The 40-tooth gear mounted to the Acrobot.

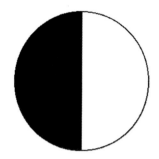

Figure 3.11
Photocopied, this wheel can be used in the Smart Acrobot.

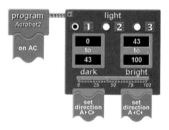

Figure 3.12
The RCX Code program that enables the Smart Acrobot to detect when it's upside down and turn the motors in different directions accordingly

one side, with one half of the paper colored black with a magic marker (B in Figure 3.10). On the other side of the gear, tape some weight such as three pennies to the outer edge, opposite the white side of the paper (C). When attached to the front of the Acrobot with an axle and a bushing, the wheel can rotate freely (D). Because the pennies are taped opposite the white side of the paper, the weight of the pennies causes the wheel to rotate such that the white side of the gear always turns to the bottom, toward the ground. When the Smart Acrobot is right side up, the light sensor sees the bottom part of the wheel, which will always be the white side. When the Smart Acrobot is upside down, the light sensor will see the top part of the wheel, which will always be the black side. To make it easier, a sample wheel has been provided in Figure 3.11.

Programming and Testing

The next task is to reprogram the RCX using the light sensor. When it's necessary to have a robot perform two different actions depending on the state of a sensor, a sensor watcher is used (see Figure 3.12). The sensor watcher continuously checks the light sensor and performs two different actions depending on its value. Before a sensor watcher can be used effectively, the values of the light and dark parts of the wheel have to be checked with the View button (see the section "LEGO Aside: The View Button," later in this chapter).

■■■■■■■■■■■■■■■■■■■■■■■■■■■■

Programming Aside: Decision Making

An RCX Code *sensor watcher*, such as the one in the Acrobot2 program, is an example of decision making in a program. In this light sensor watcher, the Smart Acrobot drives in one direction when the light sensor value is between 0 and 43, and in another direction when the light sensor value is between 43 and 100.

In other programming languages, decision-making statements are usually called *conditionals*, or *If* or *If-Else* statements. In these other programs, "if" a certain condition is met (such as the light sensor value being greater than a certain amount), then certain commands are executed (such as turning the motors in a particular direction), or "else" other commands are executed (such as turning the motors in a different direction). Because sensor watchers constantly check the value of the sensor, they are almost like an If statement inside of an infinite loop (repeat forever). The difference is that a sensor watcher executes the commands only once if the condition doesn't change.

■■■■■■■■■■■■■■■■■■■■■■■■■■■■■■■■

■■■■■■■■■■■■■■■■■■■■■■■■■■■■■■■■

LEGO Aside: The View Button

The View button on the RCX can be used to help determine the values of the light and dark parts of the wheel. Pressing the View button causes an arrow to appear on the RCX display that points to the sensor and motor ports. When the View button is pressed multiple times, the arrow on the display moves between the input and output ports. The current value of the sensor or speed of the motor shows up in the RCX display window (see Figure 3.13).

There are several points to note about working with the View button. First, the View button works only after the firmware has been installed. Viewing also works only after a program that involves the sensor that you wish to view has been run on the RCX at least once. Before the program is run, the RCX has no way of knowing which type of sensor value to display. Because built-in program number 3 involves a light sensor on port 2, the View button, pressed twice, will show you the value of the light sensor on port 2 (this works only if you haven't already erased built-in program 3 by writing one of your own programs over it).

Figure 3.13
Use the View button to determine the values of a sensor or speed of a motor.

In my testing, the value of the white part of the wheel was around 50, and the black part of the wheel was around 36. In the sensor watcher, therefore, I chose a value halfway between the two—43—to separate the different actions. The program works quite well. Once flipped over, the Smart Acrobot's black-and-white wheel turns so that the black part of the paper is facing the light sensor, causing the Smart Acrobot to then drive back where it came from. The steps involved go something like this (see Figure 3.14):

1. The Smart Acrobot climbs up a surface.

2. The Smart Acrobot flips over.

3. The black-and-white wheel turns over.

4. The light sensor sees a different color.

Figure 3.14
The Smart Acrobot approaching an obstacle (left), climbing it momentarily (middle), and then flipping over and driving away (right).

5. The Smart Acrobot drives away until encountering the next wall to climb.

6. The Smart Acrobot does it all over again.

This program is especially fun to run in between two walls, such as in a hallway. Between two walls, the Smart Acrobot performs its flipping maneuver over and over again. For the best performance, make sure that the object that Smart Acrobot runs into doesn't bend or move when Smart Acrobot tries to climb it.

A Different Design

Although this previously described adaptation to the Smart Acrobot worked, it could be improved upon. The Smart Acrobot's black-and-white wheel can sometimes take a second to turn over, and the detection should be more instantaneous. Thinking about how the toy car must have worked, I envisioned something dropping back and forth inside of the car as it turned upside down and right side up. LEGO bricks inside of a box seemed like a possible model for this kind of motion. When the Smart Acrobot flips over, the bricks in the box would drop to the top and bottom of the box. Because the light sensor is only at the bottom of the box, the light sensor would either see the bricks inside of the box when the Smart Acrobot is right side up, or just see the inside of the box when it's upside down.

Making this modification didn't take long. Leaving the light sensor in place and adding plates and beams to the existing front structure created a stable box. First, I tried filling the box with black bricks. With the View button, I determined that there wasn't enough contrast in light sensor values between upside down and right side up. With yellow bricks, there was a big difference. I executed the same program, and it worked beautifully (see Figure 3.15).

Advanced Design Considerations

As mentioned in the previous chapter, the value of the light sensor reading changes from room to room as the ambient light changes. A program for the Smart Acrobot that works in

Figure 3.15
A box filled with yellow bricks serves the same function as the spinning black-and-white gear and improves the reaction time of the Smart Acrobot.

one room might not work in another if the lighting is different. For example, if the Smart Acrobot is taken into a bright room, the "dark" reading—the black half of the wheel or the empty inside of the box—might be 43 instead of 36, and the "bright" reading—the white half of the wheel or the yellow bricks inside of the box—might be 57 instead of 50. In the current RCX Code program, the light sensor watcher needs to read a value of less than 42 to register "dark." However, in the bright room, this will never happen because the reading from the black half of the wheel is 43. This problem can be solved in two different ways, one structural and another through an advanced program.

The first way to solve the problem of different light sensor readings for different rooms is structural. In the case of the Smart Acrobot, the concern is only for the difference in reflected light between two different sides of the wheel or the difference between seeing the yellow bricks or not seeing them. To cancel the effects of different levels of ambient light in a room and rely only on the reflection from the light sensor's LED, enclose the black-and-white wheel or yellow bricks within a box made entirely of solid bricks. Using bricks instead of any beams with holes in them ensures that no light from the room will affect the light sensor reading (see Figure 3.16).

Figure 3.16

If the beams surrounding the light sensor are replaced with bricks, the light sensor reads only reflected light from its LED, and the Smart Acrobot will work in any room, even in the dark.

Advanced Programming

Although it's possible with the Smart Acrobot, solving the problem of different light sensor readings in different rooms isn't always solvable by a structural means. Oftentimes, it's necessary for the light sensor on a robot to be exposed to the open air, and it can't be enclosed inside of a light-proof box. For example, the light sensor on a line-follower robot cannot be enclosed because it needs to be able to see the line. In these cases, it's necessary to write a program that actually changes depending on the light level in the room. For the Smart Acrobot, the program would have to have the following functions:

1. Record the value of the light sensor at the beginning of the program while aimed at the white half of the wheel or

the yellow bricks inside of the box and call it the "bright" reading.

2. As long as the light sensor is within a range slightly below or above the "bright" reading, turn on the motors so that the Smart Acrobot drives forward.

3. If the light sensor reading is less than 7 points or so below the "bright" reading, turn on the motors in the other direction. (The number "7" was chosen because the difference between bright and dark in the initial tests was usually around 14 points, and 7 is halfway between.)

With RCX Code, functions 2 and 3 can be accomplished with a light sensor watcher. Unfortunately, however, function 1 cannot be accomplished with RCX Code. Recording a value and storing it for later use requires using a variable.

■■■■■■■■■■■■■■■■■■■■■■■■■■■■■■■■

Programming Aside: Variables

A piece of the RCX's memory that can record and store values for later use is called a *variable*. Sometimes the ability for a robot to store the value of a sensor in memory is called *saving state*, because the robot is saving the state of a sensor value at a certain moment in time, which it can compare to the state of the robot at a later time. Because the value of a variable can change during the course of the program, and on different executions of the program, a variable is called a *dynamic* value. Numbers that don't change are *static* values.

■■■■■■■■■■■■■■■■■■■■■■■■■■■■■■■■

To write a program for the Smart Acrobot that can be independent of room brightness, it's necessary to use a programming language that uses variables such as ROBOLAB, NQC, or Visual Basic. To learn how to take the capability of the Smart

Acrobot further with these languages, refer to Part V of this book.

Further Work

You can alter the Acrobot and make it do interesting things besides detecting when it's flipped over. The *Constructopedia* provides suggestions as to how to take the Acrobot chassis and make different designs involving such things as bump sensors and pivot wheels. The Challenges section of the RIS software offers some guided instruction on how to program those Acrobots.

PART II

At School

The three chapters in this part of the book are projects that were built either by students or their teacher in a classroom, after-school club, or summer camp.

4 The Giraffe

The Giraffe was the final project of three seventh-grade girls working together in my Technology Education class. The Giraffe, along with the Turtle and other animals (see Figure 4.1), went on to be a part of the Robotic Zoological Park '99 in Rhode Island, and Kids and Technology Day '99 at the Boston Statehouse.

Inspiration

Every year, over a hundred students gather in a gymnasium in the small town of Peace Dale, Rhode Island, for an exhibition called the Robotic Zoological Park in which they exhibit their robotic animals. These students were lucky to collaborate with the MIT Media Laboratory when they were first developing a

Figure 4.1
The robotic Giraffe discussed in this chapter (left) and its counterpart (right) made with RIS; building instructions for the RIS version of the Giraffe are on the CD-ROM.

*LEGO SYSTEM bricks (see
Figure 4.2)*

Figure 4.2
*A LEGO SYSTEM bucket of
1,200 colored bricks of different
sizes, such as the one used for the
Giraffe, goes for around $20 U.S.*

programmable LEGO brick. Many of these students got to learn
about robotics by designing and programming animals with
this MIT programmable brick before the RCX was developed!

Not only is making robotic animals a fun and educational
project for students, but it's a project that professional roboti-
cists undertake as well. Many robotics researchers in laboratories and universities try to mimic the movements and behaviors
of animals with robots. As these researchers know, and the students that work on the Robotic Zoological Park find out, designing a robotic animal is no easy task.

Investigation: Deciding on a Goal

At the start of the robotic zoo project, students are told that their
task is to design and program an animal that can somehow interact
with its environment. Students work together in small groups. After
coming up with several different animal ideas, Keenan, Catherine,
and Liz decided to make a giraffe. The girls began making sketches
of giraffes in their Design Notebook and visiting Web sites to research the kind of environment giraffes live in and the foods they
eat. They explored a variety of sites starting with a Yahoo! site on animals that I recommended: the Animals, Insects, and Pets section
of dir.yahoo.com/Science/Biology/Zoology/. They discovered, for
example, that giraffes are six feet tall when they are born!

■■■■■■■■■■■■■■■■■■■■■■■■■■■■■■

Engineering Aside:
Top-down and Bottom-up Design

Deciding on a goal and then designing something that meets
that goal is called *top-down* design. *Bottom-up* design is just
the opposite. Bottom-up design is when you look at all of the
LEGO elements in your kit and think "what can I make with
these?" Designing should always involve both top-down and
bottom-up design. Having a goal (top-down) keeps you fo-
cused on what you want the final design to do. On the other

hand, knowing what materials you have to work with (bottom-up) helps you think realistically about what you can make. Remember not to limit yourself to the materials that came in your LEGO kit. Combining your kit with things that you have around the house or that you buy at the craft store often can help you create really fun projects.

■ ■

Invention: Defining the Requirements

The next step was to think about what the animals should do. Should they move in a certain way? Follow a particular path? Interact with other animals? The students were required to think about one requirement: How would the animals interact with their environment?

The girls decided that they wanted the Giraffe to simulate eating a leaf from a tree and then bending its neck down to feed its baby. They drew sketches of what they thought this would look like (see Figure 4.3). In order to approach the tree, the Giraffe would need to be able to *move* somehow. In order to simulate eating a leaf and feeding it to the baby, the Giraffe would need to be able to *raise and lower its neck*.

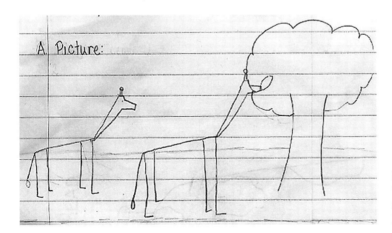

Figure 4.3
The girls' sketch of what the robotic Giraffe would do, from their Design Notebook.

How would the Giraffe do these two different things? The girls first decided to focus on the movement of the Giraffe because this, I cautioned them, might be the trickiest part.

■■■■■■■■■■■■■■■■■■■■■■■■■■■■■■

Engineering Aside: Break It Down

The best method for tackling any difficult design problem is to *break it down into smaller, easier tasks.* Don't try to build your animal all at once. Instead, start small and test single ideas one at a time.

■■■■■■■■■■■■■■■■■■■■■■■■■■■■■■

How would the Giraffe move? Someone suggested wheels, because this might be the easiest solution. Someone else replied that a rolling giraffe might not be satisfying enough to look at. What they really wanted to do was to make a giraffe with legs that could *walk*.

Coming up with Alternatives

Deciding on how to do something among alternative ideas is an early part of the design process. The great thing about designing is that there is never one right answer. There are always many different ways to satisfy your design requirements. If only school was *always* like that! Brainstorming to come up with different options can also help you be imaginative. It's even a good idea to think about possibilities that you think *wouldn't* work, so that you can narrow down the alternatives. Too often it happens that someone will start building a model from their very first idea and get stuck when it doesn't work. Taking the time to think about all of the different options beforehand allows you the freedom to think about different ways to solve a problem later on, and keeps you from going in just one direction. For example, these girls knew that they wanted to make their Giraffe walk, but they also knew that they could fall back on the option of using wheels later on, if the walking option proved to be too difficult.

Designing and Building

After deciding that they wanted the Giraffe to walk, what next? The girls were at a loss about where to begin. One of their class-mates from another group suggested looking in the *Construc-topedia*. They pointed out an example of a walking mechanism (see Figure 4.4) in the "Special Features" section on page 27.

That night, I did some research too. I went to mindstorms. lego.com/, clicked on "Search Inventions," and did a search on the word "walk". LEGO Mindstorms members have created many different walking mechanisms. Later on, when the girls ran into trouble with the Giraffe, I was able to use the information that I learned from other walking mechanisms at the LEGO Mindstorms site to help them with their design.

Figure 4.4

A walking mechanism from the Constructopedia 1.0. A similar mechanism is on page 18 of the Constructopedia 1.5.

If you cannot find a LEGO example for your robot, looking at the way that real-world objects work can be a great help, too.

LEGO Aside: Searching the LEGO Mindstorms Web Site

Looking at the LEGO Mindstorms Web site is a great way to get ideas and inspirations for designs (see Figure 4.5).

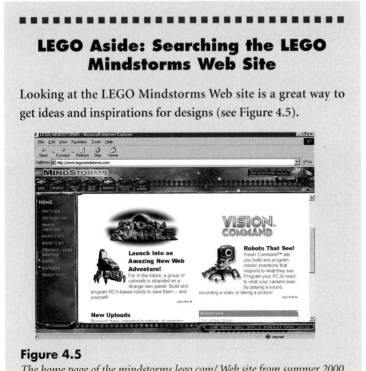

Figure 4.5

The home page of the mindstorms.lego.com/ Web site from summer 2000

When you post your own robot to your LEGO member's Web site, give it a good name so that people doing a search can find it easily. When you are searching for an example robot like the one you want to build, use keywords that you think other members might have used in their robot name. For example, a search on the word "giraffe" might not produce too many results, but a search on "walk" will.

■ ■

For example, examining the way that a real or toy wind-up animal walks can help you figure out how to make a robotic animal walk.

Right away, the girls didn't like the look of the walking mechanism from the *Constructopedia* (see Figure 4.6). It just wasn't wide enough. The body of the Giraffe, which was to be the RCX, was too long compared to the distance between its legs, so the girls decided to use the 24-tooth gear as the center gear instead of the 8-tooth gear, which required changing the placement of the axles for the 40-tooth gears. Changing the center gear caused the 40-tooth gears to spin around faster (see Figure 4.7).

Figure 4.6
The Giraffe in its early stages, using the walking mechanism from the Constructopedia *as an example.*

Figure 4.7
With five clockwise turns of the 8-tooth gear, the 40-tooth gears rotate once counterclockwise. With five turns of the 24-tooth gear, the 40-tooth gears rotate three times. Build these two mechanisms to verify this for yourself.

■ ■

Mathematical Aside: Gaining Speed with Gears

In the walking design from the *Constructopedia*, the 40-tooth gears had five times as many teeth as the center 8-tooth gear. This means that the motor had to turn around five times before the 40-tooth gears turned around once. With the first turn of the 8-tooth gear, 8 of the 40-teeth on the 40-tooth gear become meshed together with the 8-tooth gear one at a time. Because 8 out of 40 is the same as 1 out of 5 ($8/40 = 1/5$), the 40-tooth gear turns 1/5 of the way around with every full turn of the 8-tooth gear. This 1/5 of a turn is equal to 72 degrees, because 360/5 = 72. In the next few turns of the 8-tooth gear, 16, 24, 32, and finally all 40 teeth of the 40-tooth gear have gone by, for a total of five turns of the 8-tooth gear.

Five turns of the 24-tooth gear, on the other hand, will result in three turns of the 40-tooth gear. The 24-tooth gear spinning around five times is a total of 120 teeth meshing together with the 40-tooth gear one at a time, because 24 × 5 = 120. It takes only three turns of a 40-tooth gear to equal 120 teeth, because 3 × 40 = 120. Therefore, placing a gear in the center that is three times bigger results in the outer gears turning three times as fast. A 24-tooth gear is three times bigger than an 8-tooth gear, because 3 × 8 = 24.

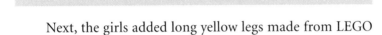

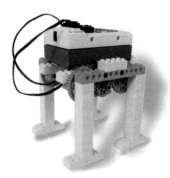

Figure 4.8
Legs are attached to the 40-tooth gears with beams and connector pegs.

Next, the girls added long yellow legs made from LEGO SYSTEM bricks (see Figure 4.8).

DESIGN NOTEBOOK

MARCH 5, 1999

Today we are working on building the legs. We are having a little bit of trouble with the rubber bands. We keep trying to make the gears turn to move the legs.

MARCH 9, 1999

Today I finally got the legs to work without using rubber bands. It shows an example of them on pg 27 in the Robotics book. But we changed it a little. Made the legs wider and the gears bigger.

Meanwhile, one of the girls was also working on making a neck with a head using the yellow system bricks (see Figure 4.9). When they attached the neck to the Giraffe during the testing sessions, it started to look a lot like a real giraffe. They put green 1x2 bricks with the cross hole at the base of the neck because these bricks can rigidly hold onto an axle. When the axle turns, the neck turns with it. They used a gearbox between the

Figure 4.9
A neck and a head made out of yellow system bricks

Figure 4.10

The gearbox was used in between the micromotor and the neck.

micromotor and the neck, because a gearbox is strong (see Figure 4.10).[1]

■■■■■■■■■■■■■■■■■■■■■■■■■■■■■■■

Scientific Aside: Gaining Strength with Gears

To understand why a gearbox is strong, it's necessary to understand what gives two gears that mesh together their strength. Before looking at meshing gears, we will examine the forces from a single gear.

To understand the forces from a single gear, think about other things that turn besides gears, like doors. When you push on a door, you know that it's harder to push the door near the hinge than near the doorknob. A physicist would say that it takes more *force* to open the door by pushing near the hinge. The same is true for seesaws. Just like the door, you have to push with more force near the middle of the seesaw (see A in Figure 4.11) to lift up your friend (wearing black with the red hat) than if you are at the end (B). In fact, you might even need a second friend to help you lift up the first friend.

---

1. The gearbox doesn't come with the Robotics Invention System kit. However, the worm gear and 24-tooth gear do, so that you are able to make your own gearbox when building your own giraffe. Two gearboxes come in the Exploration Mars expansion set. The micromotor, which also doesn't come with the RIS, is the slowest LEGO motor.

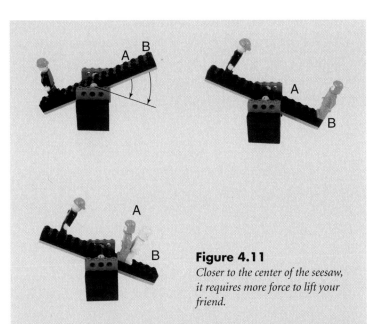

Figure 4.11
Closer to the center of the seesaw, it requires more force to lift your friend.

Why does it take more force near the center to move something that turns? A physicist would explain this by saying that it takes the same amount of *energy* to lift your friend up in the air—but that energy can be either a little force moving a long distance or a large force moving a short distance. When standing at point B on the seesaw, a larger distance is traveled before the seesaw hits the ground than when standing at point A. Likewise, opening the door near the doorknob requires you to push over a longer distance than pushing near the hinge. It's a trade-off. You can use less force, but you have to travel a longer distance. If you move a short distance, you have to use more force. The amount of energy used is the same.

Energy = Force × Distance

This situation can also be looked at in reverse. Suppose that your friend wants to lift you up in the air. Also, suppose he had to choose whether he would rather you sit near the middle of the seesaw or at the edge. If he were smart, he would want you to sit near the middle, because the seesaw can exert more force on you near the middle than near the edge. At the

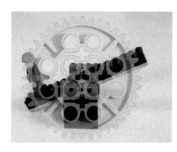

Figure 4.12
Understanding the forces of gears is similar to understanding the forces of a seesaw. Like the seesaw, a gear can exert more force from near its center than near its edge.

Figure 4.13
It takes more force to turn a gear when the force is applied near the axle. Likewise, a gear exerts more force near its axle than near its edge.

Figure 4.14
Gearing down is when a small gear turns a larger gear.

middle of the seesaw, the seesaw itself moves less distance but with more force.

Why all the talk about seesaws? A seesaw is a common thing that many people have experienced, and understanding the forces of seesaws is similar to understanding the forces of a gear (see Figure 4.12).

Both ways of looking at the seesaw are also true for spinning gears. Like trying to raise your friend up in the air, it takes more force to turn a gear by pushing it near the center of the gear than by pushing it near the edge. Like when your friend tries to lift you in the air, the reverse is also true: A spinning gear exerts more force near the center of the gear than it does at the edge (see Figure 4.13).

Gearing Down

Mechanical designers use the fact that spinning gears exert more force near the center than at the edge to their advantage. To achieve strength, all that is needed is to find a large gear and turn it by pushing it near its edge. The large force that results near the axle of the large gear can then be used to do something like lifting a weight, climbing a hill, or closing a robotic jaw. When a small gear is turning a large gear, for example, more strength results near the axle of the large gear than the force that originated near the axle of the smaller gear. This is called *gearing down* (see Figure 4.14).

Gearing down helps the motors of the walking mechanism move the heavy weight of the RCX and legs.[2] The drawback to gearing down is that the small gear must turn around many times to make the larger gear turn around once, making the large gear turn slowly. This is the trade-off between force and distance.

---

2. In the design of the Giraffe found on the CD-ROM, only one motor, instead of two, is used to make the Giraffe walk. When a 24-tooth gear was attached to the motor, the force was too weak and the Giraffe wouldn't walk at all. I had to replace the 24-tooth gear with an 8-tooth gear to make the Giraffe walk. This was the strength that results from gearing down in action!

Gearing Up

When a big gear is turning a smaller gear, the big gear is pushing on the smaller gear with a small force, because the gears are meshing near the edge of the larger gear. This is called *gearing up* (see Figure 4.15).

Although the smaller gear spins faster than the larger gear, the force, or strength, near the axle of the smaller gear is less than the strength near the axle of the bigger gear. What you've gained in speed is lost in strength. If you tied a string around the axle of the small gear, for example, you couldn't pull up that much weight.

When a gear meshes with another gear of the same size, neither speed nor strength is lost or gained (see Figure 4.16). Sometimes mechanical designers place two gears of the same size next to each other when they want only the direction of rotation to change.

Summary

Driving a small gear with a larger one is called *gearing up*. Gearing up increases speed but decreases strength. Gearing up is useful when you need speed.

Driving a large gear with a smaller one is called *gearing down*. Gearing down increases strength but decreases speed. Gearing down is useful in situations where you need strength, such as climbing up a hill and grabbing or lifting something.

The Gearbox

The gearbox is a great example of gearing down. The worm gear is like a 1-tooth gear wrapped around the axle. With each full turn of the worm gear's axle, the 24-tooth gear in the gearbox moves by only 1 tooth. It takes 24 turns of the worm gear's axle for the 24-tooth gear to turn around once. The other interesting thing about worm gears is that they cannot be made to turn by another gear. Worm gears can turn other gears only because of the way they are shaped.

■ ■

original force   force decreases

Figure 4.15
Gearing up is when a large gear turns a small gear.

force increases back to original
force decreases
original force

Figure 4.16
No speed or force is lost or gained when two gears of the same size turn each other.

Figure 4.17
Bracing the neck makes it harder for it to fall apart.

The biggest problem at this point in the Giraffe's design was that the neck and legs were breaking very easily. The neck and legs would break apart with just a slight bump. The problem was solved for the neck with a support beam that ran up the length of the back of the neck. Two of the 2x3 yellow bricks were removed and replaced by 1x2 beams and 2x2 bricks to hold the beam with connector pegs (see Figure 4.17).

DESIGN NOTEBOOK

MARCH 9, 1999 CONTINUED

Catherine made the neck stronger by adding another beam going down it. Before it would break at the base of the neck. Keenan started to build the stationary baby out of legos. She also began to build the second set of legs. Very Good Day!

By trial and error, the girls discovered that spacing the 1x2 beams exactly ten bricks apart on the back of the neck enabled them to place connector pegs 12 holes apart along the supporting beam (see Figure 4.18).

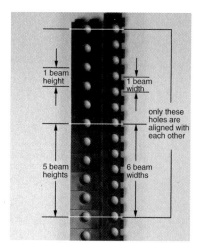

Figure 4.18
A stack of 1x2 beams alongside a 1x16 beam demonstrates that the holes line up only every fifth hole in the stack of 1x2 beams, and every sixth hole along the beam.

■■■■■■■■■■■■■■■■■■■■■■■■■■■■■■■■

Mathematical Aside: Beam Geometry

If the distance between the holes along a beam were the same as the distance between beams that are stacked up vertically, you could place connector pegs wherever you wanted to when attaching a beam to a vertical stack of beams. Instead, you have to place pegs every sixth hole along the beam and every fifth hole along the vertical stack. The space between six holes along a beam is therefore equal to the distance between five holes of beams stacked vertically. This means that the height of a beam must be larger than the distance between holes along a beam. To be precise, the distance is 6/5 (1 1/5) times larger.

> 5 holes of a vertical stack of beams = 6 holes along a beam

divide by 5 on both sides

> Distance from hole to hole on vertical stack = 6/5 × distance from hole to hole along a beam

Because the distance from one hole to the next on a vertical stack of beams is also equal to the height of a beam, you could say that:

> Height of a beam = 6/5 × distance from hole to hole along a beam

Comparing Height and Width

The width of a brick is equal to the distance between the holes along a beam (see Figure 4.19), which is also the same distance between one stud and the next.

Because the width of a beam is equal to the distance between the holes on a beam, then you could say that the height of a single brick or beam is 6/5 of the width of that brick.

> Height of a beam = 6/5 × distance from hole to hole along a beam

1 beam width

Figure 4.19
The width of a brick or beam is equal to the distance between the holes along a beam and between studs on a brick or beam.

Figure 4.20

It takes three plates to equal the height of a brick or beam and 2 1/2 plates to equal their width.

Figure 4.21

Two beams with two plates between them are equal to the exact spacing of two connector pegs placed two holes apart along a beam.

Width of a beam = Distance from hole to hole along a beam

Therefore, by substituting . . .

Height of a beam = 6/5 × width of a beam

Plates and Beams or Bricks

Using the fact that the height of a brick is 6/5 times the width of a brick, we can figure out the mathematical relationship between plates and beams. For example, if it takes three plates to equal the height of a brick or beam, then it takes only 2 1/2 plates to equal its width (see Figure 4.20). That ratio of 3 to 2 1/2 is the same as a ratio of 6 to 5.

Height of beam/width of beam = 6/5
Height of beam = 3 plates
Width of beam = ? plates
3 plates/? plates = 6/5
3 plates/2.5 plates = 6/5

Why This Is Useful

Knowing the distance relationship between beams and plates helps when trying to make a secure connection with them. Take the example of connector pegs that are two widths apart (see Figure 4.21). Suppose we want to connect beams to these two connector pegs. What spacing is required?

2 widths = ? heights
if 6 widths = 5 heights, then
2 widths = 5/3 heights (1 2/3 heights)
How can we get 1 2/3 heights? With plates!
1/2 height + 1 plate + 1 plate + 1/2 height = 1/2 height + 1/3 height + 1/3 height + 1/2 height
1/2 height + 1/3 height + 1/3 height + 1/2 height = 5/3 heights (1 2/3 heights!)

■ ■

After the neck was braced, the girls used that same idea and applied it to the legs. Instead of relying on the same spacing for every leg, they came up with some alternative distances that also worked using plates. On one leg of the Giraffe, for example, there are two connector pegs that are ten holes apart. We know, however, that the connector pegs have to be six or twelve pegs apart if they are to line up with a vertical stack of beams and bricks. The difference is in the use of plates.

At this point, the neck and head still fell off, but it fell off in one big piece instead of breaking into smaller pieces. I went to my friend Fudd's house after school that day and told him

Mathematical Aside: More Beam and Plate Geometry

The distance between the connector pegs along the beam of the front right leg is ten holes (see Figure 4.22). The vertical distance up the leg is eight bricks plus 1 plate, which is equal to 25 plates.

8 bricks + 1 plate = 8 bricks × (3 plates/1 brick) + 1 plate = 25 plates

The distance between ten holes along the beam also must be equal to 25 plates. We can check this by comparing the height of plates to the distance between holes along the beam. It takes 2 1/2 plates to equal the distance between two holes along the beam, because 2 1/2 plates is equal to the width of a brick. The distance between the holes is then:

10 widths × (2 1/2 plates/width) = 25 plates

Using the same method, it's possible to figure out why the spacing of the rear right leg works by proving that four holes along a beam is equal to the height of three bricks and 1 plate.

Figure 4.22
Each right leg shows a unique spacing using bricks and plates.

Figure 4.23

Bracing the side of the neck allowed the neck to be held onto the Giraffe even better than before, because the axle that rotated the neck passed through a hole of the bracing beam.

about the neck that kept falling off. "That's simple," he said. "Just connect a beam along the *side* of the neck and put the axle that the neck tilts on through the last hole in the beam. That way the neck will always stay connected." "Of course!" I thought. "Why didn't we think of that?" At school the next day, I told the girls, "We need to somehow connect the entire length of the neck to the axle." The solution is shown in Figure 4.23.

DESIGN NOTEBOOK

MARCH 11, 1999

Today Catherine started the body of the stationary baby. Liz finished the other set of legs and they work really well. We are almost done with almost all the building so we will probably start programming soon.

The girls were confident that their Giraffe was looking good. It seemed as if they were almost finished building the mechanics of the Giraffe. But building something and testing it are two different things! Using stronger legs and a stronger neck, the girls connected the wires to the outputs, turned on the RCX, and hit the Run button.

Implementation: Testing

Designing and building a LEGO robot and testing it out are two completely different tasks. Even if your robot looks like it will work, oftentimes you will discover that it doesn't when you test it.

DESIGN NOTEBOOK

MARCH 16, 1999

Today I got both legs on the RCX. The second I put it on the ground and tried to run it, it broke. It was not strong enough . . . . Today the baby broke. Now we are not going to have a baby. I am working on the trees which are much more important.

The very first thing that the Giraffe did was fall over. First the left set of legs touched the table, and then the right, and then the left . . . and then . . . crash! Just like a real baby giraffe, the LEGO Giraffe would take just a few wobbly steps before stumbling and falling.

Like the robotic Giraffe, every time you take a step you are slightly off balance. If you stop walking right before you are about to put down one of your feet, you'll feel unbalanced. We balance ourselves by shifting our weight back and forth onto the foot that is on the ground. When our right leg is up in the air, we shift our weight to our left foot. Shifting weight, however, isn't an easy thing for a LEGO robot to do. Even though the Giraffe looks like it has four legs, each pair of legs, left and right, is linked together as one unit. The Giraffe essentially has two legs. This was causing it to fall over.

Solving this problem required thinking back to the walking mechanism in the *Constructopedia*. What was the difference between the Giraffe and that example? If the example in the *Constructopedia* worked, why didn't the Giraffe? The two main differences were:

- The Giraffe was using the 24-tooth gear instead of the 8-tooth gear.
- The Giraffe had much longer legs.

The 24-tooth gears made the Giraffe move faster, but that wasn't causing the unbalance. I thought back to the pictures of the walking mechanisms on the Internet. One of the pictures was a caterpillar that used the very same walking mechanism from the *Constructopedia*. Thinking about how the caterpillar must have walked helped to solve the Giraffe's problem. When one set of legs was lifted up in the air, the other set of legs *and the belly of the caterpillar* must have been touching the ground. Or, if the legs moved together, the belly of the caterpillar could rest on the ground when the legs were in the air. This made the short-legged caterpillar very stable. I told the girls about the caterpillar that I had seen and explained how it worked. The girls immediately went to work on making vertical supports underneath the belly

Figure 4.24

The Giraffe with four belly supports

of the Giraffe so that the Giraffe's belly would hit the ground just like the caterpillar's did (see Figure 4.24). Real giraffes don't look like that, but *you do the best you can!* So after all, the problem was that a big heavy RCX was on top of some very long legs, making the Giraffe unstable.

DESIGN NOTEBOOK

MARCH 18, 1999

Liz is working on making the legs stronger and making them work. Catherine and I are working on the trees and next week will work on the rest of the environment. We also hope to start programming next week.

NEXT WEEK

Program and work on legs. Work on environment.

Figure 4.25

An attempt at making the Giraffe more stable by making the feet bigger

The supports made the Giraffe walk a little bit better but not perfectly. It still fell over. It just couldn't keep its balance for long. The girls had connected the two output wires and placed them on output A. They were using built-in program 1 on the RCX to make the Giraffe walk. It seemed like the motors should've made the two pairs of legs walk together, but they didn't. The legs would stay synchronized for a few seconds of walking, but then quickly get out of step with each other, which caused the Giraffe to lose its balance and fall over.

Another teacher, Mrs. Burns, came into the room to see how the animals were coming along. She looked at the Giraffe and made a suggestion, "What if the feet were bigger and wider? That might make it more stable." The girls tried it out (see Figure 4.25). The Giraffe might have stayed upright a little longer . . . it was hard to tell. But the end result was the same. The Giraffe was always falling over.

I asked them how they could make sure that the two sets of legs would stay synchronized. The solution is shown in Figure 4.26. By placing an axle between the 40-tooth gears, the two sets of legs moved together. First the legs would move, then the supports, then the legs, and the motion would repeat. It worked! Watching the little Giraffe take its very first steps that afternoon, the girls were as proud as could be.

DESIGN NOTEBOOK

MARCH 19, 1999

Today we are finishing the trees. We hope to work on the rest of the environment. Liz is making the legs stronger. She is trying to make it not wiggle so much. She added extra supports to hold it up. "It looks really cool and is coming along really well" (from Danielle from next door). We sang a lot.

APRIL 5, 1999

It works!

That last entry says it all.

Figure 4.26
Connecting the right legs to the left legs with a long axle keeps the legs synchronized.

Programming

The girls had made two trees from a dowel, chicken wire, construction paper, and masking tape. They drilled holes to hold the trees in the particleboard that we were using as the ground and painted the surface green to look like grass. They wanted their program to make the Giraffe walk forward until it reached the tree, bend its neck down to look like it was eating a leaf, raise its neck back up again, and then walk in reverse back to where it started.

Soon after the Giraffe could walk, the girls set to work on programming its movements. They connected the motor that could turn the neck to output C.

Figure 4.27 shows what the program looked like at first. The one problem with the program was that the neck never seemed to come back up to its original position. The girls had to add two seconds to the time that the motor stayed on for the way back up. This worked better but not perfectly. After a few repetitions, the neck still wouldn't come back up to the same place.

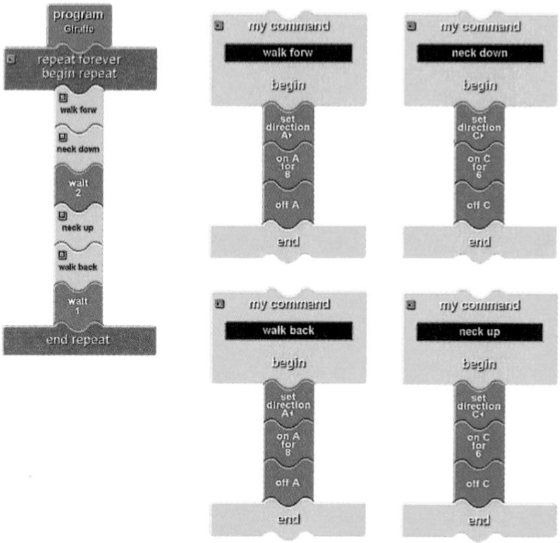

Figure 4.27
The first program for the Giraffe

Scientific Aside: Friction

When the neck is on the way down, the motor is turning the worm gear, which then turns the 24-tooth gear in the gearbox, which turns the axle, which turns the neck. This is easy for the motor to do, because the weight of the neck is helping out. On the way up, the motor is fighting to move the heavy neck and head up against the pull of gravity. A lot of the energy that the motor is pulling with is lost to heat and *friction* in the gearbox, and the head cannot be pulled up to its original position.

Friction occurs when different surfaces rub against each other. It's always a factor when designing your robots and is the cause of many different problems. Sometimes there is a problem in not having enough friction, such as when a robot gets dust on its wheels, or the surface it's driving on is too slippery. Other times there is a problem in having too much friction, such as when bushings or gears are rubbing too much on the edges of beams as they turn.

Further Work

Designing an animal can be challenging, fun, and rewarding. When you finally get your animal to work the way you want it to, what once was a pile of plastic in a bucket (or on the floor) comes to life before your eyes. It's a good idea to evaluate your project when it's finished. Does it work the way you originally wanted it to? What might you have done differently? How could it be improved? For example, if the girls had had more time, they might have added a light sensor to detect the tree instead of making the Giraffe walk for a certain amount of time. And even though the legs were braced, they still can wiggle a little bit. They could've been made stronger by adding two plates and another beam and connector peg (see Figure 4.28).

Another improvement might be to somehow keep track of the position of the neck, with an angle sensor or a light sensor, and program it so that the motor doesn't stop turning until the neck has reached its original position.

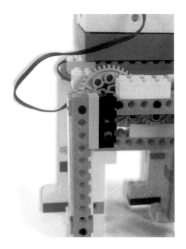

Figure 4.28

A possible improvement to the strength of the legs

5
Walking Mechanisms

Three different walking mechanisms are presented in this chapter: a Dog, a Puppy, and a Bug.

Dog

Inspiration

Seeing my students working on their walking Giraffe made me want to make a walking animal of my own. A walking animal was therefore one of the first models that I tried to make with the RCX. Even though the Giraffe is a cool robot, it really does not walk the way a real giraffe does. I wanted to create a four-legged animal that walked by putting its four feet down in the same order that a four-legged animal does.

Designing and Building

The first four-legged walking mechanism began, like the Giraffe, with the walking mechanism from the first *Constructopedia*. I placed axles between both of the 40-tooth gears on either side so that the movement of the legs would be synchronized. To hold the 40-tooth gears in place and connect them to the belly of the RCX, I used one layer of bricks and one layer of beams (see Figure 5.1). A layer of plates between the bricks and beams also works as spacing.

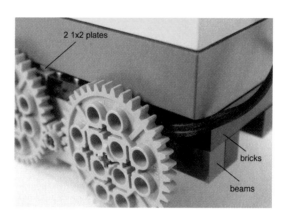

Figure 5.1
One layer of bricks and then 1x4 beams below them is good enough spacing to allow the gears to mesh. Also shown are the two 1x2 gray plates on top of one side of the motor for extra attaching strength.

Figure 5.2
Two 1x8 plates were used to help secure the motors together. These additional plates make it harder for the motors to fall off because they are one unit.

Figure 5.3
The first set of legs: 1x6 beams with one connector peg each

Figure 5.4
Securing the bottom of the walking mechanism with bricks and plates

A total of four 1x4 beams were added under the layer of bricks on the side of each motor so that the 40-tooth gears and their axle would not fall off easily if they got bumped. Bushings were also placed behind each of the 40-tooth gears to keep them from hitting the wires or the body of the RCX. After I pressed the Run button, however, the motors immediately fell off. Additional attaching strength came from adding two 1x2 gray plates to the top of each motor. I also braced the motors to each other with 1x8 plates across the bottom (see Figure 5.2).

Once I had constructed a basic structure, the first set of legs could be attempted—legs made out of beams (see Figure 5.3). I connected one 1x6 beam to each 40-tooth gear with one connector peg and tested. It walked! In fact, the kind of walking that it did was interesting. After every few steps, the walker would raise up on its hind legs! This occurred because every few steps, the beams from the front would hit the beams from the back. The only problem was that sometimes one entire set of legs would fall off. The solution was to secure both sets of legs to each other by spanning plates across the belly. After adding 2x4 bricks and 2x4 plates across each set of legs, I added two 2x10 plates and two 1x6 plates to secure the two sets of legs together (see Figure 5.4).

I attempted many different leg designs. For example, one variation was to link the legs on each side with an axle or a beam. The best results were achieved, however, when I fixed the beams onto the 40-tooth gears with two connector pegs instead of one. This synchronized the motion of the legs with the motion of the 40-tooth gears. When turned on, the walker looks as if it is starting to walk, but the back legs eventually hit the front ones. More spacing was needed between the front and back legs, so I changed the 8-tooth gear to a 24-tooth gear. The front and back legs still hit each other though, so I changed the 1x6 beams to 1x4 beams. This worked but not perfectly. Last, I added a 1x2 brick as a foot for each leg, and it worked better (see Figure 5.5).

Figure 5.5
A 1x4 beam, a 1x2 brick, and two connector pegs made a working leg and foot.

These new legs could not be placed onto the 40-tooth gears any which way, however. I had to position the legs so that they would not hit each other, and so that the feet would come down in the right order. What is the right order? My friend told me that she thought that when they walk, animals put down a front leg, then the back leg on the opposite side, and then the other front leg, and then the last back leg. This is the order in which this walking mechanism places its feet down (see Figure 5.6).

Left   Right

Figure 5.6
With the legs arranged in this manner, the Dog puts each foot down at a different time in the correct order of a walking dog.

Figure 5.7
When both sets of legs are positioned in the same manner, the Dog puts down the front feet together and back feet together, as if it were running.

The legs could be changed, however, to make the Dog move in different ways. For example, if the legs are placed as shown in Figure 5.7, the front and back legs move together, like the legs of a dog when it runs. A stronger leg can be achieved if extra 1x4 beams are available (see Figure 5.8).

Programming and Testing

The first program for the Dog is to make it walk on a leash using the long wire and a touch sensor (see Figure 5.9). The program makes the Dog walk forward when the touch sensor is

Figure 5.8
With extra 1x4 beams, the foot is less likely to fall off.

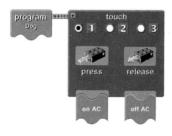

Figure 5.9
The first program for the Dog

pressed and stop when the touch sensor is not pressed. The program uses a touch sensor watcher.

This program works well. Even though the Dog cannot technically turn on its own because the front and back legs are linked together, it certainly looks like it can turn. The trick is with the leash. When you pull the leash from one side to another, the Dog is pulled by the leash and looks like it is following the person that is taking it for a walk. When you hold the leash still, it looks as if the Dog is walking in a circle. This is similar to the movement of a real dog that has one end of its leash looped around a stake in the yard.

Further Work

Like the Giraffe, lots of improvements can be made to the Dog. First, one of the motors can be removed. This second motor can be used to make a head that turns back and forth or a tail that wags. Second, one can experiment with using both motors for walking without any axles linking the two pairs of legs. This would give the Dog the ability to turn, by turning one motor forward and another backward. The disadvantage to this design is that the pairs of legs might get out of step rather quickly.

Puppy

After making the first walking mechanism, I attempted a different kind of four-legged walker. Again, the inspiration came from the *Constructopedia* walking mechanism. I thought about how the original caterpillar-style walker worked with the two outer gears connected by a beam that acted as a single large leg. I decided to make a four-legged walker based on that same principle. Although I usually don't draw sketches before I work on a LEGO design, I immediately tried to draw a sketch of this new idea to see if it would work (see Figure 5.10).

Using 24-tooth gears instead of 40-tooth gears for the outer gears, I was able to make a four-legged walking robot that worked very well (see Figure 5.11). This robot walks slower than the first Dog and wobbles a little when it walks, so I

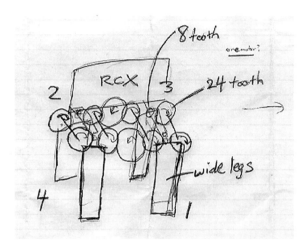

named it the "Puppy." The most interesting thing about the Puppy is that each leg can be adjusted to one of four possible positions, because a 24-tooth gear contains four different holes. Depending on the positions of the legs, the Puppy walks very differently.

Figure 5.11
The second four-legged walking model, the Puppy

Bug

After making the two four-legged walking mechanisms, I tried to make a six-legged walker that would look like a bug. I read that a six-legged walker is very stable because at least three legs are on the ground at a time. People have studied the way that six-legged insects walk and have determined that the two outer feet on one side and the center foot on the other side step down together (see Figure 5.12).

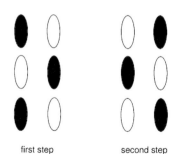

first step   second step

Figure 5.12
Six-legged creatures walk by stepping down with the center foot on one side with the front and back feet of the other side.

■ ■

Engineering Aside: Statically Stable versus Dynamically Stable

Walking mechanisms are intriguing to watch. Especially when trying to design an animal, a good walking mechanism is essential. The fewer the number of legs that the animal keeps on

Figure 5.13
Six-legged LEGO robots usually use axles connected to gears as legs. The gears rotate around, causing the axles to go up and down. A cross block keeps the axle in an upright position.

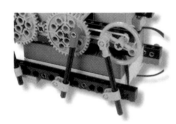

Figure 5.14
A belt slipped too often to keep the leg on the pulley wheel in sync with the other two legs.

the ground at a time, the harder it is to make because the animal is unstable. This is why many robotics researchers make insect robots with six or more legs. A six-legged walker is *statically stable*. This means that at any point in time while the insect is walking, it is always stable. Animals with fewer legs, such as humans, are *dynamically stable*. We are stable only for certain times while we are walking. Researchers at MIT have made the hardest walking mechanism of them all: one leg! This robot hops around like a kangaroo and can even do flips! It takes dynamic feedback for that robot to keep its balance.

■■■■■■■■■■■■■■■■■■■■■■■■■■■■■■■■■■

Designing and Building

I started working on the mechanics for the Bug by remembering the basic mechanics of other six-legged walkers that I had seen. The other six-legged walkers used axles for legs. Each axle was connected to a 40-tooth gear and passed through a cross block that kept the axle in a fixed range of motion (see Figure 5.13).

The biggest challenge was in figuring out how to synchronize all of the legs. For six legs, all four 40-tooth gears as well as the two large pulley wheels are needed to provide the rotational motion, because all these items are the same size. (Six 40-tooth gears can be used if they are available. The kit, however, comes with only four 40-tooth gears.) The construction began with an 8-tooth gear on the motor and two 40-tooth gears on either side of it. I then needed some way to connect the axle of one of the two 40-tooth gears to the axle of the large pulley wheel. As long as the large pulley wheel spun at the same rate as the 40-tooth gears, all three of the legs on one side would be synchronized.

I tried several different ways of connecting the axle of the large pulley wheel to the axle of the 40-tooth gear without any luck. First, I tried using a belt, but the belt slipped, and the large pulley wheel did not stay synchronized with the 40-tooth gears (see Figure 5.14).

Then I used gears to connect the axle of one of the 40-tooth gears to the axle of the pulley wheel. For the six-legged walker to walk properly, the 40-tooth gear and the pulley wheel must turn at the same speed. For this to happen, the gear ratio between the two legs must be 1:1.

■■■■■■■■■■■■■■■■■■■■■■■■■■■■■■

Engineering Aside:
Gear Ratios and Idlers

A gear ratio is expressed as

> number of turns of the driver : number of turns of the follower

where the *driver* is the first gear in the gear train, and the *follower* is the last. For example, a 40-tooth gear turning an 8-tooth gear would have a gear ratio of 1:5. One turn of the 40-tooth gear results in five turns of the 8-tooth gear. Also notice that the gear ratio could be expressed as

> number of teeth or diameter of the follower : number of teeth or diameter of the driver

(Because the number of teeth of a gear is a measure of its circumference, and its circumference is proportional to its diameter by the equation $C = \pi D$, the relationship between the number of teeth of two gears is the same as the relationship between their diameters.)

If all of the gears in a gear train are lined up in a row, then the gear ratio can be calculated simply by looking at the first and last gear. Any gears between the first and last gears are merely transferring the motion from one gear to the next, and they do not increase or decrease the overall speed or force of the gear train as a whole. These in-between gears are called *idlers*. While idlers do not change the speed or force of the overall gear train, they do affect the direction of rotation of the follower gear and the distance between the driver and the follower. You can experiment with different gears lined up to verify these concepts for yourself.

■■■■■■■■■■■■■■■■■■■■■■■■■■■■■■

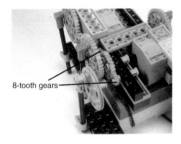

Figure 5.15
A gear train that worked to synchronize the 40-tooth gear with the large pulley wheel

Figure 5.16
The six-legged walker in its final form. The large pulley wheels are connected to the 40-tooth gears only on the opposite side.

At first, I placed various gears in front of the 40-tooth gear on its same axle. This, however, got in the way of the leg that had to be attached to the 40-tooth gear. Therefore, I placed a gear on the same axle as the 40-tooth gear behind the 40-tooth gear. Only the 8-tooth gear would fit into such a small space. The only thing left to do for the gear train was to place another 8-tooth gear on the axle of the pulley wheel to create the 1:1 gear ratio and then to choose some idler gears. A configuration that worked was one 24-tooth idler gear in between the two 8-tooth gears. Two idler gears could not be used because this would cause the large pulley wheel to turn in the wrong direction. The only problem with this setup was that the pulley wheel had to be placed farther out from the body of the walker than the 40-tooth gears (see Figure 5.15).

Then I had an insight. Why do I need to bother with connecting the large pulley wheels to the 40-tooth gears on the same side at all? Why not just connect the large pulley wheels to the 40-tooth gears on the opposite side? And that's what I did (see Figure 5.16). This is yet another example of how the best solution to a problem is often a simple one.

The disadvantage to connecting the pulley wheel to the 40-tooth gears on the opposite side is that the Bug will not be able to turn. However, as was cautioned before, the legs can get out of step with each other rather quickly when neither set of legs is connected.

I added an additional 1x2 brick and two 1x2 plates with slides to each outer gear to provide more stability. I also added plates to the top of the robot to secure the motors to each other (see Figure 5.17).

Figure 5.17
Plates and a bracing beam were added to provide more stability to the motors and outer gears.

Further Work

Once the walking mechanism is complete, it needs a program. Here are some ideas for programs:

- Attach a light sensor and write a program in which the walker walks only when it is bright.

- Attach a light sensor and write a program in which the walker walks forward until it is bright and then retreats.

- Place a touch sensor on either end of the walker so that it can sense when it has been bumped after walking into something from either direction.

- Attach a light sensor facing downward and program the walker to walk until it gets to the edge of a table and then reverse direction (use the View button first!).

6
FIRST LEGO League

This chapter describes the experiences of students involved in FIRST LEGO League (FLL), a worldwide LEGO robotics contest for students age 9–14 that takes place every year from September to December. It's a collaboration between LEGO Mindstorms and FIRST.[1] For FIRST LEGO League, teams of students design and program autonomous robots that compete against other teams in local, state, and national tournaments. For more information about how you can get involved in FIRST LEGO League as a coach or a participant, visit mindstorms.lego.com/fll.

Inspiration

During the 1998–1999 school year, my students and I participated in the pilot year of FIRST LEGO League. That fall, a little over ten cities and towns around the country had FIRST LEGO

---

1. "FIRST" stands for "For Inspiration and Recognition of Science and Technology."

Figure 6.1

The 1998 FIRST LEGO League playing field

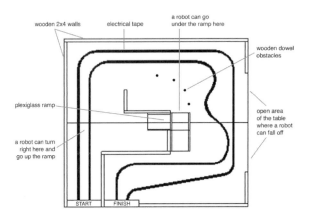

League teams. At our school in Weston, Massachusetts, there were five teams of sixth- through eighth-grade students. They met after school three days a week for six weeks to work on an autonomous robot for the competition.

The Contest

The objective of the 1998 competition was to create robots that could navigate around a playing field in the shortest amount of time (see Figure 6.1). Robots raced around the field alone and head-to-head against another robot. The playing field was made up of two pieces of 4x8-foot white melamine particleboard put together to make a square eight feet long on a side. It had long 2x4s of wood for walls and two black strips of electrical tape that wound around the course. In the middle of the field, a Plexiglas ramp allowed the robots to take a short but dangerous route to the finish line. Finally, the robots had the option of driving in a curved path and actually going under the ramp and coming out the other side.

Different teams of students approached the design problem in different ways. One team built a bumper car that used a touch sensor to detect when it had hit the wooden walls. Another team used the treads to build a tanklike vehicle to climb the ramp (see Figure 6.2). Two other teams worked on line-following programs, and one team tried the complicated route of going under the ramp.

Figure 6.2

One team used the treads to make a vehicle strong enough to climb the ramp.

Bumper Car Robot

Like every team, the Bumper Car team faced many challenges. Their biggest problem was getting the robot to go in a straight line. Even though they had programmed both motors to turn on at the same speed, the robot would stay straight for only a few feet until it started veering to one side. This didn't matter too much for the first leg of the course, but on the second leg of the course, it sent the robot right off the open end of the table where there was no wall.

The Bumper Car program drove the robot forward until the touch sensor was pressed, and then it backed up and turned to the left for a certain amount of time. The turn to the left was accomplished by slowing down the left wheel with a **set power** command while the right wheel turned backward (see Figure 6.3).

The Bumper Car team was experiencing a problem with their program, however. After bumping into the far wall, the Bumper Car wasn't turning back to the correct position. Instead, it backed up and turned too much, and headed right off the table! Even though they had timed exactly how long it took for the car to back up and face toward the next wall, they found out the hard way that *you can never rely only on time!* The Bumper Car team had a breakthrough when they noticed something interesting that happened during a trail run. They had placed their car farther to the left than usual at the starting line. This time, when the car hit the far wall and backed up to the left, it backed itself right into the left wall and straightened itself out!

There are many reasons why you shouldn't rely on "wait" time when programming your robot. Here are some examples:

- When batteries start to wear down, a robot won't go as far as it used to in the same amount of time.

- Tires encounter less friction with the table on some runs over others because of dust and other factors, causing the robot to run faster or slower on different trials.

- Different LEGO pieces shift around slightly when you hold the robot between trials, with the pieces rubbing against each other differently, getting too tight or too loose. This can cause discrepancies in the robot's performance.

Figure 6.3
The program for the Bumper Car

■ Two motors programmed to run at exactly the same speed won't necessarily do so perfectly.

These and many other small discrepancies make it impossible for a robot to perform the exact same routine over and over again when running a program, especially one based on **wait** commands. Although the Bumper Car's problem of relying on timing was solved without the use of extra sensors, it serves as a good example of how a program that uses **wait** commands isn't very repeatable.

To avoid some of the problems of timing, you should use sensors. Sensors provide the robot with necessary feedback about the environment. Without feedback, it's impossible for the robot to know how far it has moved, whether or not it has bumped into something, whether it's over a black or white line, and so on.

Thinking about how you would solve a problem with your own body can often help you think about how to program a robot to solve the same problem. Here is a problem that I gave to some FIRST LEGO League teams to get them to start thinking this way and also to illustrate the importance of using sensors: "Stand back a good distance from a wall. Remember where you start. With your arms at your sides, walk forward and count how long it takes you to get to the wall. Then go back to the same starting position and close your eyes. Now walk forward for the same amount of time that you counted the first time." Would you want to do it? Of course not! Why not? If you take bigger steps the second time, or count slower, you would walk right into the wall. When I asked this of a student at the Paraclete Center in South Boston, she closed her eyes and then put her arms out in front of her. I said "Aha! What are you doing?" She was using her hands—like a robot uses touch sensors—to give her feedback as to when she was about to hit the wall. That is exactly the kind of thing you want to do for your robot. When you are thinking about programming your robot to do something, sometimes thinking about how *you* would do it can be a big help.

Incidentally, this lesson about time-based programs was also important for the Tank robot. Because the ramp had no walls or black line of electrical tape, the tank robot couldn't use any sensors to find its way up and down the ramp. Eventually, after not being able to repeat a few successful ramp trial runs, the tank team gave up on trying to use the ramp and used a slower but more reliable line-following program.

■■■■■■■■■■■■■■■■■■■■■■■■■■■■■

Engineering Aside: Trade-Offs

These lessons about the dangers of using programs based on time are good examples of why robots need feedback. Another good lesson that it provides is about trade-offs. Engineering is all about trade-offs. A *trade-off* is when you must make a decision between two choices, and both choices have a good side and a bad side. One of the biggest trade-offs in mechanical design, as was discussed in Chapter 4, is the trade-off between having strength and having speed. A Line-Follower robot with the right program will get around the track almost every time (good), but it's slow (bad). The Tank robot can take the ramp and finish the course quickly (good) but, because it can't use feedback from sensors, is not guaranteed to make it to the finish line (bad). It's up to you as the LEGO engineer to weigh the alternatives and decide whether or not a trade-off is worthwhile.

■■■■■■■■■■■■■■■■■■■■■■■■■■■■■

The Bumper Car robot went on to do pretty well for itself. It got the award for best-looking finish because it backed out of the course in style—backward.

Line-Follower Robot

One of the few times when using your own body to think about how you would solve a problem actually gets you into trouble is when trying to make a Line-Follower robot. The main reason that the Line-Follower robot is difficult to program is because of the way we say it: "line-following." When we try to relate line-following to an activity that we've done ourselves, we think of walking along a painted line on the road, or walking along a crack in the sidewalk, where we try to stay on that line as much as possible. When most people try to create a robot that can follow a line, their first attempt is to make the robot stay on the line and go straight. This is where the confusion starts. It turns out that the easiest way for a robot to "follow" a line isn't really to stay on the line at all, but to go back and forth to one side of it.

Here is an example. Suppose that your robot is traveling straight on a piece of black electrical tape, and the light sensor reading is 35 (which you can tell by using the View button). You've programmed the robot to turn right when the light sensor reading is greater than 45 because the value of the bright surface outside of the black line is 55. You decided to make the robot turn to the right because the electrical tape that you've put down goes off to the right.

The electrical tape won't always turn toward the right, however. If the second turn of the electrical tape turns to the left and you had programmed your robot to turn to the right whenever it encounters the light surface, you can run into problems (see Figure 6.4). Chances are that the robot will keep on turning to the right, turn all the way around, see the line again, and start heading back toward the starting line. This is exactly what happened to some teams involved in FIRST LEGO League.

The problem with trying to make the robot stay straight on the black line is that you don't know which way the line will curve. Even if you knew every turn of the course ahead of time, it would be cumbersome to program the robot to navigate every turn of the course. It would also be difficult to predict exactly how your robot would follow all of the twists and turns, and exactly when it would "fall off" of the line.

There are at least two ways of trying to solve the line-following problem and still keep the robot over the center of the black line. These solutions are still more complex than the best

Figure 6.4

The first turn of the course is to the right, but the second turn is to the left.

solution of staying on one side of the line, but they are worth looking at. The first solution is to use two light sensors. When you have two light sensors, both aimed at either side of the black line, you can create a very reliable Line-Follower. When the right side light sensor senses black, you know that you should turn toward the right. When the left light sensor senses black, you know that you should turn toward the left (see Figure 6.5).

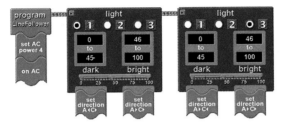

Figure 6.5
The Line-Follower program with two light sensors. This program works as long as the light sensors are far enough apart so that they don't see the black line at the same time.

Programming Aside: Multitasking

Whenever a program includes more than one sensor-watcher, each runs at the same time on the RCX. This feature of the RCX is called *multitasking*. For example, if a Line-Follower is using two light sensors, the RCX Code program checks both light sensors at the same time. Technically, the RCX doesn't execute each sensor-watcher at exactly the same time though. Instead, the RCX quickly jumps between sensor-watchers and steps through them one at a time. This usually happens fast enough so that the difference isn't noticed. The maximum number of sensor-watchers in a program is eight.

The second solution is to have the robot check for itself which way it has fallen off of the black line. First, you pick an arbitrary direction to turn when the robot falls off of the line—for example, to the right. The program will make the robot

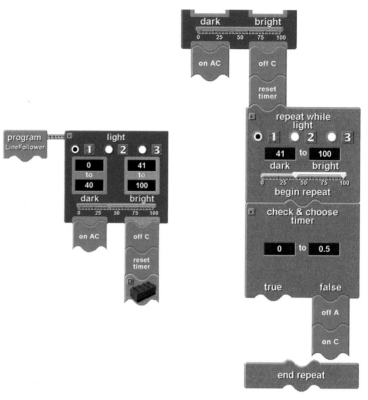

Figure 6.6

A cumbersome line-following program that never really knows which side of the line it's on

Figure 6.7

A program that will make the robot drive up to the black line and then stop

drive straight until it senses lightness and then turn right. The robot will turn to the right only for a reasonable amount of time though, maybe for a second. When that second has gone by, and the robot still doesn't find the black line, it turns back to the left and looks for the line to the left (see Figure 6.6).

This solution to the problem works, but it's very slow. This program will enable the Line-Follower robot to make the correct decision on which way to turn only part of the time. Let's go on and look at the way it should really be done.

To start thinking about how to stay on one side of the line and follow it, begin with a simple program and gradually get more complex. For example, begin with a program that will make the robot drive forward until it senses the dark line and then stop (see Figure 6.7).

This program serves as practice for having the robot tell the difference between light and dark. Next, try a program that makes the robot drive toward the black line and then back up until the light sensor sees white (see Figure 6.8).

What we are really after is a formula that we can tell the robot to repeat over and over again. A formula like this is called an *algorithm.* There is one simple formula that we can tell a robot to repeat that will cause it to follow the black line. The task is to find that formula. To write a program with a repeating formula, the repeat forever stack controller must be used. The current program can be altered to include a repeat forever (see Figure 6.9).

At this point, the robot doesn't do much more than wiggle back and forth at the edge of the black line. Instead of having the robot turned sideways to the black line, it should be facing the same direction as the black line. Next, try writing a program

Figure 6.8

A program that will make the robot drive up to the black line and then back up until the light sensor sees white

Figure 6.9

A program that will make the robot drive forward until it senses darkness, then drive backward until it senses brightness, and repeat

that will make the robot turn toward the black line and then turn away again once the light sensor detects it (see Figure 6.10).

This program is the closest so far to being able to follow a black line. However, the robot doesn't do much more than wiggle itself back and forth in a turning motion at the edge of the line. The robot doesn't make much progress forward in the direction of the line. A slight change has to be made to the program to get the robot to move forward.

The robot needs to start on one side of the line and immediately turn toward it and go forward a little bit at the same time. This kind of turn can be accomplished by turning the outer wheel faster than the inside wheel of the robot or by stopping the inside motor altogether (see Figure 6.11).

Figure 6.10

A program that will make the robot turn toward the black line and then turn back again when the line is detected

Figure 6.11

The simplest algorithm for line-following

When the robot sees the black line, it will immediately turn back toward the table surface again, and when it sees the table surface, it will turn back toward the line again, and on and on . . . zigzagging across the edge of the black line. You could apply this zigzag approach and begin with the robot on the black line as well, as long as the first thing that the robot does is to turn off of the line and not go straight.

An algorithm that makes the robot act differently depending on whether the light sensor senses brightness or darkness can best be written using a sensor-watcher. The program shown in Figure 6.11 can be greatly be simplified by using a light sensor-watcher (see Figure 6.12).

There are many ways to improve the speed of a Line-Follower. Some improvements are mechanical, and others involve changing the program. A Line-Follower that is speedy is important in a timed competition. Here are some ways to do it:

- **A securely supported swivel wheel:**

  Word spread around the Technology Education classroom pretty fast that using a swivel wheel would come in handy for a Line-Follower robot. A swivel wheel is sort of like the wheels on the front of a shopping cart that can spin around in place if they have to. They allow the shopping cart to make quick, sharp turns that an ordinary car or other vehicle couldn't do (see Figure 6.13). Several suggestions on how to make swivel wheels can be found on page 26 of the *Constructopedia* 1.0 or page 92 of the *Constructopedia* 1.5. It's important that the swivel wheel is held securely in place, too. Some teams found this out the hard way. Their swivel wheel wasn't well supported, and therefore it didn't turn smoothly and efficiently when it needed to, slowing down their robot.

- **Light sensor placement:**

  In addition to using a swivel wheel, it's also important that the light sensor be at the correct distance from the table or ground surface. A good way to find the correct distance is to hold the light sensor at various distances away from the surface from one millimeter to an inch or two and compare black and white. You will find that the

Figure 6.12
The simplest algorithm for line following, simplified

Figure 6.13
A swivel wheel improves the agility and quick-turning capability of the Line-Follower. The sandwich construction holds the swivel wheel in place securely so that the wheel can pivot easily and not drag behind.

Figure 6.14

A faster line-following algorithm can be achieved by turning on the motor on the inside of the turn at a slow speed instead of turning it off altogether.

closer the light sensor is to the surface, the greater the difference between light and dark. It's a good idea to keep the light sensor about a half an inch away from the surface. In the line-following program, you then choose a value between light and dark to help the robot decide between turning toward the line or away from it.

■ **The speed of the inside motor:**
A third consideration for line-following speed is the inside motor. If the inside motor is turned off altogether, the Line-Follower will be reliable but slow. If the inside motor speed is set to a low value, the speed of the Line-Follower will actually double or almost triple. However, if the speed of the inside motor is too fast, the robot will have the tendency to lose the line completely, especially on tight turns (see Figure 6.14).

The Competition

When our Weston teams arrived at the regional competition, we saw that many of the other teams from other schools hadn't used any sensors at all. Many of them were still learning that having the robot navigate the playing field by turning motors on and off for certain periods of time was unreliable. One team from another school had never gotten their robot to travel all of the way around the playing field once. They used the largest wheels in the kit, however, making the robot very fast. During the last few minutes before the competition, that team got very lucky. They kept practicing and changing their program little by little until the robot zipped across the playing field, banged into the far wall, zipped around the corner, and turned at the last second at the finish line for a quick finish. We couldn't believe it.

The competition got underway. Our Line-Follower robots were doing very well, scoring lots of points for making it all of the way around the playing field, and in pretty good time, too, for even more points. During the head-to-head competition, however, one of our team's light sensors got knocked off of the robot, and the robot lost sight of the line. (Let this be a lesson for readers who participate in robot competitions: Make sure your robots are crash-proof. Strengthen any weak parts that might fall off of a robot during a crash.) During the finals, the team with the quick robot using a time program was up against one of our Line-Followers. They both made it all of the way around the playing field, but the quickness of the other robot was too much for the Line-Follower. From the standpoint of scoring, the quicker robot won the competition. From the standpoint of good engineering design and programming, we came out on top.

Advanced Programming

As with the Smart Acrobot, it would be helpful if the Line-Follower were able to work under any lighting conditions. This is especially important in competitions like FIRST LEGO League, where the lighting of the competition room is likely to be different than the lighting in the classroom where the teams practice. When the students got to the FIRST LEGO League competition, everyone had to reprogram their light sensors to account for the lighting in the gymnasium. It would have been easier if the students were able to use variables that accounted for the light differences from playing field to playing field.

A Line-Follower robot is one of the cases of a problem with ambient light interference that cannot be completely solved by mechanical means. With the Smart Acrobot, a box of bricks could surround the light sensor so that ambient light doesn't affect the light sensor. With the Line-Follower robot, this isn't possible. Even if a protective box is built around the light sensor, there will always have to be one open end of the box where the light sensor has to see the table and the black line. This open end can let in light that will differ from place to place.

To write a line-following program that will work under any lighting conditions, it's necessary to use variables. The logic of the program would have to function something like this:

1. Place the robot to the right of the black line. With the light sensor over the white part of the table, record the light sensor value and store it as a variable. This is the "bright" value.

2. If the value of the light sensor is five points less than the "bright" value or higher, turn toward the left.

3. If the value of the light sensor is less than five points lower than the "bright" value, turn toward the right.

4. Repeat.

Five points was chosen as a rough estimate. If the whiteness of the table varies by more than five points, this program won't work. A slightly more sophisticated and reliable program would look like this:

1. Place the light sensor over the white table and press the touch sensor. When the touch sensor is pressed, store the light value of the white table in memory as a variable.

2. Place the light sensor over the black line and press the touch sensor. When the touch sensor is pressed, store the light value of the black line in memory as a variable.

3. Add the light value of the black line to the light value of the white table.

4. Divide that sum to obtain the average light value.

5. Run the standard line-following algorithm using this calculated light sensor value that is halfway between light and dark (similar to steps 2 through 4 in the previous list).

A program such as this one needs an advanced programming environment such as Visual Basic, ROBOLAB, or NQC. Refer to Part V of this book to learn how to write such a program. Making your robot function independently of lighting conditions is a big advantage.

PART III

At Home

The four chapters in this part of the book are projects that are intended for an adult and child or young adult working together. Chapter 7, "Tickle Me LEGO Robot," introduces the concept of taking things apart to find out how they work and modeling them with the Mindstorms Robotics Invention System (RIS) kit. Chapters 8, 9, and 10, "Animal Feeder," "Codemaster," and "Painter," involve working with tools and other materials that do not come in the Mindstorms RIS kit and require adult supervision. Different pairs of adults and children working together wrote the "Animal Feeder," "Codemaster," and "Painter" chapters.

7
Tickle Me LEGO Robot

The Tickle Me LEGO robot is an example of taking a toy apart to find out how it works and making it out of LEGO.

Inspiration

The toy that caused a craze during Christmas 1998, Tickle Me Elmo™, is an electronically enhanced stuffed animal of the Sesame Street character Elmo. Depending on how many times you press his belly he laughs, giggles, talks, and shakes uncontrollably as if you are tickling him. Tickle Me Elmo™ serves as an example of how you can take something apart to figure out how it works and then make one of your own.

Research: Taking It Apart

The mechanics that make Elmo shake are actually quite simple. A motor with a small 9-tooth gear attached to its shaft turns a larger 63-tooth gear that has a weight attached to its outer edge. Because the weight is attached to the outer edge of the gear, Elmo shakes when the gear turns and moves the weight around rapidly.

Designing and Building

Two main things were needed to make a working Tickle Me LEGO robot: a button (input) and a shaking mechanism (output). Because the shaking mechanism has a big effect on what the robot will look like, it was a good place to start. First, the RCX was placed upright and the motor connected on the bottom, facing downward, just as it is inside of Tickle Me Elmo™.

    The first test was to compare the speed of the Elmo motor with the LEGO motor. With the LEGO motor geared down in a similar fashion to the Elmo motor, a fair comparison can be made. A black connector peg placed on the 40-tooth gear helps to count rotations (see Figure 7.1). With the 8-tooth gear on the LEGO motor turning a 40-tooth gear, the Elmo motor is a lot faster! Placing the 40-tooth gear directly onto the motor shaft, however, matched the speed of the Elmo motor fairly well.

Figure 7.1

A test to compare the speed of the Elmo motor to the LEGO motor

■ ■

LEGO Aside:
The Inside of the Gear Motor

The main reason that the LEGO motor is slower than the Elmo motor is that it's already geared down on the inside! (See Chapter 4 for a discussion of the physics of gearing down.) Figure 7.2 shows what the inside of the LEGO motor looks like.

    The shaft of the motor has a 10-tooth gear. The 10-tooth gear is meshed with a 44-tooth gear. The 44-tooth gear is therefore turning approximately four times slower than the motor shaft. The 44-tooth gear also has a 12-tooth gear on the same shaft. This 12-tooth gear meshes with a hollow 37-tooth gear that fits over the motor shaft without touching it. The hollow 37-tooth gear is attached to the LEGO axle that sticks out of the plastic casing around the motor. The result of the 12-tooth gear meshing with the 37-tooth gear is that the motor speed is further slowed down approximately by another factor of 3. Ultimately, the motor shaft has been slowed down by a factor of 12 altogether.

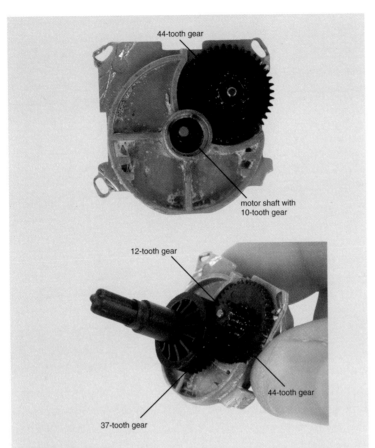

44-tooth gear

motor shaft with
10-tooth gear

12-tooth gear

37-tooth gear

44-tooth gear

Figure 7.2
*The inside of the LEGO motor, top view (top) without axle and side view
(bottom) with axle attached*

In summary:

- The 10-tooth gear on the motor shaft turns a 44-tooth
  gear next to it. The motion is slowed down by a factor of
  approximately 4.

- The 44-tooth gear has a 12-tooth gear fixed to the same
  axle. These two gears spin together at the same rate.

- The 12-tooth gear is meshed with a hollow 37-tooth gear
  that fits over the motor shaft without touching it. The
  motion of the motor is slowed down by approximately
  another factor of 3.

■ Altogether, the axle of the motor that sticks out of the plastic casing is slowed down from its original speed by a factor of approximately 12.

By internally gearing down the LEGO motor, speed is sacrificed for increased strength. The older LEGO motors are a lot faster but always must be geared down externally if strength is needed (see Figure 7.3). The original LEGO motor is very fast but not very strong. There is no internal gearing in this older motor, making its maximum speed 4,200 revolutions per minute (RPM). The maximum speed of the gear motor is 350 RPM, which is 12 times slower. For mobile, autonomous robotics applications, where the motors are used to move the heavy RCX around, gearing down the motors internally makes a lot of sense.

■■■■■■■■■■■■■■■■■■■■■■■■■■■■■

Figure 7.3

The original LEGO motor is very fast but not very strong.

The next challenge was to think of something to use as a weight. A penny was found to be about the same diameter as the weight that the Tickle Me Elmo™ designers used. A balancing scale made out of LEGO was used to determine how many pennies are necessary to achieve the desired weight. The weight on the end of the Elmo gear weighs about the same as ten pennies. Taping the pennies with masking tape makes them stay together as one unit. The 2x2 angle plates make a good housing for the pennies. The taped pennies might have stayed inside of the housing by friction alone, but I added some extra masking tape just in case (see Figure 7.4).

To attach the pennies to the 40-tooth gear, I remembered an old trick that my friend Fudd had showed me for attaching plates to gears—using four of the gray connector pegs with knobs (see Figure 7.5).

Once the weight was attached to the 40-tooth gear and the 40-tooth gear attached directly to the motor, the shaking mechanism was ready to test. When the RCX was held upright, it shook just like Tickle Me Elmo™! As always happens though, the next challenge was just around the corner. A housing was

Figure 7.4

Ten pennies are equivalent to the weight used in Elmo.

Figure 7.5
The gray connector pegs with knobs connect the plates to the 40-tooth gear.

Figure 7.6
A housing built from beams, plates, and connector pegs protects the spinning weight.

needed to protect the spinning weight, similar to the plastic container inside of Tickle Me Elmo™. A protective housing can be built around the motor and spinning weight out of beams, plates, and connector pegs (see Figure 7.6).

The last task was to add a touch sensor and big button to the contraption to finish the mechanics. Using an axle and two green 1x2 bricks with cross holes, the touch sensor was mounted facing outward from the belly of the robot (see Figure 7.7). The 6x10 gray plate serves well as the face of a big button. LEGO doesn't include springs in the Robotics Invention System kit, however, so it wasn't possible to make something that exactly matches what was inside of Tickle Me Elmo™.

When making something with LEGO that requires a spring, a rubber band usually can be used instead. Rubber bands, like springs, return to their original shape after they've been stretched out, but springs have the additional capability of returning to their original position after being *pushed in*. The springs in the button on Tickle Me Elmo™ take advantage of this pushed-in feature. If you push on a rubber band, however, not much happens! What is needed is a mechanism where a rubber band would get stretched out when the button was pushed in toward the touch sensor, and then returned to its original position away from the touch sensor.

A bump sensor was made by attaching beams to the 6x10 plate (see Figure 7.8). Gray half-beams on top of a 1x10 beam allows the bumper to slide in and out of a set of 1x10 beams with ease. Connector pegs are placed on the 1x10 sliding beam as a stopper and a holder of the rubber band. Eyeballs can be made for the Tickle Me LEGO robot with the white

Figure 7.7
The touch sensor is mounted facing outward on the belly of the robot.

Figure 7.8
A bump sensor is made using gray half-beams to allow the beams to slide back and forth.

Figure 7.9
The Tickle Me LEGO robot

parabolas and 2x2 round plates to make it complete (see Figure 7.9).

The bump sensor can be tested with built-in program 2. Program 2 turns off motor A when touch sensor 1 is pressed. I initially noticed that the motor wasn't turning off. The yellow part of the touch sensor was fitting directly inside of the holes in the back of the gray plate and wouldn't get pushed in! This problem was solved by attaching a 1x4 gray plate to the middle of the back of the large plate.

Programming and Testing

In the store, Tickle Me Elmo™ shakes and laughs when you press his belly. When you get him home and remove the tag in his back, however, he acts differently. With the tag removed, he laughs after the first press, laughs and talks after the second press, and shakes and laughs after three presses. The great thing about the Tickle Me LEGO robot is that it can be *programmed* to do different things each time its tummy is pressed!

Start with a simple program. This first program (see Figure 7.10) makes the Tickle Me LEGO robot shake and make a beep sound whenever the touch sensor is pressed.

Figure 7.10
The first program for the Tickle Me LEGO robot

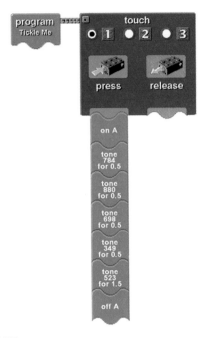

Figure 7.11
A modified first program for the Tickle Me LEGO robot plays a song when the button is pressed.

Instead of just beeping, playing a song is more fun (see Figure 7.11).

Mathematical and Scientific Aside: Making Music

Figuring out how to get the RCX to play your favorite tune in RCX Code can be tricky. It can be a lot easier, however, if you know some of the math and science of music. First, let's discuss the science.

The numbers in the program in Figure 7.11 under the word "tone" represent *frequencies*. Frequency is a word used when measuring how fast something vibrates or moves back and forth. If something moves back and forth in one second, it's said to have a frequency of 1, or 1 Hertz (named after

Heinrich Hertz). Frequencies are used when talking about sound because sound is actually created by air molecules vibrating back and forth. By the looks of the numbers in the program, they vibrate back and forth pretty quickly—up to thousands of times in one second. When the RCX creates a sound with its speaker, it's making something vibrate back and forth. The vibration of that mechanism makes the air vibrate. The vibration of the air molecules spreads outward to the other air molecules around it until it eventually reaches the air inside of your ears, and you hear it as a sound. The higher the frequency, the higher the tone, or pitch, you hear. The number underneath the frequency is the duration, or how long (in seconds) the tone lasts.

So far I've explained where the numbers come from, but I haven't told you how to figure out which numbers correspond to which notes. One way to figure out which numbers correspond to which notes on a piano (A, B, C#—C sharp—and so on) is to look them up in a table or a chart, such as the one in Appendix B. This isn't always possible, however. What if you don't have the chart in front of you, and you desperately need to program a song into the RCX? By just remembering a few numbers (instead of lots and lots of numbers), you can create your own chart.

The first number that you have to remember is that the note A is 440 Hertz. "A 440" is a standard that many musicians use. The second number to remember is 1.059. By multiplying A 440 by 1.059, you get about 466 Hertz, which is A#, the next note higher than A. By applying this pattern, or algorithm, over and over again, you can create the entire table of frequency values for notes. To get the notes below 440, divide by 1.059 instead of multiply.

This algorithm works because of the way our ears work. We hear a similar quality between notes when they vibrate in a similar kind of way. When one note is exactly twice the frequency of another note, for example, we call that an *octave*.

One note that is an octave higher than C, for example, will also be called C. One octave higher than A 440 is A 880—twice the frequency. The algorithm for obtaining the frequency of a note one octave higher is therefore to simply multiply by 2. That is a good start, but we need an algorithm to obtain a note that is only one half step higher, not a whole octave.

By convention, musicians have divided the standard octave into 12 half steps. The steps are called *half-steps* because we generally jump between notes in whole steps—A to B for example—instead of A to A#. A to A# is a half step, and A to B is a whole step. A scale—do, re, mi, fa, so, la, ti, do—is made up of steps of whole-whole-half-whole-whole-whole-half, ("do" to "re" is a whole step, but "mi" to "fa" is always a half step). Adding all of these steps makes 6 whole steps in total or 12 half steps.

From the first to the last note in an octave, the pitch, or frequency, has to make twelve identical changes that eventually result in a frequency that is twice the original. If an octave were made up of only three notes—the first, the middle, and the last—we would have to multiply the first note by the square root of 2 (approximately 1.414) to obtain the middle note. By multiplying the middle note again by the square root of 2 (1.414 again), we arrive at a number that is twice the frequency of the first. For example,

A 440 × 1.414 = 622 Hz
622 × 1.414 = 880 Hz

We know that we eventually want to arrive at twice the frequency of the original number. Because we have 12 steps to go through instead of just 2, we need to multiply the original frequency by the twelfth root of 2 to obtain the very next note. The twelfth root of 2 is about 1.059. So the only things to remember are that A is 440 and 1.059 is the multiplier.

■■■■■■■■■■■■■■■■■■■■■■■■■■■■■

Figure 7.12

Two short songs are played when the touch sensor is pressed.

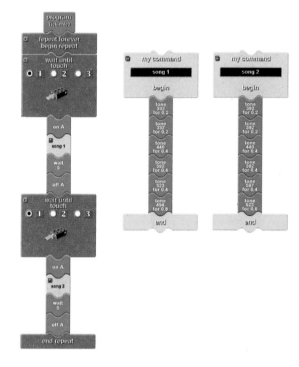

Figure 7.12 shows a program that plays two different short songs when the touch sensor is pressed multiple times.

Further Work

You can do many different things with a Tickle Me LEGO robot. By adding a light sensor, you can make the robot make sounds when somebody comes close to it, even without anyone pressing its belly! This technique was implemented by a girl at Tufts University LEGO Robotics summer camp when she made a musical Pikachu! By using the second motor, different moving features can be added to the Tickle Me LEGO robot. For example, every time the "belly button" is pressed, you could make the eyeballs spin around! The possibilities are endless!

In addition to the Tickle Me toys, think about other types of toys that you can take apart and make with your Robotics Invention System kit. Also think about toys that can be enhanced by combining them with the RIS. For example, do you own a toy castle that could use an automated drawbridge?

8
Animal Feeder

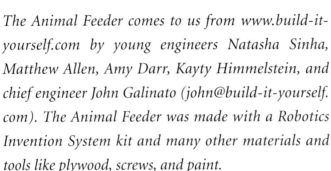

The Animal Feeder comes to us from www.build-it-yourself.com by young engineers Natasha Sinha, Matthew Allen, Amy Darr, Kayty Himmelstein, and chief engineer John Galinato (john@build-it-yourself.com). The Animal Feeder was made with a Robotics Invention System kit and many other materials and tools like plywood, screws, and paint.

Introduction

Build-It-Yourself (see Figure 8.1) is a Web site where boys and girls ages 8 through 16 can download top secret project plans; buy tools, parts, and supplies; join the Build-It-Yourself Hot Shot Inventors Crew; and show off their toy inventions. Project ideas at Build-It-Yourself have you design, invent, and build whimsical remote control and programmable toys mostly from recycled junk—remote controlled trucks, programmable robots, mechanical puppets, and many other whimsical contraptions. A combination of LEGO building elements and arts and crafts supplies make up the supply list at Build-It-Yourself. One such project at Build-It-Yourself is the Animal Feeder.

Figure 8.1
The Build-It-Yourself Laboratory

Inspiration

Lots of different kinds of animals hang out near Build-It-Yourself headquarters in Cambridge, Massachusetts, but nobody knows a lot about them. There are squirrels, pigeons and other birds, and small animals that can always be seen and heard. To study these animals, animal feeders were constructed so pictures could be taken of them.

Making the Animal Feeder in this chapter is a long process. Tools such as saws, screwdrivers, knives, and drills are needed. As an alternative to working with these materials, perhaps you can think of a way to make an Animal Feeder with only the building elements in the Robotics Invention System. When it's complete, the Animal Feeder will have a LEGO picture-taking mechanism and a homemade touch sensor see-saw. The camera mechanism for the Animal Feeder can be adapted for any kind of photobot that you can imagine. The concept of a homemade touch sensor can be adapted for a wide variety of projects.

Figure 8.2
The supporting structure for the camera mechanism

Designing and Building

Follow these ten steps to build the Animal Feeder:

Figure 8.3
The camera clicker mechanism. Building instructions are on the CD-ROM.

1. Set up the camera support piece on the base (Figure 8.2): Attach a 12" x 1" x 1/4" camera support piece to the back of a solid base (10" x 10" x 3/4") by drilling two holes and fastening them together with 1 1/4" sheetrock screws.

2. Build the LEGO camera clicker mechanism (Figure 8.3). The camera clicker mechanism operates in a similar fashion to the legs of the Bug in Chapter 5. The camera clicker is similar to one of the Bug's legs. However, the legs of the six-legged walker don't go straight up and down. To keep the axle of the camera clicker straight up and down, a second blue 0-degree angle element is needed. Keeping the axle straight, however, makes it im-

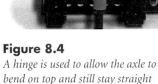

Figure 8.4
A hinge is used to allow the axle to bend on top and still stay straight on the bottom.

Figure 8.5
The front (left) and back (right) of the camera clicker mechanism, using the spiral tubing to make the axles flexible

possible to rotate around the 40-tooth gear at the upper end without bending. There needs to be some way to allow the axle to bend. One solution is to use the hinge plates and hinge tiles together with two green bricks with cross holes (see Figure 8.4). Another solution is to use one of the pieces of spiral tubing cut in half (see Figure 8.5).

3. Fasten the camera clicker mechanism to the camera support piece (Figure 8.6). Drill two holes through the LEGO camera clicker support pieces into the camera support piece. Fasten with two #4 3/4" screws.

4. Add the clicker mechanism sensor:

   ■ Cut a 12" LEGO lead in half. Separate the cut ends of both halves with an Exacto knife about 1 1/2" (see Figure 8.7).

Figure 8.6
The camera clicker mechanism fastened to the support piece

Figure 8.7
To make your own touch sensor, first cut a long wire in half and split the ends.

Figure 8.8
Stripping the insulation off of the wire can be tricky, so do it carefully.

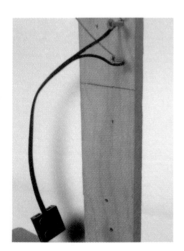

Figure 8.9
When the two wires connect to each other, it is equivalent to the touch sensor being pressed.

■ Strip the insulation off both ends of the LEGO lead pieces (see Figure 8.8).

■ Drill two holes through the camera support piece about 1" apart just below the camera clicker.

■ Cut two pieces of #20 gauge wire about 6" long.

■ Insert the ends of each wire into the camera support holes.

■ Insert both stripped ends of one of the cut LEGO leads into the two holes with the 6" wires.

■ Fasten with two #4 1/2" screws (see Figure 8.9).

■ Thread one wire to the sensor support piece on the camera clicker plunger and bend it around the hole to secure it.

■ Thread the other wire through a hole in the camera clicker beam structure piece near the plunger.

■ Bend this wire so it touches the camera plunger wire at the top of its cycle (see Figure 8.10).

■ Bend the end of this wire so no one will get accidentally stabbed.

5. Set up the fulcrum:
   Attach a 2" x 3/4" x 3/4" fulcrum piece near the front of the base. The fulcrum piece should be lined up with the camera support piece. Drill two holes and fasten with 1 1/4" sheetrock screws.

6. Set up the seesaw piece on the fulcrum:

   ■ Lay a seesaw piece (24" x 1" x 1/4"—could be a sawed-off yardstick) from the camera support piece across the fulcrum piece.

   ■ Mark the outline of the seesaw piece on the fulcrum piece (see Figure 8.11).

   ■ Drill two holes on the fulcrum piece on the outline marks of the seesaw piece. Insert screw eyes into the holes (see Figure 8.12).

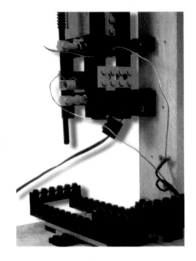

Figure 8.10
Move the 40-tooth gear around to test the point in the cycle where the wires touch each other.

- Lay the seesaw piece over the fulcrum between the screw eyes. One end of the seesaw piece should be about 1/2" from the camera support piece.

- Mark spots for holes into the edges of the seesaw piece that will allow you to insert screws through the screw eyes and into the seesaw piece. Drill the holes but don't insert the screws yet.

7. Set up the seesaw sensor:

- Drill two holes into the base 2" apart near the camera support piece and parallel to the base edge.

- Drill two holes into the seesaw piece 2" apart at one end of the seesaw piece and parallel to the length of the seesaw.

- Cut two #25 wire pieces 3" long.

- Bend the wire pieces into staple shapes (1/2" for the two vertical parts and 2" for the horizontal part).

- Insert one wire staple into the two holes in the base.

- Insert one end of LEGO stripped wire lead into one of the base holes.

- Fasten with a #4 1/2" unpainted screw. The screw must be unpainted so that it can conduct electricity.

Figure 8.11
Making the outline of the seesaw on the fulcrum

Figure 8.12
Screw eyes are inserted into the holes.

Figure 8.13
The completed seesaw sensor

Figure 8.14
Attaching the seesaw

Figure 8.15
The rubber-band helps the seesaw touch sensor return to its original closed position.

- Insert the other end of the LEGO stripped wire lead into one of the seesaw holes.

- Insert the other wire staple into the two holes in the seesaw.

- Fasten with a #4 1/2" screw.

- Bend the end of the wire staples so no one will get stabbed (see Figure 8.13).

8. Attach the seesaw:

- Drill two holes at each end of the seesaw.

- Fasten the seesaw to the fulcrum (see Figure 8.14) by inserting two #4 1/2" screws through the fulcrum screw eyes and into the seesaw holes drilled earlier.

- Insert a #4 1/2" screw into the hole at end of the seesaw near the camera support piece. Drill a hole in the base edge near the camera support piece. Use a rubber band between these two screws to force the seesaw sensor wire to touch the base wire sensor wire. Make the two staple wire pieces touch by connecting a rubber band between the two screws (see Figures 8.15 and 8.16).

- Drill a hole into the middle of a 9" plastic plate.

- Fasten the plate to the outer edge of the seesaw by inserting a #4 1/2" screw through the middle hole in the plate and into the hole at the end of the seesaw.

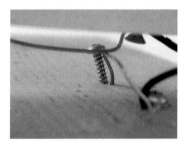

Figure 8.16
The touch sensor when there is no force on the seesaw (left) and when the seesaw is being pressed down (right)

9. Mount the camera:

▪ Attach a 6" x 3/4" x 3/4" piece to a 6" x 4" x 3/4" platform. Place the 6" strip along a 6" edge of the platform and mark a line along the edge of the strip. Drill two holes through the platform between the edge and the strip line. Insert two 1 1/4" sheet rock screws (see Figure 8.17).

▪ Attach the platform to the camera support piece with a 2" clamp (see Figure 8.18).

▪ Place a "throw away" camera on the platform so that the clicker is under the plunger.

▪ Mark an outline around the camera.

▪ Remove the platform.

▪ Build a LEGO platform to keep the camera securely in place. Use wood, paper, or foam rubber wedges between the LEGO boundary pieces and the camera such that the camera can't move (see Figure 8.19).

▪ Secure the camera by adding two 2x8 plates with holes to the base such that one hole sticks out from the base. Drill a hole through the plate holes into the platform and insert a #4 1/2" screw.

▪ Remount the camera and platform on the camera support piece with the clamp. Position the platform carefully so the plunger pushes the clicker when it's at its lowest point.

10. Add the RCX:

▪ Drill a hole into the base near the camera support piece.

▪ Insert a #4 1/2" screw into a 2x8 plate with holes in it and into the hole in the base. Put the male side up.

▪ Fasten the RCX onto this plate. Connect the LEGO sensor lead from the seesaw to sensor 1. Connect the LEGO sensor lead from the camera plunger to sensor 2. You may have to add extension leads. Connect a lead from output

Figure 8.17
The camera platform

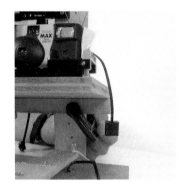

Figure 8.18
Mounting the camera

Figure 8.19
Foam prevents the camera from being able to move.

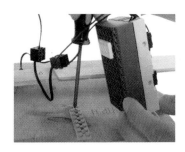

Figure 8.20
The RCX is added.

Figure 8.21
The final Animal Feeder

A to the motor (see Figure 8.20). Now the Animal Feeder is complete (see Figure 8.21).

Programming and Testing

The program for the animal feeder involves the following steps:

1. When the animal takes the food and moves the seesaw, the first touch sensor is released. When this happens, turn on the motor for the camera long enough to take a picture.

2. When the camera mechanism has gotten back to the starting position, touch sensor number 2 is pressed. At this point, shut off the motor.

This program is implemented in Figure 8.22.

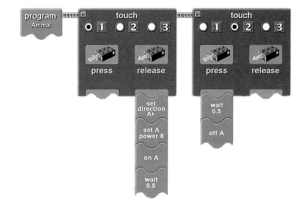

Figure 8.22
The RCX Code program for the Animal Feeder

After the Animal Feeder is programmed, it is ready for testing. Figure 8.23 shows the authors testing their Animal Feeder in the field.

Further Work

Now the Animal Feeder is ready to be taken out into the wild to capture photographs! Here are some more ideas for the Animal Feeder:

Figure 8.23
The authors (left) set up their Animal Feeders and wait for a picture (right).

- It might be wise to camouflage the Animal Feeder so that the animals don't know that it's something out of the ordinary.

- If the animals are taking the food without releasing the touch sensor, try triggering the camera with a LEGO remote control, another RCX, or a touch sensor with a very long wire, while you sit at a safe distance away.

- Try taking a picture when the light sensor detects motion instead of the touch sensor detecting a press on the seesaw.

Codemaster

The Codemaster is a robotic secret message decoder that is made using the Robotics Invention System kit. The Codemaster was designed, programmed, and written by father-and-son team Paul and Julian Kramer.

Inspiration

I gave my son Julian the LEGO Mindstorms Robotics Invention System kit for Hanukkah. The first thing he wanted to build was a car. "Okay," I said, "but what's going to be special about it? Is it just going to run from here to there? You can get a remote controlled car to do that. The whole point of the Mindstorms kit is to show you how to program . . . and not just the kind of program you can put into a remote control car (go straight one foot, turn left, go straight one foot, and so on). What makes Mindstorms unique isn't just the programming, but the sensors—the fact that a program you write can take in information, and that information will alter the behavior of what you build."

Julian came up with some ideas for more complicated cars: cars that move when the light is on, cars that move when a touch sensor is triggered, and cars that follow a path drawn on the floor. But these ideas still seemed too "step one" for me . . . like a simple algebraic expression: when x = 1, y = 2 (when light = on, car = go).

I asked him, "What complicated things in the real world use a light sensor?" (I thought the light sensor to be the coolest thing in the Mindstorms kit—much cooler than the touch sensor because just about every device we own uses touch-activated buttons.) His first suggestions were the hand dryer in the men's room that turns on when your hand breaks a beam of light and the doorbell that rings in a store when you walk in, again, breaking a beam of light.

I explained that these examples were like the light-activated car: light on, something happens; light off, something happens. I told him to really stretch his mind—try to think of something that uses light, but not just the fact that it's on or off. That's when he came up with the idea of the bar code reader. In that case, it's not just the light being on or off, but the duration of it being on or off that's being translated into information.

I thought he was on to something here: Converting on-off light information to binary information that can then be translated into other types of information seemed to be the principle behind a lot of things—like CD-ROMs, hard disks, even the Infrared Transmitter that comes with the Mindstorms kit. I wondered if we could use plastic LEGO building elements and motors, touch sensors, and a light sensor and somehow come up with a replica of a bar code scanner.

Brainstorming

The first sketch we drew was of an enormous bar code, about the size of the stripes on a convict's uniform. The idea was that the user would wave the light sensor over the striped pattern, and this on-off information would cause something else to happen. There were two problems we could see right off: We couldn't control how fast someone would pass the sensor over the stripes, and we didn't know what to do with the information we would gather.

The next improvement was the suggestion that the light sensor be put on an RCX car, which would be programmed to drive over the stripe pattern. (This reminded me of an idea I had had a long time ago: to paint bar codes on highways and equip cars with scanners on their undersides, with an onboard display that would translate the bar codes into positioning information. Cool idea, but global positioning satellites came out soon afterward, and the idea suddenly seemed quaint.) So now we could control the speed, but we still didn't know what to do with the information. Julian suggested that when the sensor read "light," a tone could sound, and in this way, the car could generate Morse code. We both agreed that the beeps would have to be very short, shorter than would probably be possible; and even if it worked, who knows Morse code anymore?

Then I suggested a Ouija board: The car could drive around a Ouija board, stopping on various letters to spell out words. But then where's the light sensor, and what's controlling the car's speed? Julian suggested putting the stripes on a record and locating the sensor on the tone arm. As the record revolved, the stationary sensor would send signals to the car, which would then drive around, spelling out words on the Ouija board. A few problems came to mind. One, the record player turns way too fast—one revolution about every two seconds. Because we would have only one revolution in which to imbed our message, this certainly didn't seem long enough to spell out one word, let alone a message. Two, if the light sensor is stationary and the RCX is moving around, how do we keep the wire connecting the two of them from getting tangled? Three, how can we send six different instructions to the car—left, right, forward, backward, stop, go—from just on-off light sensor information? How can a device spell out a word with only one instruction?

We then thought of a strip of paper on the floor with the alphabet on it; the car would drive forward or backward, stopping and starting, pausing on the letters we wanted in the order we wanted them. But we still had four instructions—forward, backward, start, stop—and we hadn't tackled the first two problems yet. Julian pointed out that "on" and "forward" could be the same instruction, and "off" and "backward" could be the same, too. So if the light sensor saw black, the car would drive forward; if it saw light, it would drive backward. But we still had the same two problems: the record revolving too fast, and the light sensor being separate from the car. I suggested we use a Mindstorms motor instead of the record player because we could have the motor spin as slowly as we wanted. And the long wires in the Mindstorms kit looked long enough to allow the car enough freedom of movement up and down the alphabet path. At this point, the sketch looked like a horizontal disk spinning slowly, with a radial pattern of light and dark sectors, a fixed light sensor peering down on the rotating disk, and nearby, an RCX car slowly driving back and forth. The problem seemed to be the distance the car would continually have to travel—from W all the way to A, back all the way to Y, just to spell the word WAY. Wouldn't it be cool if the alphabet kept repeating, so that after the car drove backward from W to A, it could just keep going backward two squares to the Y? But how many times could we repeat the alphabet, especially when the car was connected to the sensor with a wire leash?

A light bulb went on over Julian's head: Put the alphabet in a circle, just like the code disk, and the car could just drive around and around. Great, but how do we keep the wire from getting tangled? The car had to go, it seemed. It wasn't long before we hit upon the next idea: Instead of a car driving over the letters, why not just have a rotating pointer point at the letters? Now the sensor was fixed, the axle of the code disk was fixed, and the axle of the pointer disk was fixed. The wires would never have to move. Our next sketch showed two horizontal disks, like a record spinning on a turntable with another record queued up above it on the spindle, and the light sensor between the two. This was pretty much the final design; the only difference being that we ended up positioning the two disks vertically so that they resembled the big spinning roulette wheels on the wall of a carnival game booth. This design seemed to have a fun association with it, like the wheel on *Wheel of Fortune*.

Figure 9.1

The Codemaster, viewed from the side

Designing and Building

We set about constructing the thing: two motors driving two gears—on one, a code wheel; on the other, a pointer rotating in front of a fixed alphabet wheel (see Figure 9.1).

We used the worm gear on both motors to slow down the rotation as much as possible. We slowed down the code wheel more than the alphabet pointer because in one revolution of the "code," the pointer would have to make many revolutions around the alphabet. It was decided that "light" should mean "rotate pointer" and "dark" should mean "stop rotating pointer." In this way, the pointer could be made to pause on the correct letter, instead of immediately spinning back in the other direction, making the letter easier to read (see Figure 9.2).

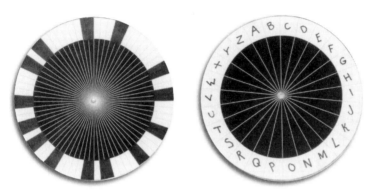

Figure 9.2
The code wheel and the alphabet wheel for the Codemaster

Programming and Testing

After we constructed the device (and decorated it with many little LEGO people in order to make the Codemaster seem really big, like a big clock in a town square), we set about writing the program (see Figures 9.3 and 9.4).

We first wrote a sketch of the program:

1. Turn on the code wheel motor when the touch sensor is pressed.

2. If the light sensor senses light, turn on the pointer motor.

3. If the light sensor sees dark, stop the pointer motor.

4. When the touch sensor is pressed again, stop the program.

Because we wanted the code wheel to spin around only once, we gave the code wheel a protrusion that would trip the touch sensor after a single revolution.

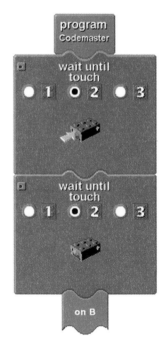

Figure 9.3
The beginning of the program waits until the touch sensor has been pressed before turning on the code wheel motor.

Figure 9.4

The full program for the Codemaster keeps checking the light sensor and turning the pointer motor on when it detects light and off when it detects darkness. When the touch sensor is pressed again by the code wheel, the loop stops, and the motors turn off.

Everything seemed to work, but at this time, the code wheel was just a white piece of cardboard, and we tested the system by manually placing a piece of black plastic in front of the light sensor. We then had to devise a way of printing out a code disk (it couldn't be drawn by hand because we envisioned two Mindstorms owners e-mailing code disks to each other for decoding). We ended up using QuarkXPress to create the code wheel. We simply drew a large circle and then divided it into 36 ten-degree sectors. We randomly placed black trapezoids on some of the sectors, to vary the lengths of the white arcs between the single black sectors. Then, placing the code on the code disk, we calibrated just how many letters would be traversed per ten-degree section. It seemed to be a relationship of ten degrees of light for every letter advanced by the pointer. From there, it was easy to construct a disk that would actually cause the pointer to spell out the message. (The message we tested was: "Let's go Mets.") We tested it, and it worked with about 85 percent accuracy. On the one hand, we were disappointed that the machine made mistakes (sometimes overshooting or undershooting the desired letter), but on the other hand, we had a proof of concept, and it seemed only a matter of detail to improve the accuracy.

Further Work

A lot of the inaccuracies of the Codemaster probably result from the two different motors not spinning at the exact same speed. The accuracy of the Codemaster might be improved if the code wheel and the pointer were driven by a single motor. In addition, an angle sensor or a second light sensor could be used to ensure that the pointer wheel has rotated to the proper place.

Next, we hope to come up with a way to generate random code disks and then substitute "fortune-telling sayings" for the alphabet on the pointer's disk. In this way, someone could ask the machine a question, and the answer would be randomly generated based on the randomly generated light/dark pattern on the code disk.

We knew the thing we built had no practical application, but we were happy to have constructed a device that translated light and dark pulses into human-readable information. We were able to take advantage of the LEGO motors, touch sensor, and light sensor, plus, on the programming side, we learned how to use while loops and repeats. It was a great learning experience.

10
Painter

The Painter is an artistically inclined robot designed, programmed, and written by father-and-son team Tom and Brendon Kellner.

Inspiration

Some of the most interesting tools or machines we've been admiring over the past several years have been computer-driven laser cutters. A friend proudly showed us a computer-driven router that moves in a three-dimensional space 3 x 4 x 2-feet high over a vacuum hold-down table. We once spent many hours on a CAD program entering data to cut a model boat hull; our effort wasn't successful because the software was incompatible with that of the router. On the flip side, we also saw a machine designed for taking the lines off (making a plan) of a model boat hull. The machine is a three-dimensional plotter in the sense that it has a pointer that moves around in a three-dimensional space. The pointer is lined up with the surface of the shape that is transferred to a digital image; the point gets registered digitally to create a surface with compound curves.

We considered making a three-dimensional plotter in which the RCX would move around according to its program in a 3D box using worm gears and/or pulleys. Then the desire for simplicity set in, and we decided to make a two-dimensional mobile robotic plotter if we could find a way for it to leave a trail

Figure 10.1

The RCX Code program for driving in a circle

as it moved. The RCX seemed perfectly suited to drawing geometric designs, and the programming capabilities could easily be set to draw repeating patterns. On several occasions, we had admired the Greek keys of the Roman mosaics at the Worcester Art Museum in Massachusetts. Tom's goal was to make a link back in time to when ancient Greeks, Romans, and Egyptians used repeating patterns to decorate their environments. Brendon wasn't as specific in his goal; he enjoyed the exploration and building.

Designing and Building

Brendon immediately built a robot that ran, stopped, and turned. The robot took several moments to accelerate and often ran too fast and turned unpredictably. Brendon then consulted the *Constructopedia* and constructed the robot with caterpillar treads, which moved slower due to the geared-down treads. We were able to quickly program it to move in a circle (see Figure 10.1) or trace an outline of a box from a couple of inches to 20 feet.

To get the robot to drip paint, some sort of container and valve was needed to allow the paint to drip and not drip as needed. We used a yogurt cup as the container (see Figure 10.2). Brendon tried to build a valve out of LEGO elements, but it kept leaking even with silicon putty around it. He then used a real plumbing valve connected to the yogurt container with silicon putty (see Figure 10.3).

Figure 10.2

A yogurt cup was used as the paint container.

Figure 10.3

Silicon was placed around a plumbing valve to allow the paint to slowly drip out of the yogurt cup without leaks.

Figure 10.4

Water was used instead of paint for testing.

Figure 10.5

A figure eight can be made with the right RCX Code program.

Figure 10.6

With green paint and paper, permanent art is created.

At first Brendon placed the yogurt container on one end of the robot. It was too heavy on that side so he added a counterweight (a spice jar filled with water). The jar combined with the RCX was too heavy, and the robot fell apart. We moved the yogurt cup so that was centered above the treads, and we took the extra jar filled with water out of the design.

When the plumbing valve is turned by hand, liquid slowly drips out of the yogurt container and onto the floor. To test the Painter, we used water instead of paint (see Figure 10.4). Different shapes were made (see Figure 10.5). If it were adjusted just right, the Painter could leave a string of half-inch drops every inch of its trail. With paint and paper, we ran it around on the floor, and it left a trail of drops or puddles all over the place (see Figure 10.6).

Having a robot that can leave a trail of drops behind is fun, but we thought it would be even more fun if the robot could open and close its own valve so that it could decide when to paint and when not to paint. We decided to use a pulley system so that the belt could slip if the valve got too tight and the motor was still trying to shut the valve. By sawing the large pulley wheel down the middle, we were able to pull it apart far enough to place the copper pipe through its center. With the large pulley wheel attached to the valve, a micromotor could turn the valve on and off with a belt (see Figures 10.7 and 10.8).

Figure 10.7

The valve for the Painter consists of a large pulley wheel connected to the metal valve and a belt that goes to the micromotor. The pulley on the micromotor is small, making the large pulley wheel slow and strong.

Figure 10.8

A close-up of the valve

Figure 10.9

The center of this image shows the copper pipe inside of a 1x8 gray plate at the underside of the Painter.

Figure 10.10

The Mindstorms remote control was used to have the Painter make creations—and messes.

Figure 10.11

It was a lot of fun to command the RCX to draw a design just by pressing some buttons.

We drilled a hole through a 1x8 gray plate to hold the pipe in place so that the yogurt cup wouldn't tip over (see Figure 10.9).

At first we used the Mindstorms remote control to turn on and off the micromotor to allow the water or paint to flow (see Figures 10.10 and 10.11).

The Painter was not without problems, however. With the weight of the RCX, cup of fluid, and LEGO structure, the gears from the motor to the treads kept slipping. We had to keep squeezing the construction back together every couple of minutes of movement. It was often difficult to get the robot to move in a straight line because more friction was on one side than the other. Also, when the Painter rode over its own tracks, it got paint on the treads and left three trails.

Programming and Testing

Programming the movement at first seemed easy: We programmed the Painter to run both tracks at the same power level, and it would go fairly straight for a while. Cutting back the power level on the motor to one side made it turn in that direction tracing the arc of a circle. When we turned off one side completely, the RCX would spin in place. We thought of more complicated shapes that we could program the robot to draw, such as a figure eight or a spiral (see Figure 10.12).

Making a figure eight is almost like making two circles. First the robot makes half of a circle, turns in the opposite direction and makes a full circle, and then turns back again and finishes the first circle. Because the first part of making a figure eight is the same as the last part, it makes sense to use My Commands (see Figure 10.13).

■■■■■■■■■■■■■■■■■■■■■■■■■■■■■■

Programming Aside: My Commands

The second program for the figure eight uses yellow code blocks called "My Commands." A My Command is made up of a series of other commands. Once a My Command is defined, it can be used over and over again in a program, which can save time when you want to do the same set of steps over and over again. My Commands are also useful for saving screen space, such as with the Giraffe and Tickle Me LEGO robot programs, making a program easy to read, and for making new My Commands out of other My Commands! In other programming languages, My Commands are often called *subroutines*.

■■■■■■■■■■■■■■■■■■■■■■■■■■■■■■

To make a spiral, we made a long string of commands to make the robot keep increasing the length of time that it would drive after turning (see Figure 10.14). In this case, we used a My Command to make the program easier to read on the screen.

Figure 10.12
A program for a figure eight

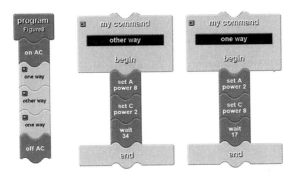

Figure 10.13
A program for a figure eight using My Commands

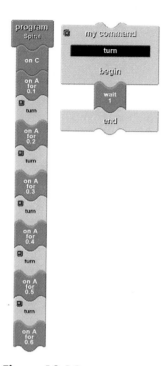

Figure 10.14
The RCX Code program for a spiral

After a while, writing a program for a spiral gets very long. To write a simpler program that will make a good spiral requires variables. (For information on variables, see Part V and the Programming Aside about variables in Chapter 3.) Tom was interested in having the robot paint repeating patterns in addition to figure eights and spirals. He drew a Greek key design on a scrap of paper.

In the program for the Greek key and the spiral, we used My Commands for quicker and simpler writing of complex repetitive steps. The command **square key**, for example, is made up of other My Commands such as **left**, **right**, and **straight** (see Figure 10.15).

We also made some attempts at painting patterns on the road (see Figure 10.16).

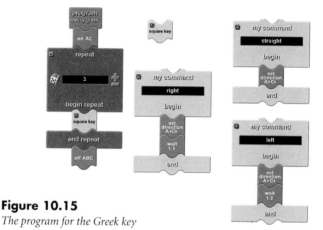

Figure 10.15
The program for the Greek key

Further Work

Tom still wants to program the Painter to draw repeating patterns geometrically and accurately. With time for drying between each color, layers of tracings of the same design would show the variability of the machine and a more complex visual composition. Another option, using the light sensor, would be to program the Painter to follow a flashlight and paint a trail.

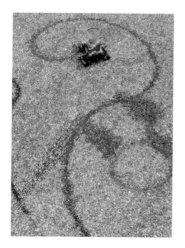

Figure 10.16
The Painter making patterns in the road

PART IV

At Work

The four chapters in this part involve models that were designed and created while their inventors were at work, either on grants that involved the use of LEGO or displaying LEGO robots as freelance work.

11
Kinetic Sculptures

Kinetic sculptures are artistic sculptures that move. Perhaps you've seen a kinetic sculpture in a museum, an airport, a public park, or on television. They are fun to watch and sometimes can mesmerize you for a long time as you try to figure out their motion or just sit back and experience them. This chapter describes four different LEGO kinetic sculptures: a Bubble Machine, a model of a museum sculpture, a robot with a funny motion, and a model of a sculpture from a famous artist.

Yes . . . the way the world is supposed to work.

> —Mitch Resnick, MIT Media Lab, after seeing an early proto-
> type of the LEGO bubble machine, commenting on the fact
> that bubble wands fit perfectly into a LEGO connector peg

EXTRA BUILDING ELEMENTS

Propeller, nine-volt motor, small yellow baseplate (optional), yellow bricks (optional) (see Figure 11.1)

Figure 11.1
The propeller and the nine-volt motor are used in the Bubble Machine.

Bubble Machine

Inspiration

My first kinetic sculpture was a Bubble Machine. The book *Designing Everyday Things, Integrated Projects for the Elementary*

Figure 11.2

The first sketch of the Bubble Machine

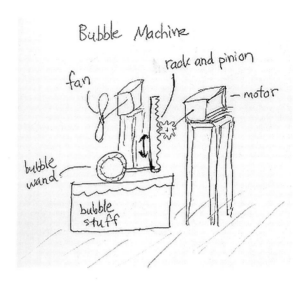

Classroom includes a section on bubbles. In these bubble activities, students are encouraged to investigate and experiment with designing different bubble-blowing devices. Reading this section made me think, "Hey! I can build that with LEGO!"

Designing and Building

After deciding to make a kinetic sculpture, you should make a sketch. Figure 11.2 shows a sketch of a Bubble Machine that has a *rack and pinion* to dip the bubble wand down into some bubble solution and then up to a fan.

A rack and pinion is one of the best ways to transfer rotational motion into back-and-forth motion (see Figure 11.3). It's used in most steering systems. The gear that makes the rack move is called the *pinion*. The rack and pinion was a natural first idea for the Bubble Machine because this is the way that we blow bubbles ourselves: We use our hand to dip the bubble wand down into the solution and bring the wand straight up to our mouths, where we can blow the bubbles. Using the rack and pinion for this motion, however, would be a slow process, and there would be a long pause between one stream of bubbles and the next. The second idea was to use several bubble wands circling around (see Figure 11.4).

Figure 11.3

A rack and pinion translates the rotational motion of the steering wheel into the back-and-forth motion of the tires on a car.

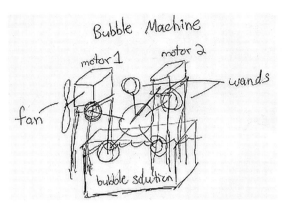

Figure 11.4
The second sketch of the Bubble Machine

Engineering Aside:
Form Follows Function

When first beginning a design, it's tempting to mimic something from the real world as closely as possible. Although in the case of the bubble wands, it probably would have worked, this approach often isn't the best way to do things. One example in history involves the invention of the airplane. Early inventors tried to make flying machines that mimicked birds. Birds get both forward motion, or *thrust*, and upward motion, or *lift*, by flapping their wings. These early flying machines also tried to get thrust and lift from flapping wings. All of these efforts failed. Instead of looking at the particular manner in which a bird flies, the Wright brothers thought about what the different *functions* of a bird's wings are: thrust and lift. They decided to have separate physical components, or *forms*, for each function: an engine to provide thrust and wings (that didn't have to flap because they didn't have to provide thrust) to provide lift. So remember this lesson from history when you design something: It's usually better to think about the *function* first and the *form*, or the physical components, second.

Figure 11.5

A first attempt at making a fast fan involved a compound gear train.

The first problem to concentrate on for constructing the Bubble Machine was the fan; Getting the LEGO fan blades to blow a strong burst of air was going to be a big challenge. Knowing that I needed the fan to go very fast, I first tried to gear up the motor as much as possible (see Figure 11.5). The older, faster nine-volt LEGO motor was used for maximum speed.

Mathematical Aside: Compound Gear Trains

When people talk about gears meshing together, they sometimes use the term *compound gearing* to describe the system of gears. Compound gearing is taking advantage of the multiplying effect of having two gears on the same axle. Compound gearing was used on the six-legged walker described in Chapter 5 and is used on the inside of the gear motor. In the case of the six-legged walker, compound gearing was used only as a matter of convenience to connect one axle to another. In the case of the inside of the gear motor, however, compound gearing allows the motor to be geared down twice in a compact space.

As was discussed in Chapter 4, different-sized gears can be meshed together to create speed with less strength, or slowness with more strength. As we saw with the Giraffe's neck, the worm gear turning another gear is one of the strongest and slowest gear combinations there is by using only two gears. But there are ways to get even slower and stronger (or faster and weaker) gears by using more than one gear on the same axle. Consider the gear train in Figure 11.6.

When the motor turns the first 40-tooth gear (gear A in Figure 11.6) once, the first 8-tooth gear (B) turns 5 times. When the first 8-tooth gear has turned 5 times, the second 40-tooth gear (C) has also turned 5 times, because they are both on the same axle. When the second 40-tooth gear turns 5 times, the second 8-tooth gear (D) turns 25 times. In other words, the overall speed has increased by a factor of 25.

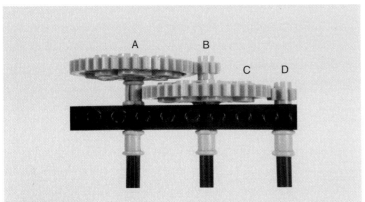

Figure 11.6
A compound gear train with a gear ratio of 1:25 increases the speed by a factor of 25.

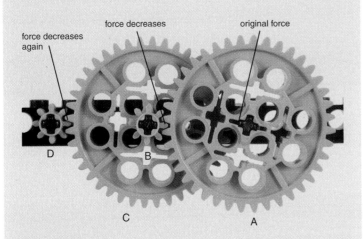

Figure 11.7
The compound gear train has the effect of decreasing the strength, or force, that the turning axle can supply.

We can also examine the forces at various points along the gear train, in a similar manner to the analysis we performed with the Giraffe's gears (see Figure 11.7). The force provided by the motor is first decreased by a factor of 5 at the junction of the first 8-tooth gear, and then it's decreased again by a factor of 5 with the junction of the second 40-tooth gear and second 8-tooth gear. Overall, the force has decreased by a factor of 25, and the speed has increased by a factor of 25. The reverse would be true if the motor were connected to the 8-tooth gear (D), in which case the motor would be geared down instead of geared up.

■ ■

The compound gear train that was used to make the fan turn quickly and move lots of air was inspired by the inside of the Bubble Copter toy (see Figure 11.8).

The way the Bubble Copter works is this:

1. You push hard on the handle of the Bubble Copter, and the wheels start to turn.

2. The motion of the wheels turns a big gear, which in turn is geared up with a compound gear train until it's turning a fan (at the center) extremely fast to blow some bubbles.

Using all of those gears in the Bubble Machine posed a big problem though—weight and friction. There is always friction between two gears that are meshing together, causing them to spin slower than you would expect. The extra gears put an addi-

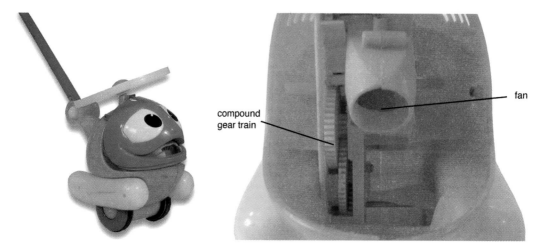

Figure 11.8
The Bubble Copter (left) uses a complicated compound gear train (right) inside of it to get the fan to turn fast enough to blow bubbles.

tional *load* on the motor, causing it to turn slower. With the Bubble Copter, the friction is overcome by pushing hard on the handle. When you try to push the Bubble Copter on the ground, you can feel the resistance caused by the friction in between the gears. You can overcome the friction by pushing harder on the Bubble Copter, forcing the wheels to move on the ground, which then forces the gears to spin quickly. With the Bubble Machine, unfortunately, you can't do that. The LEGO motor can spin only as fast and as strong as provided by the electrical power. The friction and extra weight of the compound gear train of the Bubble Machine fan was causing the fan to turn too slowly to blow a bubble. I temporarily gave up on working on the fan and moved back to the wands.

Getting the bubble wands to move slowly wasn't as challenging as getting the fan to move quickly. While working on making a slow-moving gear train, I also worked on how to connect bubble wands to the gear train. After experimenting with a couple of different all-LEGO bubble wands without success (see Figure 11.9), I cut off the ends of some plastic bubble wands that come inside bottles of bubble solution to use as wands. It just so happens that the cut-off bubble wand fits directly into the end of a connector peg very well (see Figure 11.10).

In the process of getting the bubble wands to move slowly, friction works in favor of the bubble wands. Wanting the bubble wands to move slowly, I geared down the motor as much as possible. The compound gear train from the Mathematical Aside,

Figure 11.9
All-LEGO wands made from beams and pegs or a modified large pulley wheel were tested.

Figure 11.10
The standard bubble wand fits well into the LEGO connector peg and is held in place by friction. Cross blocks and connector pegs with axles were used to connect the wands to the slow-moving 40-tooth gear.

Figure 11.11

A compound gear train is used to gear down the motor for the bubble wands.

Figure 11.12

The LEGO micromotor is the slowest LEGO motor at a maximum 30 RPM.

Figure 11.13

*The **set power** command changes the speed of the LEGO motor.*

"Compound Gear Trains," earlier in this chapter —used in reverse—is the gear train used in the Bubble Machine to make the bubble wands turn slowly and with enough strength to force them through the thick bubble solution (see Figure 11.11).

There are alternatives to gearing down when trying to get something to move slowly. One alternative solution to having the wands spin slowly would have been to use the micromotor—the slowest LEGO motor there is (see Figure 11.12). The micromotor isn't always the best alternative to gearing down, however. While the micromotor is slow, it's not necessarily as *strong* as another motor that is geared down. Before using a micromotor for a certain application, test the maximum strength that is necessary for the micromotor to withstand.

Another alternative for changing motor speed is to change it from within RCX Code with the **set power** command (see Figure 11.13). Unlike gearing down, using **set power** makes the motor spin slower but not stronger. If both motors are set to power 1 on a robot, it's possible that the robot won't move at all, and instead only the humming noise of the stalled motors will be heard. If this happens, it's a sign that too much load is on the motors, and the power level should be higher.

■ ■

Engineering Aside: Pulse Width Modulation

In most cases, such as when very little load is on the motor, using **set power** doesn't have an effect at all. The reason that **set power** has such a limited effect has to do with the way that the RCX controls the speed of the LEGO motors. When the **set power** command is used to lower the speed of the motor, the RCX turns the motor on and off very quickly—over 100 times a second. This is called *pulse width modulation* (PWM). During one of the fractions of a second that the motor is turned off, the motor will keep spinning on its own because of its inertia. *Inertia* describes the property of all things to stay in motion once they are set in motion, unless acted on by an outside force. Because of the inertia of the inside of the motor, once the motor starts being pulsed—turned on and off—the motor quickly picks up enough speed to be close to equal the speed of power level 8. This applies only when little load, or outside force, is on the axle of the motor, however. With a bigger load on a motor, such as when the tires are trying to climb a ramp or go over rough terrain, the motor cannot gain enough inertia to have a considerable speed when **set power** is low. This is proven with datalogging in Chapter 21.

LEGO Aside: Plastruct

I also investigated making a bubble solution dish out of LEGO bricks. On the first try, bubble stuff leaked out of the cracks. Using silicon gel on the inside of the case helped, but there were still small leaks in places. My friend, LEGO Mindstorms Master Builder Anthony Fudd, then told me about Plastruct (see Figure 11.14).

Plastruct is the product that LEGO engineers use when they want a model to stay together. It helped me to make a leak-proof LEGO bubble solution dish. You probably don't want to ever make a robot stay together permanently, but there might be cases, such as with the bubble solution holder, when you need a tight seal. Plastruct is a liquid that you brush on the plastic pieces (see Figure 11.15), and it actually fuses the two pieces of plastic together. It can be found in arts and crafts supply stores.

You can brush on Plastruct as you are building or after something has been built. A thicker form of Plastruct is used for the very large models, such as those found in FAO Schwarz or LEGOLAND.

Warning: The vapors of Plastruct are harmful, and you must use it in a ventilated area, such as near an open window.

Figure 11.14
Plastruct welds LEGO elements together.

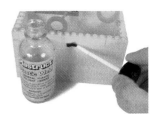

Figure 11.15
Plastruct can be brushed on the outside of LEGO bricks after the construction is finished or between the LEGO bricks when the construction is underway.

Figure 11.16

The gear train for the fan was simplified to a lower gear ratio. The lower gear ratio actually turned the fan faster than the higher one.

Figure 11.17

The motor was moved farther from the propeller to allow the propeller to blow air more efficiently without interference.

Figure 11.18

An axle turns more efficiently when held in place properly.

Figure 11.19

The axle of the propeller was vibrating too much to turn the propeller at a good speed.

After constructing a working system of slowly turning bubble wands, my attention was turned back to the fast motor and fan. As was mentioned earlier, too much friction and weight was in the compound gear train to make the fan turn quickly. The problem was solved by simplifying the gear train. Instead of a compound gear train, a 24-tooth gear meshing with an 8-tooth gear was used instead (see Figure 11.16).

It turns out that the fan actually turns faster with these two gears than with a compound gear train, even though the motor isn't geared up as much. The reason is that less weight and friction is involved with only two gears. When a bubble wand with solution in it was held up to the fan to test it, it almost worked! A bubble started to form in the bubble wand, and the motor had been geared up by only a factor of three. Even though it still wasn't working, "almost" having success made me excited. Next, I moved the propeller out farther along the axle, and I moved the motor backward so that more air could be drawn through the fan (see Figure 11.17).

This helped, but there were still no bubbles. For inspiration and ideas, I found Fred Martin's paper "The Art of LEGO Design" (ftp://cherupakha.media.mit.edu/pub/people/fredm/artoflego.pdf).

"The Art of LEGO Design" offers many tips on good LEGO construction. One topic in the paper is about axles binding, or rubbing, inside of the LEGO beams. It mentions that a good solution to this problem is to put the axle through two beams and brace the beams with a plate to ensure that the axle stays straight (see Figure 11.18). I turned on my fan motor and looked at the axle from the side. Sure enough, it was vibrating (see Figure 11.19). In fact, the vibration was made worse by having the propeller farther along the axle away from the motor. With the fan axle through a beam, and the beam secured to the Bubble Machine, I tested it again (see Figure 11.20).

It blew a bubble! It was one of the proudest LEGO building moments I've ever had, because I had worked so hard for it and solved so many problems. Streams of bubbles came out of the bubble wands every time they passed in front of the fan. It was great fun.

Programming and Testing

The Bubble Machine can be programmed many different ways. One idea is to program it to turn on and off when the touch sensor is pressed (see Figure 11.21).

Figure 11.20
Placing the LEGO axle through a beam stopped the axle from vibrating too much and allowed the fan to spin faster and blow bubbles.

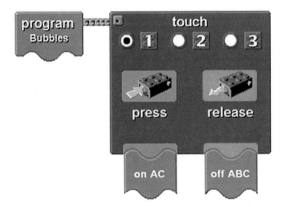

Figure 11.21
A touch sensor-watcher doesn't act like an on-off switch.

The touch sensor-watcher turns on the Bubble Machine when the touch sensor is pressed and turns it off when it's not pressed. This doesn't act like a real on-off switch, however. A better program would be to wait for the touch sensor to be pressed, turn on the motors, wait for the touch sensor to be pressed again, and then turn off the motors (see Figure 11.22).

This new program doesn't work well, however. The reason is because the RCX processes commands very quickly, one right after the other. For example, when the touch sensor is pressed and then released, it takes a small amount of time to press the touch sensor. In that small amount of time, the RCX turns on motors A and C and then checks again if the touch sensor is pressed. If your finger is still on the touch sensor when the RCX checks the touch sensor again fractions of a second later, it turns the motors off. The solution to this problem is to add commands that will wait until the touch sensor has been released (see Figure 11.23).

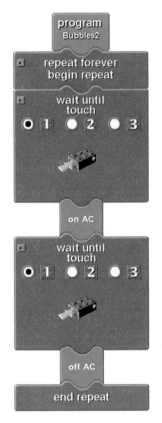

Figure 11.22
A better program for the Bubble Machine that attempts to act like an on-off switch

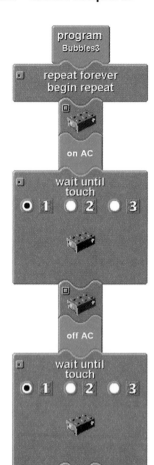

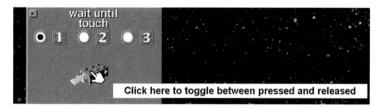

To make the **wait for touch sensor** command wait for a release, click on the image of the touch sensor (see Figure 11.24).

Figure 11.24

To change a touch sensor command from pressed to released, click on the image of the touch sensor.

Besides a toggle switch, more interesting programs can be written for the Bubble Machine. Once during a conference presentation, I programmed the Bubble Machine to turn on when the temperature in the room reached 70 degrees (see Figure 11.25).

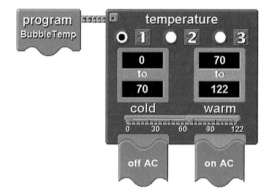

Figure 11.23

Adding commands that will wait until the touch sensor is released before checking for a new action makes the touch sensor act like a real on-off switch.

Figure 11.25

A program that uses the LEGO temperature sensor to turn on the Bubble Machine when the temperature rises above 70 degrees

A program can also be written that turns on the Bubble Machine when someone gets close to it, by using the light sensor. It's possible to write a program that simply uses a sensor-watcher to wait until the light level is above ambient room light and turn on the motors. However, this program doesn't work when the person approaching the Bubble Machine is wearing black clothing. In this case, the light sensor senses a value darker than the ambient room light. What is really needed is a program that will do the following:

- If the light sensor value is below ambient light, turn on the motors.

- If the light sensor value is around ambient light, do nothing (turn off the motors).

- If the light sensor value is above ambient light, turn on the motors.

To accomplish this, the Bubble Machine should sense a change in the value of the light sensor, and not just "do something when bright" and "do something when dark." A sensor watcher in combination with a continuous **check and choose** command will accomplish this "change detection." A **check and choose** command is similar to an If-Else statement, in the same way that a sensor-watcher is similar to an If-Else statement inside of an infinite loop (see Figure 11.26).

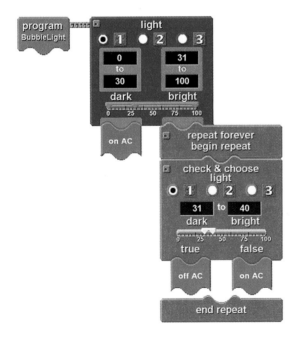

Figure 11.26

A program that turns on the Bubble Machine when someone gets close to it

In the example shown in Figure 11.26, the ambient light level in the room is 35. If the light remains within the range of 31–40, the motors will be off. If the light falls below 31 (someone wearing a dark outfit is approaching) or above 40 (someone wearing a bright outfit is approaching), the motors will turn on.

One cautionary note should be added about the Bubble Machine. It does matter which direction the propeller is turning. If it turns in the wrong direction, the air blows the wrong way!

The Bubble Machine received a nomination to the mindstorms.lego.com Hall of Fame in August 1999 and got second place in its category.

Further Work

Here are some more ideas for your Bubble Machine:

- Make a rolling Bubble Machine on wheels.
- Add a pivot to the Bubble Machine and use the second gear motor to automatically tip the Bubble Machine up and down periodically, so that it can blow bubbles high up into the air and then redip by itself.

Mathematica

In December 1999, while at the Boston Museum of Science for the Massachusetts FIRST LEGO League competition, I saw a kinetic sculpture that inspired me to make a model of it out of LEGO (see Figure 11.27).

Here is the note that was next to the sculpture:

A linkage. Until 1873, most mathematicians thought it impossible to make a linkage where circular motion is converted into straight-line motion without any sliding. Peaucellier was awarded a prize for his solution in that year. A solution that Sarrus had published 20 years earlier (shown here) went completely unnoticed.

The model was an example of how an early designer (Sarrus) figured out a way to turn rotational motion into up-

Figure 11.27
A kinetic sculpture at the Mathematica exhibit at the Boston Museum of Science

Figure 11.28
The linkage system from the Boston Museum of Science realized in LEGO. A worm gear on the motor slowly turns a 40-tooth gear.

and-down motion. Unlike the rack-and-pinion alternative, this transfer of motion happens without any sliding. Some people had said that it couldn't be done, but he proved them wrong. Using a worm gear and the largest white hub, I made a model of this sculpture out of LEGO (see Figure 11.28).

Twisting and Turning

Inspiration

One day while I was thinking about worm gears, I came up with the idea for a model that I call "Twisting and Turning" (see Figure 11.29). I was thinking about how remarkable it is that when a motor shaft is turning a worm gear, another gear can be meshed with the worm gear either horizontally or vertically, or any other way! I wanted to explore a motion that would use gears mounted parallel to the table, because most every other model I had made used gears that were upright.

Further Work

Twisting and Turning moves in a strange pattern across a surface. Here are some more ideas for Twisting and Turning:

- Attach a pen or marker to the robot and trace the path that it travels.

- Program the robot to change motor direction every so often at random time intervals.

- Use the second motor to create another kind of motion on top of the robot that responds to changes in light level.

Figure 11.29
Twisting and Turning is a kinetic sculpture that moves in a random pattern over a table or floor.

Figure 11.30
Arthur Ganson's "Machine with Concrete"

Machine with Minifig

Many artists make kinetic sculptures. Arthur Ganson, for example, has a permanent exhibit at the MIT Museum in Cambridge, Massachusetts, of his kinetic works of art. One of my favorite pieces is "Machine with Concrete" (see Figure 11.30).

In a lot of Mr. Ganson's work, he solders and bends metal in intricate ways, including making his own gears, to achieve the desired movements in a piece. Other works, like "Machine with Concrete," use manufactured gears and can easily be duplicated with LEGO building elements (see Figure 11.31).

Mr. Ganson's design uses 12 pairs of worm gears meshed with 50-tooth gears. The motor turns at 212 RPM. The first 50-tooth gear therefore turns at 212/50 RPM or 4.24 RPM. The second 50-tooth gear turns at 4.24/50 or 0.0848 RPM or 0.0848 × 60 = 5.088 revolutions per hour! At this rate, Mr. Ganson calculates, the last gear will turn around once in 2.191 trillion years!

Figure 11.31
A piece that I call "Machine with Minifig"

■■■■■■■■■■■■■■■■■■■■■■■■■■■■■■

Mathematical Aside:
Major Gear Ratios

Here's how to calculate how long it will take for the last gear in the gear train to turn around once:

> If the first gear pair of worm gear and 50-tooth gear slows the rotation rate down by a factor of 50, then the very last axle is slowed down by 12 factors of 50.
> $(1/50) \times (1/50) \times (1/50) \times (1/50) \times (1/50) \times (1/50) \times (1/50) \times (1/50) \times (1/50) \times (1/50) \times (1/50) \times (1/50) = (1/50)^{12}$

$(1/50)^{12} = 0.0000000000000000000004096 = 4.096 \times 10^{-21}$ revolutions of last gear per one revolution of motor.

212 RPM of the motor $\times$ 4.096 $\times$ 10^{-21} revolutions of last gear per revolution of motor = 8.68352 $\times$ 10^{-19} revolutions of last gear per minute

8.68352 $\times$ 10^{-19} revolutions per minute $\times$ 60 minutes in an hour = 5.210112 $\times$ 10^{-17} revolutions per hour

5.210112 $\times$ 10^{-17} revolutions per hour $\times$ 24 hours in a day = 1.25 $\times$ 10^{-15} revolutions per day

1.25 $\times$ 10^{-15} revolutions per day $\times$ 365.25 days in a year = 4.57 $\times$ 10^{-13} revolutions per year

By taking the inverse of this number (dividing it into the number 1), we can figure out how many years per revolution instead of revolutions per year:

$(1/4.57 \times 10^{-13}) = 2.19 \times 10^{12}$ years per one revolution = 2,190,000,000,000 years for one revolution!!!

The same analysis can be applied to the Machine with Minifig. The speed of the motor can be estimated, or calculated, by attaching an angle sensor and using the data log (see Figure 11.32). See Chapter 20 for details on data logging.

Alternatively, you can watch the first 40-tooth gear spin, figure out its speed, and then multiply by 40 to get the speed of the motor. The calculated speed of the motor in Figure 11.32 is 300 RPM. (The official published speed from LEGO is 350 RPM without any loading.) Using the same method as before, it can be calculated that the Minifig will move one full rotation in 106.3 billion years.

Figure 11.32
Using the data log, the speed of the motor can be calculated with the angle sensor.

■■■■■■■■■■■■■■■■■■■■■■■■■■■■■■■■

Further Work

The next time that you are visiting a museum, playing with a kinetic toy, or passing by a publicly displayed work of art, stop and think if it can be made out of LEGO. The best part about the LEGO Mindstorms system is that the kinetic sculptures that you make can be interactive as well. Not only can your kinetic sculptures move in funny and interesting ways, they also can be triggered to move by the light sensor detecting motion or the touch sensor detecting a press. A LEGO kinetic sculpture can be set up in your house for a party or even in a local art museum.

12
Keep On Moving

Over the years, a number of toys have been sold that can drive around a room, backing up when they bump into walls. This chapter is about a LEGO model that duplicates that same behavior: Keep On Moving.

Inspiration

Matthew Miller is a fellow Mindstorms enthusiast in the Boston area. He is extremely technically savvy and a creative engineer. You can see Matt's creations online at www.mattdm.org/mindstorms/. One of Matt's creations inspired the Keep On Moving robot.

I got a chance to see some of Matt's LEGO creations in person at a local event. I found one model most interesting. It was a bumper car of sorts, but there was no bumper. The robot would bump into something, recognize that it had bumped into it after a couple of seconds, and then back up, turn, and move forward again, all without using any touch sensors. Matt explained how he did it: He put an angle sensor inside of the robot (see Figure 12.1).

Matt then wrote a program for his robot that used the angle sensor to detect when the robot had stopped moving, and

Figure 12.1
Angle sensors, like the one that Matt used in his bumper car, sell for around $16.50 U.S.

then it would back up, turn with rack-and-pinion steering, and move forward again.

This method of making a "bumper car," Matt explained, is better than the typical bumper car that uses touch sensors. Regular bumper cars that use touch sensors can get caught when they bump into a soft object that doesn't provide enough force to push in the bumper. In these cases, the regular bumper car simply gets stuck forever, while Matt's bumper car figures out that it was stuck and tries to get out of the situation.

Designing and Building

Even if you do not own an angle sensor, you can make a robot similar to Matt's. First, begin with any robot body that can move forward, backward, and turn. A robot with caterpillar treads is a good start (see Figure 12.2).

The Torbot from page 39 of *Constructopedia* 1.0 or the Tracks from page 21 of *Constructopedia* 1.5 are both good places to begin. For the purposes of Keep On Moving, the motors need to be able to spin freely when the robot gets stuck on something for a couple of seconds. As was mentioned in Chapter 1, if a robot gets stuck and the motors get locked in position while they are trying to spin, the batteries will drain quickly. Unfortunately, neither the Torbot nor the Tracks in the *Constructopedia*s have this important feature. One way to ensure that the motors will be able to spin freely if the robot is stuck is to use belts and pulley wheels (see Figure 12.3).

Figure 12.2

A robot with treads is a strong and durable robot that can go forward, backward, and turn in place.

Figure 12.3

If the robot gets stuck, having belts and pulleys enables the motor to spin freely. When one pulley wheel gets stuck, the pulley closer to the motor will be able to keep spinning, and the belt will slip over both of them.

In this case, the bigger pulley will get stuck if the treads get stuck, while the belt, the smaller pulley wheel, and the motor will still be able to spin freely. In RIS 1.5, the white clutch gear can also be used instead of using belts and pulleys. The center of the white clutch gear can still turn even when the teeth of the gear are stuck (see Figure 12.4).

Figure 12.4
The clutch gear is found in RIS 1.5.

■■■■■■■■■■■■■■■■■■■■■■■■■■■■■■■■

Scientific Aside: Torque

You may have noticed "2.5–5.0 N cm" written on the side of the clutch gear. This stands for "2.5 to 5.0 Newton[1] centimeters." A Newton centimeter is a measure of *torque*, which is the ability of a force to cause something to turn. This writing on the side means that when this clutch gear must turn something heavy, or when there is a lot of friction, the clutch gear won't be able to handle the load somewhere between 2.5 and 5.0 Newton centimeters' worth of torque. When the torque reaches this level, the inner and outer parts of the gear will turn independently of each other. If the teeth of the gear are stuck, the inner part of the gear will keep turning, and if the axle is stuck, the outer part of the gear will keep turning.

A torque is a "Newton centimeter" because two factors are involved in the ability to cause something to turn. The first factor is the force that is applied to something, which can be measured in Newtons. The second factor is the distance away from the center of the object that is turning, which can be measured in centimeters.

Torque, the ability to cause rotation, is affected by force *and* distance.

---

1. A *Newton* is a unit of measurement for force, just like the British unit of pounds. We usually think of pounds as a measurement of how much something weighs. Weight is also a force. Weight is the measurement of how much force we exert on the earth, and the earth exerts on us, because of the existence of gravity.

Torque = Force × distance

Why didn't they just print the maximum force on the side of the gear instead of the maximum torque[2]? Here's an example that explains why. First, calculate the maximum force that the clutch gear can take. The teeth of the white clutch gear are approximately one centimeter away from the center of the gear. Therefore, we can say that the teeth get stuck and the gray clutch spins when the clutch gear is trying to use between 2.5 and 5 Newtons of force to turn something.

2.5–5.0 Newtons × 1 centimeter = 2.5–5.0 Newton centimeters

The edge of the axle, on the other hand, is approximately a fourth of a centimeter away from the center of the gear. Therefore, we can say that the white part of the gear spins outside of the inner gray part of the gear when the force acting on the edge of the axle is between 10 and 20 Newtons.

10–20 Newtons × 0.25 centimeters = 2.5–5.0 Newton centimeters

The maximum force that causes the clutch gear to take effect is different depending on whether the force is applied at the axle or at the edge of the gear. The maximum torque, however, is the same for both. This is probably why the print on the side of the gear concerns torque and not force. It is easier just to print one number range.

---

2. It would be more accurate to say that torque equals the force acting in a direction perpendicular to the edge of the gear or other body times distance.

■■■■■■■■■■■■■■■■■■■■■■■■■■■■■■■

The next step is to make your own angle sensor using the light sensor and a half-black half-white circle. A circle with 1 5/8-inch diameter is roughly the same size as the 40-tooth gear. Half of a white piece of paper can be colored black with a magic marker, in a similar fashion to the wheel made for the Ac-robot in Chapter 3, or a painting program on a computer can be used (see Figure 12.5).

A hole must be punched in the center to accommodate a connector peg or axle. The spinning motion of one of the motors then must be transferred to the motion of the black-and-white wheel through a pulley or clutch gear. In Figure 12.6, where the treads have been removed for clarity, two crown gears transfer the motion from the pulley wheel to the 40-tooth gear. The light sensor then rests on top of the RCX and is aimed at the black-and-white wheel.

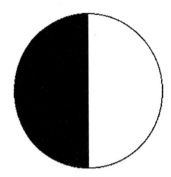

Figure 12.5
When photocopied, this wheel will fit over the 40-tooth gear.

Figure 12.6
Making an angle sensor out of a light sensor and a black-and-white wheel

Programming and Testing

The program for the Keep On Moving robot has three tasks that execute simultaneously. The first task starts a timer and then turns on the motors to make the robot drive forward (see Figure 12.7).

The second task, the timer-watcher, keeps track of how long it has been since the light sensor has seen the black part of the wheel. When the timer reaches two seconds, the robot backs up for one second, turns for one second, and then drives forward again after resetting the timer to zero (see Figure 12.8).

The third and last task is the light sensor-watcher (see Figure 12.9). When the light sensor senses the black side of the

Figure 12.7
The first task makes the robot drive forward.

Figure 12.8

When the timer reaches two seconds, the robot backs up, turns, and drives forward again.

wheel, it resets the timer. Because of the way the light sensor-watcher works, the timer isn't continually reset the entire time that the light sensor senses the black half of the wheel. The timer is reset only when the light sensor changes from the white half to the black half. Meanwhile, if the timer reaches two seconds before the light sensor detects the change, then the robot assumes that it is stuck and backs up and turns (see Figure 12.10).

Further Work

Here are some ideas for using or enhancing your Keep On Moving robot:

- Add a touch sensor for an extra, quicker obstacle detector. The black-and-white wheel then becomes a backup obstacle detector.

- Design a maze of obstacles for Keep On Moving to navigate.

- Alter the program such that after backing up, Keep On Moving randomly chooses between turning to the left or to the right. (Hint: After backing up straight, use a **repeat random** between 1 and 2, with only an **add to counter** inside of it, followed by a **check and choose** counter between 1 and 1.)

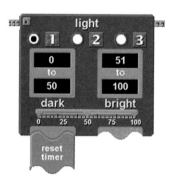

Figure 12.9

The light sensor-watcher resets the timer every time the light sensor sees the black part of the wheel again.

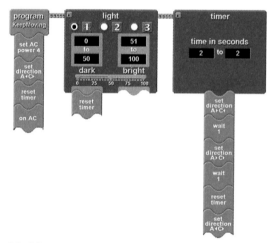

Figure 12.10

The entire program with all three tasks for Keep On Moving

13
Flashlight
Follower

*Most light-seeking robots move slowly, scanning the
area for the brightest region and then moving toward it.
The Flashlight Follower is not like most light-seeking
robots. The Flashlight Follower responds quickly to
changes in the position of a flashlight beam on the floor,
and is easy to build and to program.*

Inspiration

The idea for making a Flashlight Follower robot came from
watching kids make Line-Follower robots at summer camp at
Tufts University. During the line-following activity, we ran into
a problem. Some campers wanted to use their robots in the hallway where a dark rug covered the floor. They were having trouble programming the light sensor to tell the difference between
the black electrical tape and the rug. To solve this problem, we
found some white electrical tape. The kids were then able to
program their Line-Follower robots with ease.

    The white tape gave me an idea. If somebody were to pro-
gram a robot to follow a white line of tape on a dark rug, then
how about the spot created by a flashlight beam on the rug? The
advantage of a flashlight over tape is that the object that the robot

is following is not fixed—you can keep changing where the spot is by waving the flashlight around, and you can make the robot follow it.

Designing and Building

A robot with treads was the first model of the Flashlight Follower. Building ideas came from the *Constructopedia*. The light sensor was placed on the robot with an angle plate (see Figure 13.1).

Using the program for the Line-Follower robot (see Figure 13.2), I tested the robot with the flashlight, with very little success.

Figure 13.1
The first model of the Flashlight Follower used treads.

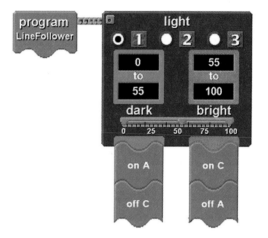

Figure 13.2
At first, the program for the Line-Follower robot was used for the Flashlight Follower.

At this point, the biggest problem with the Flashlight Follower was that it could lose the flashlight spot very easily if I wasn't careful. When the light sensor no longer detected the flashlight spot, I would have to wait a few seconds for the robot to spin around in a large circle before I could aim the flashlight at one side of the light sensor again. There clearly had to be a different solution.

I thought that one possible solution would be to make a robot that quickly turns in place, scanning back and forth in a small arc while looking for the light, but not moving forward or turning all of the way around. The robot would move forward only when it is definitely near the light. This seemed like a good solution.

Construction began for this new idea by putting the two motors in the middle of the underside of the RCX with the yellow hubs and medium-sized tractor tires attached. I had seen this configuration before on the LEGO Dacta Bumper Car model, and I remembered that it could turn around in place very fast, because the motors were in the center of the RCX (see Figure 13.3).

Figure 13.3
The LEGO Dacta Bumper Car, designed for the Amusement Park kit

After adding two layers of bricks and beams, I attached a skid plate attached to a 1x2 brick to either end of the underside of the RCX for balance. Last, I used an angle plate and a 2x8 plate to attach the light sensor to one side of the RCX (see Figure 13.4).

Figure 13.4
A new Flashlight Follower robot that could make a tight turn in place

Programming and Testing

The first step in writing the light-scanning program was to find out how long it took for the robot to sweep out a good area to search for the flashlight spot. After experimenting with different wait times, I decided that 3/10 second at the slowest speed resulted in a pretty good area for the robot to sweep out back and forth in a short amount of time (see Figure 13.5). The time and speed varied depending on whether the robot was operating on a smooth or carpeted surface.

Next, I wanted to incorporate the light sensor into the program. If the robot encountered the flashlight spot while it was scanning, I wanted the robot to react by driving forward (see Figure 13.6). When running this program, the robot did not react to the flashlight. Because of the way RCX Code works, the action underneath a sensor-watcher is performed only once if the condition doesn't change. Merely switching the direction of the motors momentarily was not enough to make the robot drive straight. Instead, the robot needed to be driving straight as long as it still saw the flashlight, until the spot was lost. A

Figure 13.5
A program that causes the robot to sweep back and forth in place in a small arc

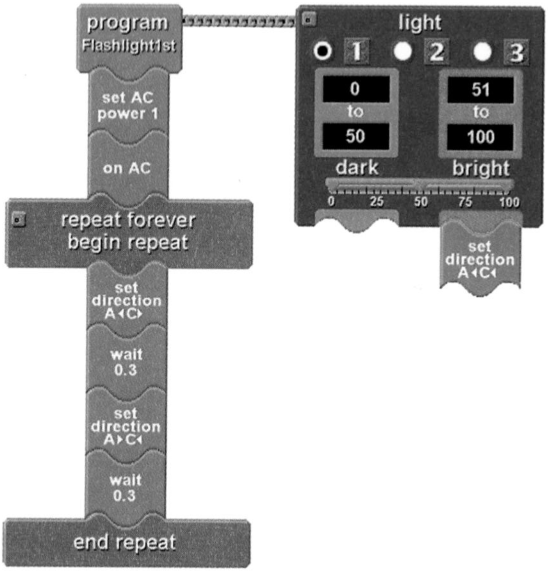

Figure 13.6
Using the light sensor-watcher to make the robot drive straight when it sees the flashlight

Programming Aside: The Repeat While Loop

The final program for the Flashlight Follower robot used a repeat while stack controller. The repeat while stack controller executes the commands that are inside of the loop repeatedly as long as a certain condition is true. In the case of the Flashlight Follower, that condition is that the light sensor value is bright. This makes the loop into a *repeat while light* loop. In other programming languages, a *repeat while* loop is just called a *while loop*. When used in combination with a sensor-watcher, *repeat while* loops turn the sensor-watcher into an If-Else statement inside of an infinite loop.

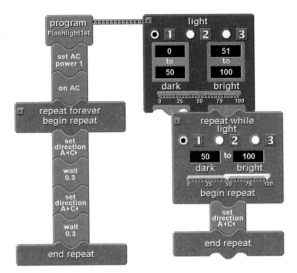

Figure 13.7
The final Flashlight Follower program

repeat while loop was inserted into the program to provide this function (see Figure 13.7).

Now the Flashlight Follower worked excellently. When the robot does not see the flashlight, it scans back and forth in a small arc. When the robot does see the flashlight, it drives forward until losing the light. This simple algorithm enables the robot to respond quickly to changes in the direction of the flashlight spot, making it a very efficient and fast Flashlight Follower.

Further Work

Here are some ideas for the Flashlight Follower:

- Play a game with a friend and a second flashlight. Start with the Flashlight Follower at an even distance between you, faced sideways. The object of the game is to make the robot come to you by directing it with your flashlight.

- Try using colored bulbs or color filters over a regular flashlight to create spots with different colors. Program the Flashlight Follower to react differently to different colors (play different tones, follow or don't follow, and so on).

- Put a second light sensor on the other side of the robot, so that the Flashlight Follower can respond differently to either light sensor.

- Make a second robot that holds a bright flashlight aimed down at the floor behind it. The Flashlight Follower robot will then follow the second robot.

- Add a touch sensor bumper to the Flashlight Follower so that it can avoid obstacles as well as follow a light.

Advanced Programming

Like the Smart Acrobot and the Line-Follower robot from FIRST LEGO League, the Flashlight Follower is a robot that can benefit from variables. In the beginning of the Flashlight Follower program, the light sensor value of the floor can be recorded. The robot can then be programmed to move only when a higher value has been reached. For an example of such a program, read Part V of this book.

14

RCX-to-RCX Communication

RCXs can communicate with each other with infrared (IR) messages. With more than one RCX, two robots can be programmed to send messages to each other and perform different actions depending on the messages they receive. If you do not want to purchase a second Robotics Invention System (RIS) or do not have a friend with an RIS, a second RCX can be purchased separately. In this chapter, two different communication projects are presented: IR Tag and Remote Control.

IR Tag

Inspiration

When I was younger, there was a toy called Laser Tag that you could play with your friends. It included a gun that sent an infrared signal across the room, and an infrared receiver was implanted inside of a vest. If the gun was "fired" toward the vest, then the person wearing the vest was "hit." Laser Tag is a game that can be copied with two RCXs.

Designing and Building

Laser Tag can be imitated with two RCXs, two touch sensors, and a friend. Here is one possibility for a set of rules:

- A touch sensor is used to send a unique IR message.

- Receiving your own IR message does not count as a "hit."

- The first two times that your RCX is "hit" by an opponent, you play a beeping sound.

- After the third time you're hit, you play a "dead" sound, and you're out of the game.

Programming and Testing

Figure 14.1 shows the RCX Code program for RCX 1.

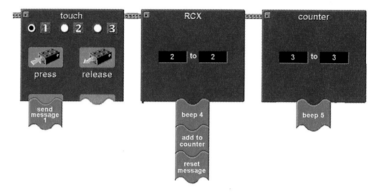

Figure 14.1
A program that sends a message when the touch sensor is pressed and responds with "dead" or "alive" beeping sounds when a message is received from RCX 2

Note: *Make sure that only one RCX is turned on at a time when programming multiple RCXs, or communication errors may result.*

When the touch sensor is pressed, a message 1 is sent out of the RCX's infrared transmitter. When a number 2 is received from RCX 2, a beeping "hit" sound is made, and the counter is increased by 1. Because of the way RCX Code works, the message must be reset so that the RCX will perform the same actions if another identical message from RCX 2 is received. After the counter reaches 3, a "dead" sound is played. The program for RCX 2 looks identical to the program shown in Figure 14.1, except that the RCX sensor-watcher would say "1 to 1" instead of "2 to 2," and it would **send message 2** instead of **send message 1** when the touch sensor is pressed.

There are a couple of problems with this program. The first problem is that after RCX 1 is "dead," it can still send out IR messages. To prevent this from happening, the touch sensor-watcher must be modified (see Figure 14.2).

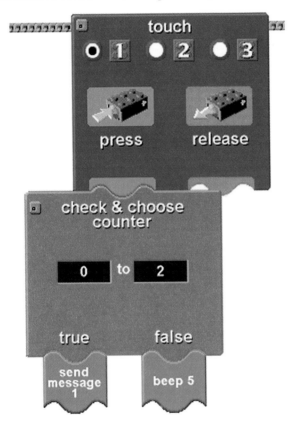

Figure 14.2
A check & choose counter in combination with the touch sensor-watcher makes sure that the RCX cannot send an IR message when it is "dead."

With this modified program, the RCX checks to see if the counter is between 0 and 2. If it is, then an IR message is sent. If not, then a "dead" sound reminds the player that he or she is out of the game.

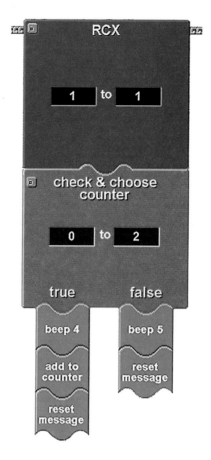

Figure 14.3

A check & choose counter added to the RCX-watcher helps to determine what to do when a message is received, depending on whether the receiving RCX is "dead" or "alive."

The next problem is that after an RCX is "dead," it still makes "hit" beeping sounds if it receives an IR message after the third hit. As a solution, a **check & choose** can be added to the RCX-watcher (see Figure 14.3).

Further Work

IR Tag is a fun game that can be improved in different ways. For example, specific IR reflectors can be set up that bounce the IR messages around the room. A sheet of aluminum foil serves as a good reflecting surface. Second, a motor with a spinning wheel or a lamp can be added to the RCX so that a visual as well as auditory cue indicates when an RCX is "dead." Third, different techniques can be used to prevent cheating. For example, in order for the game to begin, a message from a second touch sensor must be sent and received from both RCXs. Afterward, each player has a certain time in which to run and hide. This prevents players from restarting the program themselves after they have been hit three times.

A warning should be given about IR communication. The distance that an RCX can send a message to another is highly dependent on the battery level inside of the RCX. To make any IR game fair, the battery level of each RCX should be equal.

Remote Control

Inspiration

When thinking about possible applications for RCX-to-RCX communication, I thought of other devices in the world that use infrared communication. The most obvious one is a remote control. Another great use for RCX-to-RCX communication, then, is to make your own custom RCX remote control. Depending on sensor values, different messages can be sent from one RCX to another. The second RCX can be programmed to change actions depending on the message received.

Designing and Building

One kind of remote control can be built using a light sensor and a circle with different shades of gray on it (see Figure 14.4). The circle can be taped onto the side of a 40-tooth gear. When inserted into the side of the RCX with a connector peg with axle, an easy-to-use controller is created. The different commands that you want to send to the second RCX can be written on the back of the wheel (see Figure 14.5).

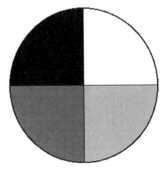

Figure 14.4

A wheel with four different shades of gray can be used in combination with a light sensor to make a four-state Remote Control.

Figure 14.5
The commands that you wish to send to the second RCX can be written on the back of the wheel for clarity.

Programming and Testing

Unlike the programs for IR Tag, the programs for the two RCXs for Remote Control are very different. The program for the Remote Control RCX will only send messages, and the program for the mobile robot will only receive them. Figure 14.6 shows the program that will send different messages depending on the light sensor values.

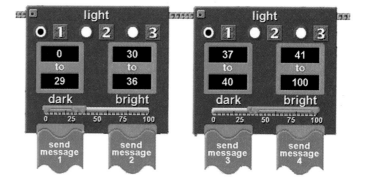

Figure 14.6
The Remote Control RCX will send a 1, 2, 3, or 4 depending on whether it sees the black, light medium gray, light gray, or white part of the wheel.

If the light sensor reading is . . . then . . .

0–29	Black	Send message 1
30–36	Medium gray	Send message 2
37–40	Light gray	Send message 3
41–100	White	Send message 4

After the program has been downloaded and run on the RCX, the View button should be used to test the values of the different colors of the wheel. After the light sensor values are known, the program can be modified accordingly. The ranges provided in the previous table were chosen because the actual light sensor values were those shown in the following table:

Black: 25

Medium gray: 33

Light gray: 38

White: 42

The program for the receiving RCX uses a series of RCX-watchers (see Figure 14.7).

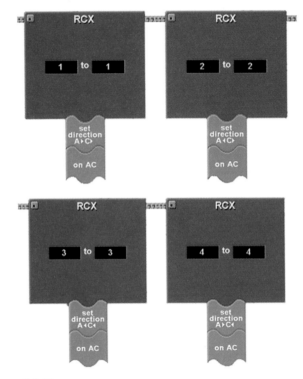

Figure 14.7
The program for the mobile robot that is receiving commands from the Remote Control

The motors are set to drive the robot forward, left, backward, and to the right depending on the message received, as shown in the following table:

0–29	Black: receive message 1	Go forward
30–36	Medium gray: receive message 2	Turn left
37–40	Light gray: receive message 3	Go backward
41–100	White: receive message 4	Turn right

There is one problem with these programs: There is no command to make the mobile robot stop moving. One possible solution is to add another shade of gray to the wheel. This would be tricky, however, because the light sensor values of the four shades are already close to each other. Also, sometimes stopping a mobile robot can require a split-second decision. If the robot is about to drive into danger—at the top of a set of steep stairs, for example—the stop command should be able to be executed quickly. You don't want to be fumbling around with turning a joystick wheel to the proper position to get the robot to stop in this case. A good solution is to add a touch sensor stop button (see Figure 14.8).

The programs for both the sending and receiving RCXs must be modified to incorporate the touch sensor (see Figure 14.9 and 14.10).

Figure 14.8
Adding a touch sensor stop button helps out in times of trouble.

Figure 14.9
A number 5 is sent when the touch sensor is pressed.

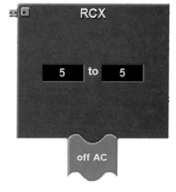

Figure 14.10
When a number 5 is received, the motors stop.

Further Work

The Remote Control can be used for a wide variety of projects. In addition to controlling a mobile robot, the four-color joystick wheel can be reprogrammed to control almost any of the robots in this book. Also, a mobile robot can execute much more sophisticated sets of commands other than "turn left," "go forward," and so on. For example, when a message 1 is received, the robot can drive forward until it sees a dark line (see Figure 14.11).

Another idea is to send "secret messages" from across the room to another person with an RCX. Turning the Remote Control dial to different colors on the wheel can make a motor spin a dial on the receiving RCX that pointed to different secret messages.

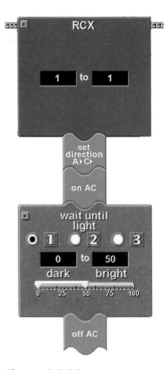

Figure 14.11

Instead of merely driving straight, the mobile robot can drive straight until encountering a dark line when a message 1 is received from the Remote Control RCX.

PART V

Advanced Programming

The seven chapters in this part of the book cover programming topics for the RCX that go beyond the capabilities of RCX Code. Programming features such as variables and data logging are described. Three new software environments are discussed:

1. Visual Basic, one of the possible environments for taking advantage of the Mindstorms Spirit control.
2. LEGO Dacta ROBOLAB, the graphical programming environment for Macs and PCs. A demonstration copy can be found on the CD-ROM.
3. Not Quite C (NQC), a C-like compiler written by Dave Baum for Macs and PCs, available on the CD-ROM.

15

Visual Basic

This chapter introduces you to Visual Basic, the programming environment used with the documentation of the official LEGO Mindstorms Software Developer's Kit (SDK). This chapter will not cover every possible programming command, so it is recommended that you obtain the SDK documentation if you wish to write your own programs in the Visual Basic environment. This documentation, which provides a list of how every command for the RCX appears in Visual Basic code, can be found at mindstorms.lego.com/ or on the ROBOLAB 2.0 CD-ROM.

Introduction

In order to run the Visual Basic examples in this chapter, the Spirit.ocx file must be registered on your computer. This file gets installed and registered automatically when you install the LEGO Mindstorms Robotics Invention System or PITSCO-LEGO Dacta Red Rover software. The Spirit.ocx file also comes on the ROBOLAB 2.0 CD-ROM, although it does not get installed or registered automatically. If you obtain the Spirit.ocx file from this or another outside source, you must place the Spirit.ocx file in the Windows\System directory, and go to the Start menu, select Run, and type "regsvr32 C:\Windows\System\

Spirit.ocx" (without the quotes). To use the Software Developer's Kit, you must have a PC.

The quickest way to begin programming your RCX with a more sophisticated language than RCX Code is to program it with Visual Basic. You do not even need to own a copy of Visual Basic to use it. Microsoft Office programs come with Visual Basic for Applications, or VBA, which is sufficient. To set up VBA to be able to program the RCX, follow these steps:

1. Open Microsoft Word and select Tools | Macro | Visual Basic Editor.

2. Select Insert | UserForm to bring up a Form window.

3. Select Tools | Additional Controls.

4. Scroll down the list and select Spirit Control to place the Spirit Control, in the form of a LEGO logo, on your Toolbox palette.

5. Place this Spirit Control on the Form by selecting it from the Toolbox palette (see Figure 15.1).

6. Save the program in this state as a template for any and all Visual Basic programs that you write for the RCX.

Now that VBA is ready to send programs to the RCX, you can begin to write and download programs. To begin program-

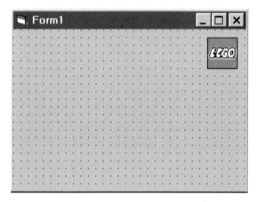

Figure 15.1
Placing the Spirit Control on the Form window allows programs to be sent from VBA to the RCX. This is required of every program written for the RCX.

ming, select Insert | Module. To test a simple program, type the text from the test program that follows into the Module window. This program will turn on motors A and C. The comments, which are the statements after the single quote marks, are not required for the program to be able to download. The name "test" can be any name. Indentations and white space can be changed, but keeping indentations makes the program easier to read.

```
Sub test()
  UserForm1.Spirit1.InitComm        ' Initialize communication
                                    '  with the RCX
  UserForm1.Spirit1.BeginOfTask 0   ' Mark the start of the
                                    '  first task
  UserForm1.Spirit1.On "02"         ' 0 is Motor A, 2 is Motor C
  UserForm1.Spirit1.EndOfTask       ' Mark the end of the first
                                    '  task
End Sub
```

■■■■■■■■■■■■■■■■■■■■■■■■■■■■■■■

Programming Aside: Comments

The sample program that turns on motors A and C makes use of Visual Basic's capability of including comments in a program. Every programming environment for the RCX except for RCX Code allows the use of comments. Comments enable you to add statements about your program inside of the program itself. This is helpful for someone else who may be reading your program. Comments also help you to remember what your program does if you haven't worked on it for a while. It is a good habit to always add comments to your programs.

Different programming environments use different commenting styles. Visual Basic uses the single quote character (') to mark a comment. In Not Quite C (NQC), you place comments after // or between /*and */. In ROBOLAB, you use a text tool to add comments onto the programming window.

■■■■■■■■■■■■■■■■■■■■■■■■■■■■■■■

With the RCX on and the Infrared Transmitter connected, click the Run button at the top of the screen. If all goes well, VBA will download a program into the current program slot.

Press the Run button on the RCX, and motors A and C should turn on indefinitely.

There are several possible changes to this test program to note. First, because every command in the program is a subset of UserForm.Spirit1, the **With** command can be used to simplify the program. A cleaner, neater version of the test program would look like this:

```
Sub test()
 With UserForm.Spirit1
  .InitComm       ' Initialize communication with the RCX
  .BeginOfTask 0 ' Mark the start of the first task
  .On "02"        ' 0 is Motor A, 2 is Motor C
  .EndOfTask      ' Mark the end of the first task
 End With
End Sub
```

Second, without the **BeginOfTask** and **EndOfTask** commands, the program would have executed on the RCX directly instead of downloading it. Sometimes executing a program directly on the RCX is a good way to test part of a program. Third, the UserForm and Spirit1 names can be changed to whatever names you like by clicking on them and editing the (Name) property in the Properties window. The new names then replace UserForm.Spirit1 in the program. Fourth, if an error message ever appears on your screen saying that macros are disabled, go to Tools | Macro | Security and set the Security Level to low or medium instead of high.

Earlier in Chapters 3, 6, and 13, I discussed a light sensor program that could adjust itself to the lighting conditions of the room, which required the use of variables. In Chapter 10, I explained that variables simplify the lengthy RCX Code program considerably for making a spiral. In the rest of this chapter, we'll examine those new programs.

Smart Acrobot

Before rewriting the program for Smart Acrobot to include an adjustment for different lighting conditions, let's examine what the original Smart Acrobot program would look like translated into Visual Basic (see the code that follows). The sensor-watcher is represented by an If-Else statement inside of an infinite loop.

```
' The original Smart Acrobot Program translated into Visual
'   Basic
Sub SmartAcrobot()
 With UserForm1.Spirit1
  .InitComm
  .BeginOfTask 0
  .SetSensorType 0, 3 ' Set Input 1 to be a light sensor
  .On "02"            ' Turn Motors A and C on
  .Loop 2, 0          ' Loop forever
   .If 9, 0, 0, 2, 43 ' If light sensor on Port 1 is greater
                      '   than 43
    .SetFwd "02"      ' Set Motors A and C to the forward
                      '   direction
   .Else              ' or Else,
    .SetRwd "02"      ' Set Motors A and C to the reverse
                      '   direction
   .EndIf
  .EndLoop
  .EndOfTask
 End With
End Sub
```

There are several differences between the original RCX Code program and this Visual Basic program. The first difference to notice is the **SetSensorType** command. In RCX Code and ROBOLAB, it is not necessary to specify which sensors are plugged onto which ports at the beginning of the program, but it is required in Visual Basic and NQC. The other big difference is the use of numbers to represent everything. For example, .Loop 2, 0 marks the beginning of an infinite loop. The 2 indicates that the number of times to loop will be a constant number, and the 0 represents "forever." More will be said later about how to interpret these numbers.

Now that we know how to write the basic program for the Acrobot with Visual Basic, we can use Visual Basic to solve the problem of having different light levels in different rooms. The original program for the Smart Acrobot turns on the motors backward or forward when the value of the light sensor is greater or less than 43. The number "43" may not be the dividing point between light and dark in every room, however. An all-purpose program that works under any lighting conditions requires variables. Here are the requirements for such a program from the Smart Acrobot chapter:

- Record the value of the light sensor at the beginning of the program while aimed at the white half of the wheel or the yellow bricks inside of the box. This is the "bright" reading.

- As long as the light sensor is within a range slightly below the "bright" reading and higher, turn the motors on so that the Smart Acrobot drives forward.

- If the light sensor reading is less than 7 points or so below the "bright" reading, turn the motors on in the other direction. The number "7" was chosen because the difference between bright and dark in the initial tests was usually around 14 points, and 7 is halfway in between.

The following shows what this program would look like in Visual Basic:

```
'Smart Acrobot with a Variable
Sub SmartAcrobot()
 With UserForm1.Spirit1
   .InitComm
   .BeginOfTask 0
   .SetSensorType 0, 3 ' Set Input 1 to be a light sensor
   .On "02"             ' Turn Motors A and C on
   .SetVar 0, 9, 0      ' Set Variable 0 to light sensor value
                        '  on Port 1
   .SubVar 0, 2, 7      ' Subtract the number 7 from variable 0
   .Loop 2, 0           ' Loop forever
    .If 9, 0, 0, 0, 0   ' If the light sensor on Port 0 >
                        '  variable 0
     .SetFwd "02"       ' Set Motors A and C to the forward
                        '  direction
    .Else               ' or Else,
     .SetRwd "02"       ' Set Motors A and C to the reverse
                        '  direction
    .EndIf
   .EndLoop
   .EndOfTask
 End With
End Sub
```

If you are not familiar with Visual Basic, these programs might seem rather confusing at first glance. It is especially confusing because numbers are used to define everything, such as using 02 to represent Motor A and Motor C. This can be fixed by defining some constants for the program, such as OUTPUT_A = 0. After this constant is defined, for example, we can use the word OUTPUT_A instead of 0 when we want to refer to Motor A.

■■■■■■■■■■■■■■■■■■■■■■■■■■■■■■■

Programming Aside: Constants

In computer programming and mathematical terminology, a *constant* is a number that does not change its value like a variable does. Like variables, however, constants use names to refer to numbers. Constants are usually given names that have all capital letters. Constants that are used in a program are usually defined at the beginning of the program. A constant definition such as SENSOR_1=0 at the beginning of a program enables you to use SENSOR_1 instead of typing 0. When reading through a program, it is much clearer to understand what SENSOR_1 means than 0.

■■■■■■■■■■■■■■■■■■■■■■■■■■■■■■■

The file getstart.zip that can be downloaded from the LEGO Mindstorms Software Developer's Kit Web site, mindstorms.lego.com/sdk/ (also on the ROBOLAB 2.0 CD-ROM), contains a data file called RCXdata.bas that is filled with lots of example constants. To use these constants in your program, select File | Import File and then select the RCXdata.bas file. This file is added as a module in your program file, and every constant can then be used in your program. Alternatively, you can define your own constants at the top of your program each and every time you write a new one. Although this takes more time than importing the RCXdata.bas file, I have done that here for clarity. Here are some constants taken from that file and added to the Smart Acrobot program to make it a little easier to read:

```
' Smart Acrobot with a Variable and constants defined
Option Explicit

Public Const SENSOR_1 = 0
Public Const LIGHT_TYPE = 3
Public Const OUTPUT_A = 0
Public Const OUTPUT_C = 2
Public Const GT = 0      ' Stands for Greater Than
Public Const SENVAL = 9 ' Sensor Value
Public Const VAR = 0     ' Variable
Public Const CON = 2     ' Constant

Sub SmartAcrobot()
 With UserForm1.Spirit1
  .InitComm
  .BeginOfTask 0
  .SetSensorType SENSOR_1, LIGHT_TYPE ' Set Input 1 to Light
                                      ' Sensor
  .On OUTPUT_A
  .On OUTPUT_C                        ' Turn Motors A and C
                                      ' on
  .SetVar 0, SENVAL, SENSOR_1         ' Set variable 0 to the
                                      ' value of the light
                                      ' sensor on Port 1
  .SubVar 0, CON, 7                   ' Subtract the number 7
                                      ' from variable 0
  .Loop CON, 0                        ' Loop forever
   .If SENVAL, SENSOR_1, GT, VAR, 0   ' If the light sensor
                                      ' on Port 1 is
                                      ' greater than
                                      ' variable 0
    .SetFwd OUTPUT_A                  ' Set Motor A forward
    .SetFwd OUTPUT_C                  ' Set Motor C forward
   .Else                             ' or Else,
    .SetRwd OUTPUT_A                  ' Set Motor A reverse
    .SetRwd OUTPUT_C                  ' Set Motor C reverse
   .EndIf
  .EndLoop
  .EndOfTask
 End With
End Sub
```

This program is now much easier to understand. I have used only the constants that are provided with the SDK. However, you can make up your own constants to make the program even easier to read. For example, you could add Public Const FOREVER = 0 to the beginning of your program so that you could say .Loop CON, FOREVER in your program. The variable should be given a better name than 0 as well.

Line-Follower Robot

The program for the Line-Follower robot (which follows) is very similar to the Smart Acrobot program:

```
' The Original Line Follower Program Translated into Visual
'  Basic
Option Explicit

Public Const SENSOR_1 = 0
Public Const LIGHT_TYPE = 3
Public Const OUTPUT_A = 0
Public Const OUTPUT_C = 2
Public Const GT = 0        ' Stands for Greater Than
Public Const SENVAL = 9 ' Sensor Value
Public Const VAR = 0       ' Variable
Public Const CON = 2       ' Constant

Sub LineFollower()
 With UserForm1.Spirit1
   .InitComm
   .BeginOfTask 0
   .SetSensorType SENSOR_1, LIGHT_TYPE ' Set Input 1 to Light
                                       '  Sensor
   .Loop CON, 0                        ' Loop forever
   .If SENVAL, SENSOR_1, GT, CON, 45   ' If the light sensor
                                       '  on Port 0
                                       '  is greater than 45
    .On OUTPUT_A                       ' Turn on Motor A
    .Off OUTPUT_C                      ' Turn off Motor C
   .Else                               ' or Else,
    .On OUTPUT_C                       ' Turn on Motor C
    .Off OUTPUT_A                      ' Turn off Motor A
   .EndIf
  .EndLoop
  .EndOfTask
 End With
End Sub
```

As discussed in Chapter 6, a line-following program that will work under any lighting conditions must use a variable. The logic of the program would have to function something like this:

■ With the light sensor over the white part of the table, to the right of the black line, record the light sensor value. This is the "bright" value.

■ If the value of the light sensor is 5 points less than the "bright" value or higher, turn toward the left.

■ If the value of the light sensor is less than 5 points lower than the "bright" value, turn toward the right.

The Visual Basic program for this is almost identical to the Smart Acrobot program:

```
' A line follower program that will work under any lighting
'  conditions
Option Explicit

Public Const SENSOR_1 = 0
Public Const LIGHT_TYPE = 3
Public Const OUTPUT_A = 0
Public Const OUTPUT_C = 2
Public Const GT = 0        ' Stands for Greater Than
Public Const SENVAL = 9 ' Sensor Value
Public Const VAR = 0       ' Variable
Public Const CON = 2       ' Constant

Sub LineFollower()
 With UserForm1.Spirit1
  .InitComm
  .BeginOfTask 0
  .SetSensorType SENSOR_1, LIGHT_TYPE        ' Set Input 1 to
                                             '  Light Sensor
  .SetVar 0, SENVAL, SENSOR_1                ' Set variable 0 to
                                             '  the value
                                             '  of the Port 1
                                             '  light sensor
  .SubVar 0, CON, 5                          ' Subtract the
                                             '  number 5 from
                                             '  variable 0
  .On OUTPUT_A                               ' Turn Motor A on
  .Loop CON, 0                               ' Loop forever
   .If SENVAL, SENSOR_1, GT, VAR, 0          ' If the light
                                             '  sensor on Port
                                             '  1 > variable 0
    .On OUTPUT_A                             ' Turn on Motor A
    .Off OUTPUT_C                            ' Turn off Motor C
   .Else                                     ' or Else,
    .On OUTPUT_C                             ' Turn on Motor C
    .Off OUTPUT_A                            ' Turn off Motor A
   .EndIf
  .EndLoop
  .EndOfTask
 End With
End Sub
```

To be even more accurate, it is necessary to record both the value of the table and the value of the black line. The command to record the value could be triggered by a touch sensor on Port 3. This procedure could also be applied to the Smart Acrobot.

```
' An extremely accurate line follower program that will
'  always work under various lighting conditions

Option Explicit

Public Const SENSOR_1 = 0
Public Const SENSOR_3 = 2
Public Const SWITCH_TYPE = 1
Public Const LIGHT_TYPE = 3
Public Const OUTPUT_A = 0
Public Const OUTPUT_C = 2
Public Const GT = 0      ' Stands for Greater Than
Public Const EQ = 2      ' Equal to
Public Const SENVAL = 9 ' Sensor Value
Public Const VAR = 0     ' Variable
Public Const CON = 2     ' Constant


Sub LineFollower()
 With UserForm1.Spirit1
  .InitComm
  .BeginOfTask 0
  .SetSensorType SENSOR_1, LIGHT_TYPE  ' Set Input 1 to Light
                                       '  Sensor
  .SetSensorType SENSOR_3, SWITCH_TYPE ' Set Input 3 to Touch
                                       '  Sensor
  .While SENVAL, SENSOR_3, EQ, CON, 0  ' Wait until the touch
                                       '  sensor is pressed
  .EndWhile
  .SetVar 0, SENVAL, SENSOR_1          ' Set variable 0 to
                                       '  the value of the
                                       '  light sensor on
                                       '  Port 1
  .While SENVAL, SENSOR_3, EQ, CON, 1  ' Wait until the
                                       '  sensor is released
  .EndWhile
  .While SENVAL, SENSOR_3, EQ, CON, 0  ' Wait until the touch
                                       '  sensor is pressed
                                       '  again (over the
                                       '  line)
  .EndWhile
  .SetVar 1, SENVAL, SENSOR_1          ' Set variable 1 to
                                       '  the value of the
                                       '  light sensor on
                                       '  Port 1
  .SumVar 0, VAR, 1                    ' Add the dark
                                       '  variable to the
                                       '  light variable
```

```
        .DivVar 0, CON, 2                    ' Divide the sum of
                                             '  light and dark in
                                             '  half
        .On OUTPUT_C                         ' Turn Motor C on
        .Loop CON, 0                         ' Loop forever
          .If SENVAL, SENSOR_1, GT, VAR, 0   ' If the light sensor
                                             '  on Port 0 is
                                             '  greater than
                                             '  variable 0
            .On OUTPUT_A                      ' Turn on Motor A
            .Off OUTPUT_C                     ' Turn off Motor C
          .Else                              ' or Else,
            .On OUTPUT_C                      ' Turn on Motor C
            .Off OUTPUT_A                     ' Turn off Motor A
          .EndIf
        .EndLoop
        .EndOfTask
    End With
End Sub
```

Spirals

The original program in Chapter 10 for Painter to make a spiral
looks like the following in Visual Basic:

```
' A program for making a Spiral with the Painter robot

Public Const CON = 2
Public Const OUTPUT_A = 0
Public Const OUTPUT_C = 2

Sub SpiralOrig()
 With UserForm1.Spirit1

   .InitComm

   .BeginOfSub 0   ' The Wait One Second Subroutine
   .Wait CON, 100
   .EndOfSub

   .BeginOfTask 0

   .On OUTPUT_C     ' Turn on Motor C and keep it on forever

   .On OUTPUT_A     ' Turn on Motor A
   .Wait CON, 10    ' Wait for a tenth of a second
   .Off OUTPUT_A    ' Turn off Motor A
   .GoSub 0         ' Call the Wait One Second Subroutine
   .On OUTPUT_A     ' etc...
```

```
        .Wait CON, 20
        .Off OUTPUT_A
        .GoSub 0
        .On OUTPUT_A
        .Wait CON, 30
        .Off OUTPUT_A
        .GoSub 0
        .On OUTPUT_A
        .Wait CON, 40
        .Off OUTPUT_A
        .GoSub 0
        .On OUTPUT_A
        .Wait CON, 50
        .Off OUTPUT_A
        .GoSub 0
        .On OUTPUT_A
        .Wait CON, 60
        .Off OUTPUT_A
        ' and on and on...
        .EndOfTask
    End With
End Sub
```

In this program, a subroutine (the equivalent of a "My Command") of "Wait 1 Sec" is created and then reused for every turn. By changing the subroutine, the time taken for every turn also will be changed. Although this subroutine makes changing the turn time easier, the time that the robot drives straight still has to be changed manually at every turn. Even just five successive turns makes this program cumbersome. By using a loop and a variable, this program can be greatly simplified. A variable can be created that holds the value for the amount of time that the robot drives straight. By adding 0.1 seconds to the variable every time through the loop, the program, which follows, becomes much shorter:

```
' A program for the Spiral using a variable

Public Const CON = 2
Public Const OUTPUT_A = 0
Public Const OUTPUT_C = 2
Public Const VAR = 0        ' Variable

Sub Spiral()
 With UserForm1.Spirit1
```

```
        .InitComm

        .BeginOfTask 0

        .SetVar 0, CON, 100    ' Set variable 0 to the value of 1
                               '  second
        .On OUTPUT_C
        .Loop CON, 0           ' Loop forever

          .On OUTPUT_A         ' Turn on Motor A
          .Wait VAR, 0         ' Wait for the value of variable 0
          .Off OUTPUT_A        ' Turn off Motor A
          .Wait CON, 100       ' Wait for one second
          .SumVar 0, CON, 10   ' Increase the value of variable 0 by
                               '  a tenth of a second before looping
                               '  again

        .EndLoop
        .EndOfTask
      End With
    End Sub
```

This new and improved program waits for an additional 0.1 seconds (ten 100ths of a second) after every time through the loop. It will loop forever.

Flashlight Follower

The Flashlight Follower in Chapter 13 is another robot that can benefit from the ability to use variables. First, the following shows the RCX Code program translated into Visual Basic:

```
' The Original Flashlight Follower program translated into
'  Visual Basic
Option Explicit

Public Const SENSOR_1 = 0
Public Const LIGHT_TYPE = 3
Public Const OUTPUT_A = 0
Public Const OUTPUT_C = 2
Public Const GT = 0              ' Stands for Greater Than
Public Const SENVAL = 9         ' Sensor Value
Public Const CON = 2           ' Constant

Sub FlashlightFollower()
 With UserForm1.Spirit1
  .InitComm
  .SetSensorType SENSOR_1, LIGHT_TYPE
```

```
' Scan back and forth task
.BeginOfTask 0
.StartTask 1
.SetPower OUTPUT_A, CON, 1      ' Power Level 1
.SetPower OUTPUT_C, CON, 1
.On OUTPUT_A                    ' Turn on Motor A
.On OUTPUT_C                    ' Turn on Motor C
.Loop CON, 0                    ' Repeat Forever
 .SetFwd OUTPUT_C               ' Scan back and forth
 .SetRwd OUTPUT_A
 .Wait CON, 30
 .SetFwd OUTPUT_A
 .SetRwd OUTPUT_C
 .Wait CON, 30
.EndLoop
.EndOfTask

' Go towards the light task
.BeginOfTask 1
.Loop CON, 0                              ' Repeat Forever
 .If SENVAL, SENSOR_1, GT, CON, 50        ' If the light
                                          '  sensor > 50,
  .While SENVAL, SENSOR_1, GT, CON, 50 ' Keep on driving
  .SetRwd OUTPUT_A                         '  towards the light
  .SetRwd OUTPUT_C
  .EndWhile
 .EndIf
.EndLoop
.EndOfTask

End With
End Sub
```

One unique thing to notice about this program is that it is a multitasking program. In RCX Code, different tasks are represented by vertical columns of commands. In Visual Basic, each task is designated by **BeginOfTask** and **EndOfTask** commands. Also, Task 1 has to be explicitly started within Task 0 with the **StartTask** command. Like the Smart Acrobot and the Line-Following robot, variables can help make the Flashlight Follower program more universal, as follows:

```
' The Flashlight Follower program using a variable
Option Explicit

Public Const SENSOR_1 = 0
Public Const LIGHT_TYPE = 3
Public Const OUTPUT_A = 0
```

```
Public Const OUTPUT_C = 2
Public Const GT = 0        ' Stands for Greater Than
Public Const SENVAL = 9 ' Sensor Value
Public Const VAR = 0       ' Variable
Public Const CON = 2       ' Constant

Sub FlashlightFollower()
 With UserForm1.Spirit1
  .InitComm
  .SetSensorType SENSOR_1, LIGHT_TYPE

  ' Scan back and forth task
  .BeginOfTask 0
  .StartTask 1
  .SetVar 0, SENVAL, SENSOR_1    ' Set variable 0 to the value
                                 ' of the light sensor on
                                 ' Port 1
  .SumVar 0, CON, 5
  .SetPower OUTPUT_A, CON, 1      ' Power Level 1
  .SetPower OUTPUT_C, CON, 1
  .On OUTPUT_A                    ' Turn on Motor A
  .On OUTPUT_C                    ' Turn on Motor C
  .Loop CON, 0                    ' Repeat Forever
   .SetFwd OUTPUT_C               ' Scan back and forth
   .SetRwd OUTPUT_A
   .Wait CON, 30
   .SetFwd OUTPUT_A
   .SetRwd OUTPUT_C
   .Wait CON, 30
  .EndLoop
  .EndOfTask

  ' Go towards the light task
  .BeginOfTask 1
  .Loop CON, 0                             ' Repeat Forever
   .If SENVAL, SENSOR_1, GT, VAR, 0        ' If the light sensor
                                           ' value is greater
                                           ' than the variable

    .While SENVAL, SENSOR_1, GT, VAR, 0
     .SetRwd OUTPUT_A                      ' Drive towards the
                                           ' light
     .SetRwd OUTPUT_C
    .EndWhile
   .EndIf
  .EndLoop
  .EndOfTask

 End With
End Sub
```

Further Work

To use the examples in the preceding sections, you do not need to download anything from the Mindstorms Web site. However, to go beyond these examples and create your own Visual Basic programs, it is necessary to download two files from the mindstorms.lego.com/sdk Web site. The pbrick.zip file unzips to become pbrick.pdf, which is a 109-page document that covers the syntax and usage of each Visual Basic command that can be used with the RCX. The getstart.zip file unzips to several files that make up an introductory Visual Basic project (see Figure 15.2).

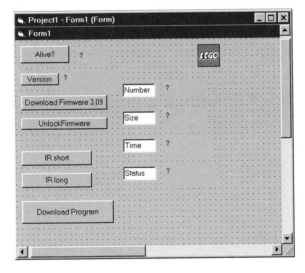

Figure 15.2
A sample Visual Basic project file can be downloaded from the Software Developer's Kit Web site.

The "Getting Started" project demonstrates the power of the Software Developer's Kit. Not only can you type Visual Basic code that can be downloaded into the RCX, but you can create your own customized graphical user interface (hopefully designed a lot better than the one in the "getting started" project) for your own programming use. Many Mindstorms enthusiasts have created such interfaces that can be downloaded from the Internet. One such interface is BotCode (see Figure 15.3).

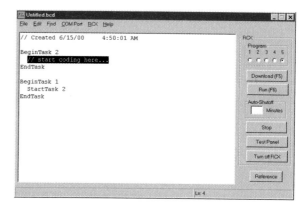

Figure 15.3

BotCode is one of the Visual Basic interfaces created using the SDK.

A full listing of these interfaces can be found at news.lugnet.com/robotics/rcx/.

16
ROBOLAB

This chapter provides an introduction to LEGO Dacta ROBOLAB, the Mindstorms for Schools. As with Chapters 15 and 17, this chapter includes example programs that enhance some of the programs from robots found earlier in the book. A demonstration copy of ROBOLAB 2.0 can be found on the CD-ROM that accompanies this book.

Introduction

ROBOLAB is the most versatile and advanced programming environment available for the RCX. In addition to accessing all of the capabilities of the RCX, as with Visual Basic or NQC, ROBOLAB offers a set of additional programming features. With ROBOLAB, you have the ability to:

- Convert programs into HTML pages and JPG images to create a Web site
- Send messages and share information with other RCXs over the Internet by using the ROBOLAB Server

- Gather, graph, and manipulate data collected from both LEGO and DCP sensors such as humidity, pH, and voltage.[1]

- Professionally analyze data with LabVIEW[2] programs

These advanced features of ROBOLAB such as data manipulation, Internet publishing, and Internet control are discussed in later chapters. In this chapter, the use of variables to improve upon programs for the Smart Acrobot, Line-Follower robot, and Flashlight Follower, and for making spirals will be described.

ROBOLAB (see Figure 16.1) was designed as the Mindstorms for Schools for LEGO Dacta, the educational division of the LEGO Group. Like RCX Code, it is a graphical programming environment that allows students to easily write programs for their robotic creations. ROBOLAB can also be used in the FIRST LEGO League competitions. Unlike RCX Code, ROBOLAB can run on Macintosh computers and enables full access to the capabilities of the RCX such as variables, data logging, and using more than one timer.

Another unique feature of ROBOLAB is its use of different levels and different ways of programming. There are two main divisions of ROBOLAB, Programmer and Investigator. Investigator extends the capabilities of programming robots to include the ability to gather data with sensors and plot that data with graphs. Programming in ROBOLAB is done in one of three different code environments. The Programmer portion of ROBOLAB contains two different programming environments, Pilot and Inventor. Pilot (see Figure 16.2) is an introductory programming environment that enables only sequential programs to be written where things happen in a

Figure 16.1
The opening screen of ROBOLAB

---

1. A LEGO DCP adapter available from the LEGO Dacta distributor in your country is required. In the United States, contact PITSCO-LEGO Dacta at 1-800-362-4308 or www.pldstore.com/.

2. "LabVIEW" stands for "Laboratory Virtual Instrumentation Engineering Workbench." LabVIEW contains a graphical programming language called "G," which was used to create ROBOLAB.

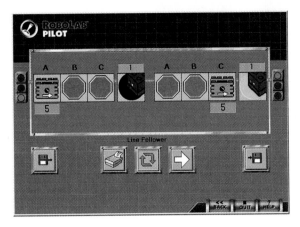

Figure 16.2

A line-following program written in Pilot Level 3

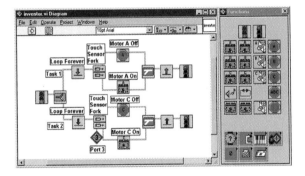

Figure 16.3

An Inventor Level 4 program that controls the two motors of a walking mechanism independently with two touch sensor leashes

fixed order. Inventor programs (see Figure 16.3) are written like a flowchart and have full programming flexibility.

Both Pilot and Inventor are divided into four different levels of increasing capability. The third and last type of programming environment is G Code (see Figure 16.4), contained within the Investigator portion of ROBOLAB. With G Code, you can write sophisticated programs to analyze data that has been collected by the RCX. For the details of this programming example, read Chapter 20.

Programming levels that resemble Pilot and Inventor also exist within ROBOLAB Investigator for writing the programs to gather data (see Figure 16.5). The Inventor-style program in

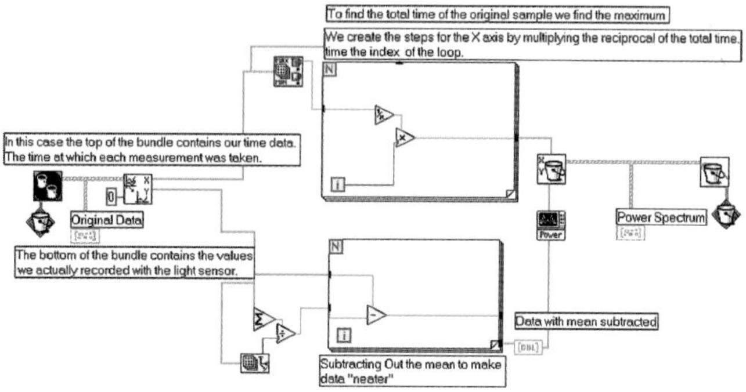

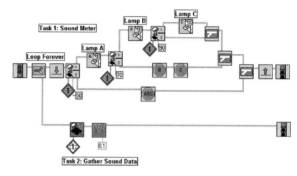

Figure 16.4
A G Code program in Investigator that calculates the speed of the motor from light sensor data from a spinning black-and-white wheel

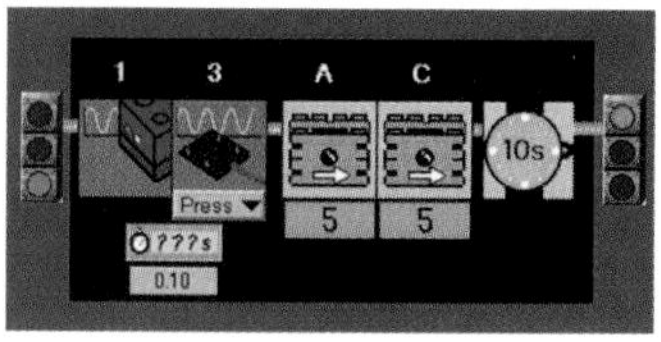

Figure 16.5
A Pilot-style program within Investigator that collects light and air pressure data every 0.1 seconds for 10 seconds while motors A and C are on

Figure 16.6
An Inventor-style program within Investigator

Figure 16.6 collects sound level data from the DCP microphone every 0.1 seconds. While the data is being collected, a simple sound meter made out of three LEGO lamps displays the decibel level. Lamps A, B, and C light up if the sound level has reached 50, 70, or 90 decibels.

Smart Acrobot

In ROBOLAB, there are two different ways to approach programming the Smart Acrobot to work independently of the light level in the room. The first method involves using Inventor Level 2 and the **Wait for Darker** and **Wait for Brighter** commands (see Figure 16.7). The red **Jump** and **Land** (up and down) arrows represent a *repeat forever* loop. First the motors are turned on in the forward direction. Then, a **Wait for Darker**

Figure 16.7

A Smart Acrobot program that responds to changes in light level independently of the light in the room without using variables

command is used. **Wait for Darker** takes the current light sensor reading and then waits for 5 points darker than that reading. When the light sensor reads five points darker than the opening bright reading, the motors are turned on in the reverse direction, and then the **Wait for Brighter** command is used. **Wait for Brighter** waits for a light level 5 points brighter than the dark reading. This same program could be written with Pilot Level 3.

The second method for writing the Smart Acrobot program involves using the variables in Inventor Level 4 (see Figure 16.8). The program in Figure 16.8 behaves in an identical manner to the Inventor Level 2 program in Figure 16.7. After the motors are turned on, the value of the light sensor is saved in a

Figure 16.8

An Inventor Level 4 program for the Smart Acrobot uses a variable, which is called a "container" in ROBOLAB.

container, which is the ROBOLAB term for a variable. Then the number 5 is subtracted from that variable, and the **Wait for Dark** command waits for a light sensor reading that is darker than that variable. In ROBOLAB, the number 5, and anything else that is placed below a command, is called a *modifier*. Modifiers provide information about command attributes, such as port numbers. Although these two programs function in an identical manner, using variables provides more flexibility and capability to ROBO-LAB programs. For example, the touch sensor can be used to trigger the RCX to record both the bright and dark values and store them in different containers. Then, the midway point between these two values can be found, and that number used in the equivalent of a light sensor-watcher (see Figure 16.9).

The program in Figure 16.9 is identical to the Visual Basic version in the previous chapter. The Visual Basic If statement is

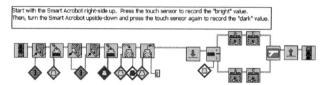

Figure 16.9

An extremely accurate Smart Acrobot program records both the bright and dark values, finds the value that is midway between them, and uses that value in the equivalent of a light sensor-watcher.

called a *fork* in ROBOLAB. This is where the program forks in two different directions depending on the value of the light sensor. Like Visual Basic, ROBOLAB programs can have comments written into them to help other people read about what your program can do.

Line-Follower Robot

The line-following program is almost identical to the Smart Acrobot program, except that only one motor is on at a time. For better performance, this other motor can be turned on at the lowest speed instead (see Figure 16.10).

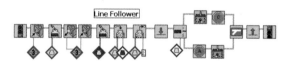

Figure 16.10

The program for the Line-Follower robot using variables

Spirals

The original program for the Painter to make a spiral looks like the one shown in Figure 16.11 in ROBOLAB. In this program, a subroutine of **Wait 1 Sec**, like a "My Command," is created and then reused for every turn. By changing the subroutine,

Figure 16.11

A program to make Painter drive in a spiral

the time taken for every turn will also be changed. Although this subroutine makes changing the turn time easier, changing the time that the robot drives straight still has to be changed manually at every turn. Even just five successive turns makes this program cumbersome. By using a loop, and adding 0.1 seconds to the amount of time that the robot drives straight every time through the loop, this program can be greatly simplified (see Figure 16.12). The new and improved program waits for an additional 0.1 seconds (ten 100ths of a second) after every time through the loop. It loops forever.

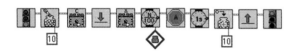

Figure 16.12

A greatly simplified spiral program that spirals forever

Flashlight Follower

This image shown in Figure 16.13 is the original Flashlight Follower program translated into ROBOLAB. The top task causes the Flashlight Follower to scan back and forth every 0.3 seconds. The bottom task causes the robot to drive straight while the

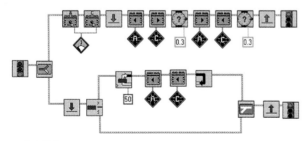

Figure 16.13

The original Flashlight Follower program translated into ROBOLAB

light sensor value is above 55 (the default value). Multitasking programs such as this one have the orange **Task Split** command at the beginning of the program. The **set direction** commands used in this program appear in the ROBOLAB palette only after the Extras folder has been installed. To install Extras, go to the Project menu and select Install (Remove) Extras. Then click on Install Extras and restart ROBOLAB. The improved version of this program, using a variable to record the light level in the room, is shown in Figure 16.14.

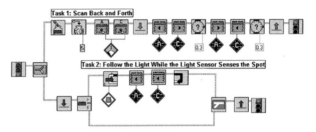

Figure 16.14

The Flashlight Follower program using a variable to account for light variation from room to room

Further Work

The Pilot level programs in this chapter can be executed with the ROBOLAB 2.0 demo found on the CD-ROM. Demonstration movies and other information about ROBOLAB can be found on the CD-ROM as well. See Appendix E for a list of ROBOLAB commands and their descriptions.

17
NQC

This chapter covers Not Quite C (NQC), the C-like programming language for the RCX written by Dave Baum. Copies of NQC, MacNQC, and RcxCC, a graphical interface for NQC, can be found on the CD-ROM that accompanies this book.

Introduction

One of the most popular ways of programming the RCX among techie adults is NQC. NQC stands for "Not Quite C" and was developed by Dave Baum. NQC is like the popular computer language C, without some of the confusing aspects of the C language. Like ROBOLAB, NQC is a programming environment that was developed specifically for the RCX, can be used on a Macintosh computer, and does not require the Spirit.ocx file to be present on your computer. Like Visual Basic, NQC is a textual language, meaning that the programs are written in words that conform to certain rules, or syntax.

As with Visual Basic, there are two different ways to use NQC. NQC programs can be written in "bare" form, such as from an MS-DOS prompt window, or as a part of a graphical user interface (GUI). Unlike Visual Basic, NQC is a program that has to be downloaded from the Internet before you can use it. NQC can be found on the CD-ROM that comes with this book, and the latest version can always be downloaded from www.enteract.com/~dbaum/nqc/. The two GUIs that exist for NQC are RcxCC and MacNQC, both of which can be found on the CD-ROM. The latest version of RcxCC and MacNQC can also be found on the main NQC site. After installing NQC, you are ready to write NQC programs for the RCX. Although NQC does not require that the Spirit.ocx file be installed and registered on your computer, RcxCC does. If you have not installed either the LEGO Mindstorms Robotics Invention System or PITSCO-LEGO Dacta Red Rover software, then you may not have the Spirit.ocx file registered on your computer. The Spirit.ocx file is also found on the ROBOLAB 2.0 CD-ROM in the LEGO Mindstorms OCX folder. When copying from the ROBOLAB CD, copy Spirit.ocx into C:\Windows\System\ Spirit.ocx, go to the Start menu, select Run, and type "regsvr32 C:\Windows\System\Spirit.ocx" (without the quotes).

To start writing "bare" NQC programs without RcxCC in Windows, bring up any text editor such as Notepad, WordPad, or Word. Type the following program in that editor:

```
// A Simple Program to turn on Motor A


task main()
{
 On(OUT_A); // Turn on Motor A
}
```

The // at the beginning of the line denotes a comment, like the single quote mark (') in Visual Basic or using the Text Tool in ROBOLAB. A semicolon is required at the end of each command line. Save the program as motora.nqc in the same folder where nqc.exe resides. Then, on a PC, go to Start | Programs | MS-DOS Prompt and change directories with the **cd** command until you are at the folder where the nqc.exe file and the motora.nqc file are located. For example, if nqc.exe is in C:\NQC, then you type the following (if you're not already at the C drive):

```
>C:
```

Then type the following:

```
C:\>cd NQC
```

Then type the following line at the MS-DOS Prompt:

```
C:\NQC>nqc -d motora.nqc
```

The -d stands for "download." Press the Run button on the RCX, and Motor A should turn on.

Smart Acrobot

The original program for the Smart Acrobot consisted of only a light sensor-watcher switching the motor directions back and forth if the Smart Acrobot was upside down or right-side up. The following shows that program translated into NQC:

```
// NQC translation of original Smart Acrobot program

task main()
{
 SetSensor(SENSOR_1, SENSOR_LIGHT); // There is a light
                                    //  sensor on Port 1
 On(OUT_A + OUT_C);     // Turn on Motor A and C

 while(true)            // Begin an infinite loop
  {
   if (SENSOR_1 < 43)   // If the light sensor < 43
    Fwd(OUT_A + OUT_C); // Turn the Motors forward
   else                 // or Else,
    Rev(OUT_A + OUT_C); // Turn the Motors reverse
  }
}
```

There are some similarities and differences to note between NQC and Visual Basic. First, the port and type of sensor that we are using is specified at the beginning of the program. Next, the motors and sensors can be referred to by shortcut names like OUT_A and SENSOR_1. Unlike Visual Basic, however, these shortcut names are built into NQC. There is no need to specify these constants at the beginning of a program or in a separate file. The while(true) statement is NQC's way of using a *while* loop to create an infinite loop. Finally, note that brackets {} are required at the beginning and end of loops and the main program itself.

The following is a more sophisticated NQC program that involves using a variable to record the bright ambient light sensor value:

```
// Smart Acrobot with a variable

task main()
{
 int bright; // initialize a variable called bright that
             //  will be an integer

 SetSensor(SENSOR_1, SENSOR_LIGHT);
 bright = SENSOR_1 - 5;   // Set the variable to the light
                          //  sensor value minus 5
 On(OUT_A + OUT_C);

 while(true)
 {
  if (SENSOR_1 < bright) // If the light sensor value
                         //  is less than the variable
    Fwd(OUT_A + OUT_C);
  else
    Rev(OUT_A + OUT_C);
 }
}
```

Line-Follower Robot

The algorithm for following a line is only slightly different from that of the Smart Acrobot. The difference is that only one motor is on at a time (see the code example that follows). Notice that if the number of commands following an If or Else statement is greater than one, then brackets are needed around the statements.

```
// Line Follower with a variable

task main()
{
 int bright;
```

```
SetSensor(SENSOR_1, SENSOR_LIGHT);
bright = SENSOR_1 - 5;

while(true)
{
 if (SENSOR_1 < bright)
 {
  On(OUT_C);  // Turn on Motor C
  Off(OUT_A); // Turn off Motor A
 }
 else
 {
  On(OUT_A);  // Turn on Motor A
  Off(OUT_C); // Turn off Motor C
 }
 }
}
```

To improve the accuracy of the Line-Follower even further, the light sensor value of the black line can be measured in addition to the bright surface. This can be accomplished most easily with a touch sensor trigger, as follows:

```
// Line Follower with touch sensor to trigger the collection
//  of dark and bright values

task main()
{
   int bright;           // The light value of the surface
   int dark;             // The light value of the dark line
   int bright_plus_dark; // Light plus dark
   int half_way_between; // Half-way between light and dark

   SetSensor(SENSOR_1, SENSOR_LIGHT);
   SetSensor(SENSOR_3, SENSOR_TOUCH); // There is a touch
                                      // sensor on Port 3

 // Put the light sensor over the surface

 until(SENSOR_3 == 1); // Wait until the touch sensor is
                       //  pressed, and then
 bright = SENSOR_1;    // Set the bright variable to the
                       //  light sensor value

 until(SENSOR_3 == 0); // Wait until the touch sensor is
                       //  released
 // Put the light sensor over the dark line
```

```
    until(SENSOR_3 == 1); // Wait until the touch sensor is
                          // pressed again
    dark = SENSOR_1;                  // Set the dark variable
                                      //  to the light sensor
                                      //  value
    bright_plus_dark = bright + dark;
    half_way_between = bright_plus_dark / 2; // The value of
                                             // half-way
                                             // between
                                             // light and
                                             // dark

  while(true)
  {
   if (SENSOR_1 < half_way_between)
   {
    On(OUT_C);
    Off(OUT_A);
   }
   else
   {
    On(OUT_A);
    Off(OUT_C);
   }
  }
}
```

This technique of using a touch sensor trigger could also be applied to the Smart Acrobot.

Spirals

The following code example shows the original program for the Painter to make a spiral translated into NQC:

```
// Spiral

void turn()
{
 Wait(100); // Wait one second
}

task main()
{
 On(OUT_C);

 OnFor(OUT_A, 10);
 turn();
 OnFor(OUT_A, 20);
 turn();
```

```
OnFor(OUT_A, 30);
turn();
OnFor(OUT_A, 40);
turn();
OnFor(OUT_A, 50);
turn();
OnFor(OUT_A, 60);        // and on and on
}
```

In this program, a subroutine of **Wait(100)** is created and then reused for every turn. A subroutine is created by using the term void instead of task. By changing the subroutine, the time taken for every turn will also be changed. Although this subroutine makes changing the turn time easier, the time that the robot drives straight still has to be changed manually at every turn. Even just five successive turns makes this program cumbersome. By using a loop, and adding 0.1 seconds to the amount of time that the robot drives straight every time through the loop, this program can be greatly simplified, as follows:

```
// Spiral using a variable and a loop

task main()
{
 int duration=0;

 On(OUT_C);

 while(true)
 {
  OnFor(OUT_A, duration); // Go straight
  Wait(100);              // Turn by only having motor C on
  duration += 10;
 }
}
```

This new and improved program waits for an additional 0.1 seconds (ten 100ths of a second) after every time through the loop. It will loop forever.

Flashlight Follower

The following is the original program for the Flashlight Follower translated into NQC:

```
// Flashlight Follower

#define SCAN_TIME 30 // Define a constant

task main()
{
 SetSensor(SENSOR_1, SENSOR_LIGHT);

 SetPower(OUT_A + OUT_C, 1); // Set the power level to 1
 On(OUT_A + OUT_C);

 start scan;        // Start the scan task
 start check_light; // Start the check_light task
}

task scan()
{
 while(true)
 {
  Fwd(OUT_C);
  Rev(OUT_A);
  Wait(SCAN_TIME);   // Wait for the amount of time defined
                     //  by the constant SCAN_TIME

  Fwd(OUT_A);
  Rev(OUT_C);
  Wait(SCAN_TIME);
 }
}

task check_light()
{
 while(true)
 {
  if (SENSOR_1 > 50)
  {
   while(SENSOR_1 > 50)
   {
    Rev(OUT_A + OUT_C);
   }
  }
 }
}
```

Several new features of the NQC syntax show up in the Flashlight Follower program. The first is #define SCAN_TIME 30. The **#define** command is helpful at the beginning of NQC programs to declare any constants. Calling Wait(SCAN_TIME) in the program instead of Wait(30) helps to remember what the Wait time is referring to. Also, if this time ever must be changed, it has to be changed only at the top of the program in one place because of the **#define** command, instead the two places that it shows up in the program.

The next new piece of syntax is the **start** command. The Flashlight Follower program is a *multitasking* one, which means that it is running two different processes at once. The first task is to scan back and forth, and the second task is to drive forward when the light sensor detects the flashlight spot. As with Visual Basic and its **StartTask** command, different tasks in NQC must be started with a special command.

To make the Flashlight Follower more universal and able to be used under different lighting conditions, it is necessary to use a variable. The easiest way to do this is to add a variable to the check_light task, as follows:

```
task check_light()
{
 int ambient_light;

 ambient_light = SENSOR_1;

 while(true)
 {
  if (SENSOR_1 > ambient_light + 5)
  {
   while(SENSOR_1 > ambient_light + 5)
   {
    Rev(OUT_A + OUT_C);
   }
  }
 }
}
```

In NQC, variables are either local to the task—meaning that they can be used only in one particular task—or they are global—meaning that the variable can be used in any task in the entire program. The ambient_light variable in this program is a local variable. To make ambient_light a global variable, it must be placed above the task main():

```
int ambient_light

task main()
```

Further Work

NQC is a widespread language that is used by many LEGO enthusiasts. It is even used in some college classes as an introduction to the C programming language. Numerous resources
about NQC are available. One of the best is news.lugnet.com/
robotics/rcx/nqc/.

18
Going the Distance

Going the Distance is yet another robot in this book that makes use of the spinning black-and-white wheel. Going the Distance can be programmed to drive for a certain distance and, with a counter, even remember that distance.

Inspiration

After building Keep On Moving, I realized that there were other uses for a spinning black-and-white wheel acting as an angle sensor. In addition to the Smart Acrobot and Keep On Moving, a third use for the black-and-white wheel is for programming a robot to go for a certain distance. Instead of programming a robot to turn on its motors for a certain amount of time with an **on for** command, a robot can be programmed to turn its motors on until the black-and-white wheel has spun around a certain amount of times.

Designing and Building

This robot is also almost identical to the Keep On Moving robot. The only difference is that the pulleys and belts are replaced by the original 24-tooth gears. A slip in the belts would cause the robot to veer away from going straight, which is the goal of this robot.

Programming and Testing

The program for the Going the Distance robot is almost identical to the program for Keep On Moving. The only difference is that the timer is replaced with the counter. The timer-watcher in Keep On Moving kept track of how much time had elapsed since the light sensor last saw the dark half of the wheel. Similarly, in Going the Distance, the counter-watcher counts how many times the light sensor has seen the dark half of the wheel. The program shown in Figure 18.1 tells the robot to go forward until the black-and-white wheel has spun around ten times before stopping.

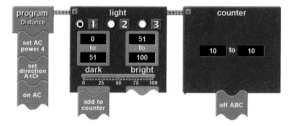

Figure 18.1
The program for Going the Distance

When I tested the program for Going the Distance, the robot went approximately 27 inches in the ten turns of the black-and-white wheel. When the program was run repeatedly, the robot would always travel approximately the same distance. There were a couple of problems though. One problem was that programming a distance using the spinning wheel did not seem any more accurate than simply programming with **on for** commands. This was mostly due to the fact that the robot would not always go straight. Another problem was that when the light sensor started while aimed at the black part of the wheel, the counter would immediately be set to 1 even before the robot started moving. This resulted in the robot traveling a distance equivalent to only nine turns of the black-and-white wheel. When the light sensor started while aimed at the white part of the wheel, the wheel would spin around only 9 1/2 times before stopping.

To solve both of these problems, changes had to be made to both the mechanics and the program. First, to make the wheel for the light sensor more accurate, I tried creating different wheels divided up into more than two sections (see Figure 18.2).

Figure 18.2
New black-and-white wheels were created with additional divisions.

The real LEGO angle sensor, however, is divided up into sixteenths of a rotation. Without using a protractor, accurately creating a wheel that has more divisions than sixteen requires using a painting program on the computer. If you photocopy the graphic shown in Figure 18.3 and cut it out, you will have a wheel suitable for taping to a 40-tooth gear.

When using these wheels, the number that the counter-watcher waits for in the program must be increased. There is a problem in using a wheel with 32 divisions on it, which is that the wheel can spin so fast that the light sensor cannot keep up. The solution to this problem is to gear down the wheel (see Figure 18.4). The robot, however, still drives at its original speed.

The last mechanical improvement was to make the robot drive straight. I connected together the axles of both sides of the robot with an axle extender, and then it drove straighter than when the two treads were independent of each other. Any discrepancies in the motors themselves, or in the amount of friction that each motor encounters from tight axles, and so on, are cancelled out by each other when the two motors are interconnected. The major trade-off with this change is that now the robot is no longer able to make turns.

The next improvement I made was to the program. Because I added an **add to counter** command on the bright side of the

Figure 18.3
A black-and-white wheel with 32 divisions

Figure 18.4
With another 40-tooth gear and an 8-tooth gear, the black-and-white wheel is now slower by a factor of five, allowing the light sensor plenty of time to keep up.

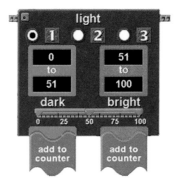

Figure 18.5

*Adding the **add to counter** command to the bright side of the light sensor-watcher improves the repeatability of the robot.*

light sensor-watcher (see Figure 18.5), the counter increases every time the wheel transitions from black to white in addition to when it transitions from white to black. Now, with a 32-division wheel, the light sensor will truly count 32 divisions for one rotation. To program the wheel to turn all of the way around, however, requires a counter value of 33, because the very first section of the wheel is counted even before the robot starts moving. Using the program shown in Figure 18.5, it no longer matters which color the wheel starts out on because the resulting distance is the same. With all of these improvements, the robot can be programmed to start and stop at a specified distance with pretty good accuracy.

Advanced Programming

At this point, Going the Distance can travel only backward and forward. To do something interesting with the robot requires some imagination. One possibility is to make Going the Distance into a smart robot scout that can remember and repeat a certain distance. By combining the features of Keep On Moving and Going the Distance, you can make a robot scout that can remember where it has encountered obstacles. The program could go something like this:

1. Drive forward until hitting an obstacle, while adding to a counter the entire time.

2. Remember the counter value of where the obstacle exists and retreat.

3. When the program is run again, drive that same distance again.[1]

If this robot is sent into a room with an obstacle at an unknown distance, the robot will hit the obstacle and then retreat back to base. When the program is run again back at base in safe territory, the path of the distance to the obstacle can be witnessed.

---

1. If the RCX is shut off before the program is run again, the counter value will not be remembered.

To write this program requires that the robot save the counter value in its memory, which can be done only with Visual Basic, ROBOLAB, or NQC.

Visual Basic

The following is the Visual Basic translation for the original Going the Distance program:

```
' Going the Distance

Option Explicit

Public Const SENSOR_1 = 0
Public Const LIGHT_TYPE = 3
Public Const OUTPUT_A = 0
Public Const OUTPUT_C = 2
Public Const GT = 0            ' Stands for Greater Than
Public Const LT = 1            ' Stands for Less Than
Public Const SENVAL = 9        ' Sensor Value
Public Const VAR = 0           ' Variable
Public Const CON = 2           ' Constant

Sub GoingTheDistance()
 With UserForm1.Spirit1
  .InitComm
  .BeginOfTask 0
  .StartTask 1
  .SetSensorType SENSOR_1, LIGHT_TYPE ' Set Input 1 to Light
                                      '  Sensor
  .SetPower OUTPUT_A, CON, 3
  .SetPower OUTPUT_C, CON, 3
  .SetFwd OUTPUT_C
  .SetRwd OUTPUT_A
  .On OUTPUT_A
  .On OUTPUT_C
  .SetVar 0, CON, 0                     ' Set Counter 0 to 0
  .Loop CON, 0
   .If SENVAL, SENSOR_1, GT, CON, 50
    .SumVar 0, CON, 1
    .While SENVAL, SENSOR_1, GT, CON, 50
    .EndWhile
   .Else
    .SumVar 0, CON, 1
    .While SENVAL, SENSOR_1, LT, CON, 51
    .EndWhile
   .EndIf
  .EndLoop
  .EndOfTask

  .BeginOfTask 1
  .Loop CON, 0
```

```
      .If VAR, 0, GT, CON, 10
       .Off OUTPUT_A              ' Stop if the desired distance has
                                  '  been reached
      .Off OUTPUT_C
     .EndIf
    .EndLoop
    .EndOfTask
 End With
End Sub
```

The program can be modified to keep track of the counter value that it has reached when it encounters an obstacle with the touch sensor as follows:

```
' Remember the Distance

Option Explicit

Public Const SENSOR_1 = 0
Public Const SENSOR_2 = 1
Public Const LIGHT_TYPE = 3
Public Const SWITCH_TYPE = 1
Public Const OUTPUT_A = 0
Public Const OUTPUT_C = 2
Public Const GT = 0               ' Stands for Greater Than
Public Const LT = 1               ' Stands for Less Than
Public Const EQ = 2               ' Stands for Equal To
Public Const SENVAL = 9           ' Sensor Value
Public Const VAR = 0              ' Variable
Public Const CON = 2              ' Constant

Sub GettingStarted()
 With UserForm1.Spirit1
  .InitComm

  .BeginOfTask 0
  .SetVar 0, CON, 0                        ' Set the counter to
                                           '  zero
  .StartTask 1
  .SetSensorType SENSOR_1, LIGHT_TYPE
  .SetSensorType SENSOR_2, SWITCH_TYPE ' A touch sensor on
                                           '  Port 2
  .SetPower OUTPUT_A, CON, 3
  .SetPower OUTPUT_C, CON, 3
  .SetFwd OUTPUT_C
  .SetRwd OUTPUT_A
  .On OUTPUT_A
  .On OUTPUT_C
  .Loop CON, 0
   .If SENVAL, SENSOR_1, GT, CON, 50       ' If the light sensor
                                           '  value is greater
                                           '  than 50,
```

```
        .SumVar 0, CON, 1                    ' Add 1 to the
                                             '  counter
        .While SENVAL, SENSOR_1, GT, CON, 50
        .EndWhile
      .Else
        .SumVar 0, CON, 1
        .While SENVAL, SENSOR_1, LT, CON, 51
        .EndWhile
      .EndIf
    .EndLoop
    .EndOfTask

    .BeginOfTask 1
    .Loop CON, 0' Loop forever

      .If SENVAL, SENSOR_2, EQ, CON, 1 ' If the touch sensor is
                                       '  pressed
        .SetVar 1, VAR, 0              ' Remember what the
                                       '  distance is in a
                                       '  different variable,
                                       '  VAR 1

        .Off OUTPUT_A' Stop
        .Off OUTPUT_C
      .EndIf

      .If VAR, 0, EQ, VAR, 1           ' If the counter is
                                       '  approaching the
                                       '  obstacle distance,
        .Off OUTPUT_A                  ' Stop
        .Off OUTPUT_C
      .EndIf

    .EndLoop
    .EndOfTask
  End With
End Sub
```

ROBOLAB

Figure 18.6 shows what the original RCX Code program for Going the Distance looks like in ROBOLAB.

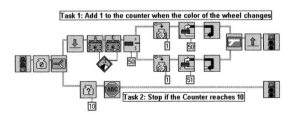

Figure 18.6
The original Going the Distance program in ROBOLAB

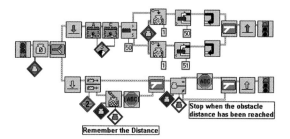

Figure 18.7
A ROBOLAB program that can keep track of how far the robot has traveled before bumping into something and then repeat that distance again later

To keep track of the distance traveled with a variable, the program needs to be modified (see Figure 18.7).

NQC

The following is the original program for Going the Distance:

```
// NQC translation of original Going the Distance program

int counter;

task main()
{
 SetSensor(SENSOR_1, SENSOR_LIGHT);

 On(OUT_A + OUT_C);
 Fwd(OUT_C);
 Rev(OUT_A);
 SetPower(OUT_A + OUT_C, 3);
 counter = 0;

 start counting;
 start wait_for_count;
}

task counting()
{
 while(true)
 {
  if (SENSOR_1 > 50)
  {
   counter += 1;
   while(SENSOR_1 > 50)
   {
   }
  }
  else
```

```
      {
        counter +=1;
        while(SENSOR_1 < 51)
        {
        }
      }
    }
  }
}

task wait_for_count()
{
  until(counter == 10);
  Off(OUT_A + OUT_C);      // Stop if the counter distance has
                           //  been reached
}
```

With a touch sensor added to record distance, the NQC program becomes the following:

```
// Remember the Distance

int counter;
int distance;

task main()
{
  SetSensor(SENSOR_1, SENSOR_LIGHT);
  SetSensor(SENSOR_2, SENSOR_TOUCH);

  On(OUT_A + OUT_C);
  Fwd(OUT_C);
  Rev(OUT_A);
  SetPower(OUT_A + OUT_C, 3);
  counter = 0;

  start counting;
  start wait_for_touch;
}

task counting()
{
  while(true)
  {
    if (SENSOR_1 > 50)
    {
      counter += 1;
      while(SENSOR_1 > 50)
      {
      }
    }
```

```
    else
    {
     counter +=1;
     while(SENSOR_1 < 51)
      {
      }
     }
    }
   }
  }

task wait_for_touch()
{
 while(true)
 {
  if(SENSOR_2 == 1)
  {
   distance = counter;
   Off(OUT_A + OUT_C);
  }

  if(counter == distance)
   Off(OUT_A + OUT_C);    // Stop if the obstacle distance
                          //  has been reached
 }
}
```

Further Work

There is one big problem with the programs in the preceding section. There isn't a way to reset the distance variable! The programs must be modified so that if a second touch sensor is pressed, the distance variable will reset itself. Some other ideas include:

- Send the counter variable to another robot in an infrared message, warning it of the dangers ahead.

- Make the treads independent again and give the robot the ability to turn. Then, program the robot to solve a simple maze. After bumping into various walls and remembering the distances to them, the robot will "learn" how to solve the maze faster and faster each time.

19
Elevator

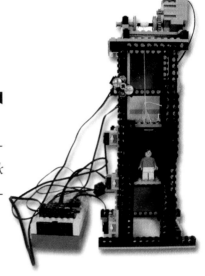

The Elevator demonstrates a LEGO model of a real-world object. It is one of the few models in this book where the focus is on programming rather than designing and building.

Inspiration

The inspiration for the Elevator came from two different sources. On the first day of an introductory digital systems laboratory class, when the professor showed a video of former students' final projects, I was inspired by one project that was an elevator made out of LEGO beams and bricks, with a LEGO minifig riding in it. The elevator was programmed to respond to the press of buttons in the same manner that a real elevator works. My second inspiration was in a seminar class called "The Way Things Work" at Tufts University; a student built a LEGO elevator complete with working elevator doors. I wanted to challenge myself to build a working elevator on my own.

Designing and Building

To push the limits of what can be done with one RCX, I constructed an elevator with four floors and four touch sensors. Each of the first three touch sensors for floors one through three were connected to ports 1 through 3 on the RCX. The fourth touch sensor was custom made with nuts and bolts.

Figure 19.1
The fourth touch sensor is a custom-made sensor connected to both ports 2 and 3.

Figure 19.2
The wire connected to port 3 is connected to two bolts along the main beam of the Elevator.

Figure 19.3
The complete touch sensor for the fourth floor

■■■■■■■■■■■■■■■■■■■■■■■■■■■■■■

LEGO Aside: Four Touch Sensors on Only Three Ports

The Elevator uses four touch sensors for its four floors. The RCX, however, has only three sensor ports to use. One trick to using four touch sensors is to make your own touch sensor that will register a press on two ports simultaneously. The program for the robot can then take this into account.

First, a long wire was cut in half and stripped (see Chapter 8 for instructions on how to cut and strip wire). The two wires were then connected to ports 2 and 3 on the RCX (see Figure 19.1). I wrapped the bare ends of the wire connected to port 3 around two separate bolts and secured them tightly with two nuts (see Figure 19.2). The other end of the wire connected to port 2 was also connected to bolts in the same manner using a 1x4 beam (see Figure 19.3). When the 1x4 beam is rotated, a metal-to-metal connection is made for both wires, and a touch sensor press is registered for both port 2 and port 3.

■■■■■■■■■■■■■■■■■■■■■■■■■■■■■■

Programming and Testing

The first program for the Elevator was to send it to the floor for which the button was pressed. Different tasks watch each sensor. If the second-floor or third-floor touch sensor was pressed, the second-floor and third-floor touch sensors were also checked to determine if the request was in fact for the fourth floor, represented by a press of ports 2 and 3 (see Figure 19.4).

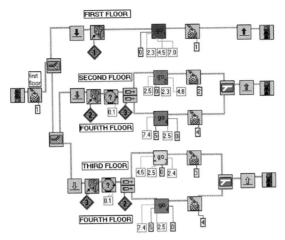

Figure 19.4
The first program for the Elevator sends it to a different floor depending on which touch sensor was pressed.

■■■■■■■■■■■■■■■■■■■■■■■■■■■■

Programming Aside: Creating SubVIs in ROBOLAB

Each command that sends the Elevator to the proper floor is a ROBOLAB SubVI. SubVIs enable you to compact a large portion of a program that is taking up a lot of space into a single icon. The Create SubVI option on the Edit menu, Edit | Create SubVI, is available after the ROBOLAB Extras have been installed. Go to Project | Install (Remove) Extras and follow the instructions.

To create a SubVI, use the mouse to drag a box around the commands that you want to compress into one command. Make sure that the first and last commands in the group are already connected to other commands before and after them. Any values that you want to remain as modifiers for the new SubVI should be kept out of the box. After the area has been selected, select Edit | Create SubVI, and a new command is created.

By double-clicking on the icon of the SubVI and selecting Windows | Show Diagram, the contents of the SubVI can be viewed. For the Elevator SubVIs (see Figure 19.5), the motor that raises the Elevator is turned on for various amounts of time and in various directions depending on where the Elevator currently is and where it is going. The current position of the Elevator is held in memory with a container (variable).

The names of the modifiers can be changed by right-clicking (command-clicking on a Mac) on the representation of the modifier and selecting Show | Label. The pop-up can then be modified with the cursor. You can create your own Help menu for your new SubVI by double-clicking on its icon, selecting Windows | Show VI Info, and entering a description for the SubVI (see Figure 19.6). This description and the new names of the modifiers will then be displayed when Help | Show Help is selected. Finally, the icon itself can be edited by double-clicking on the image of the icon in the upper-right corner of the programming window. By default, the icon reads "Inventor."

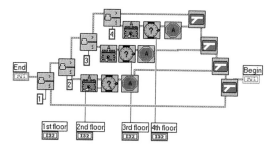

Figure 19.5
The contents of the go1.vi SubVI

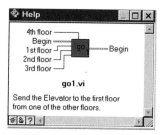

Figure 19.6
Custom help menus can be created for new Sub VIs.

The program that turns on the motor for different times and directions depending on the starting and ending floor is not adequate. Because of inaccuracies in the motor and the friction and slack in the string, the motor does not necessarily return to the same place every time. As an attempt at improving the Elevator, I added a light sensor and black-and-white wheel to keep track of the Elevator's position (see Figure 19.7). I wrote a new program to account for the addition of the light sensor (see Figure 19.8).

Figure 19.7
A light sensor was added to keep better track of the position of the Elevator.

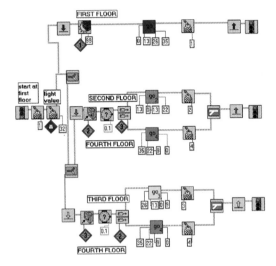

Figure 19.8
The updated program for the Elevator has a light sensor on port 1.

■■■■■■■■■■■■■■■■■■■■■■■■■■■■■■

LEGO Aside: A Light Sensor and a Touch Sensor on the Same Port

Normally only one sensor can be attached to a port on the RCX at one time. There are some exceptions however. For example, when two touch sensors are attached to one port and either one is pressed, a press is registered with the RCX. Another trick is to have a light sensor and a touch sensor on the same port.

In the Elevator, the light sensor is stacked on top of the touch sensor already on port 1. When the RCX is configured to have a light sensor on port 1 and a touch sensor on port 1 is pressed, it registers a value of 100 to the RCX. In this new program, the **wait for bright** command waits for a value greater than 99 on port 1 as a signal for the first-floor touch sensor. The SubVIs were also changed to reflect the addition of the light sensor (see Figure 19.9). Of course, this would not work if the light sensor sensed a value of 100 during normal operation. Then the RCX would think that the touch sensor had been pressed.

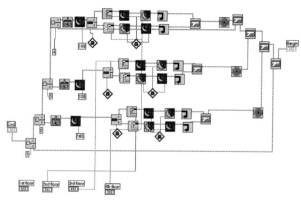

Figure 19.9
The new SubVI for sending the Elevator to the first floor

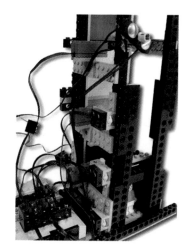

Figure 19.10
The updated Elevator has a light sensor on the first three floors.

Instead of waiting for a certain amount of time, the modifiers for the SubVIs now specify the number of black-and-white sections of the wheel to wait for.

This updated program and mechanics did not make a noticeable change in the accuracy of the Elevator. It still would not return to exactly the same spot every time. It still needed improvement. To make the Elevator more accurate, I added two additional light sensors to ports 2 and 3, and I used the original light sensor down on the first floor (see Figure 19.10). I also added a yellow 1x2 brick to one side of the elevator car so that the three light sensors could detect when the car had arrived at

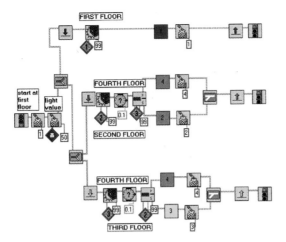

Figure 19.11

The final program for the Elevator

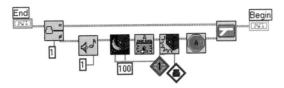

Figure 19.12

The final SubVI to send the Elevator to the first floor

the floor. I wrote a new program to reflect these changes (see Figure 19.11).

Figure 19.12 shows an example of one of the new SubVIs. When the Elevator is at the first floor and the touch sensor on port 1 is pressed, nothing happens. When the Elevator is on any other floor, the RCX makes a beep sound, waits for the touch sensor to be released, and then turns on the motor until the light sensor on the first floor detects the Elevator. I added the beep to the program to give the RCX time to process the press of the touch sensor. Without the beep sound, the RCX has trouble keeping up with so many tasks and sometimes can ignore the touch sensor press. For the fourth floor, the Elevator is simply sent upward until it reaches the light sensor on the third floor, and then for two seconds more. On the way back down, one of the three light sensors can detect it. Modifiers are no longer necessary.

Visual Basic

The following is the program for the Elevator in Visual Basic:

```
' Elevator
Option Explicit

Public Const VAR = 0
Public Const CON = 2
Public Const SENVAL = 9
Public Const SENSOR_1 = 0
Public Const SENSOR_2 = 1
Public Const SENSOR_3 = 2
Public Const LIGHT_TYPE = 3
Public Const OUTPUT_A = 0
Public Const GT = 0
Public Const LT = 1
Public Const EQ = 2
Public Const NE = 3


Sub Elevator()
 With UserForm1.Spirit1
  .InitComm

   ' Go to the first floor routine
   .BeginOfSub 1
   .If VAR, 0, NE, CON, 1 ' As long as the car is not already
                           ' on the first floor
    .PlaySystemSound 0     ' Make a beep sound
    .While SENSOR_1, SENVAL, GT, CON, 99 ' Wait for the touch
                                          ' sensor
    .EndWhile
    .SetRwd OUTPUT_A
    .On OUTPUT_A
    .While SENSOR_1, SENVAL, LT, VAR, 1 ' Wait for the
                                         ' yellow brick
    .Off OUTPUT_A
   .EndIf
   .EndOfSub

   ' Go to the second floor routine
   .BeginOfSub 2
   .If VAR, 0, NE, CON, 2  ' As long as the car is not
                            ' already on the 2nd floor
    .If VAR, 0, GT, CON, 2 ' If the elevator is on 3 or 4
     .PlaySystemSound 0
     .While SENSOR_2, SENVAL, GT, CON, 99
     .EndWhile
     .SetRwd OUTPUT_A
     .On OUTPUT_A              ' Go down to the 2nd floor
     .While SENSOR_2, SENVAL, LT, VAR, 1
     .EndWhile
```

```
 .Off OUTPUT_A
.Else                  ' If the elevator is on 1st floor
 .PlaySystemSound 0
 .While SENSOR_2, SENVAL, GT, CON, 99
 .EndWhile
 .SetFwd OUTPUT_A      ' Go up to the 2nd floor
 .On OUTPUT_A
 .While SENSOR_2, SENVAL, LT, VAR, 1
 .EndWhile
 .Off OUTPUT_A
 .EndIf
.EndIf
.EndOfSub


' Go to the third floor routine
.BeginOfSub 3
.If VAR, 0, NE, CON, 3  ' As long as the car is not
                        ' already on the 3rd floor

 .If VAR, 0, GT, CON, 3 ' If the car is on the 4th floor
  .PlaySystemSound 0
  .While SENSOR_3, SENVAL, GT, CON, 99
  .EndWhile
  .SetRwd OUTPUT_A
  .On OUTPUT_A          ' Go down to the 3rd floor
  .While SENSOR_3, SENVAL, LT, VAR, 1
  .EndWhile
  .Off OUTPUT_A
 .Else                  ' If the car is on the 1st or 2nd
                        ' floor
  .PlaySystemSound 0
  .While SENSOR_3, SENVAL, GT, CON, 99
  .EndWhile
  .SetFwd OUTPUT_A
  .On OUTPUT_A          ' Go up to the 3rd floor
  .While SENSOR_3, SENVAL, LT, VAR, 1
  .EndWhile
  .Off OUTPUT_A
 .EndIf
.EndIf
.EndOfSub


' Go to the fourth floor routine
.BeginOfSub 4
.If VAR, 0, NE, CON, 4
 .PlaySystemSound 0
 .While SENSOR_2, SENVAL, GT, CON, 99
 .While SENSOR_3, SENVAL, GT, CON, 99
 .EndWhile
 .EndWhile
 .SetFwd OUTPUT_A
 .On OUTPUT_A
```

```
                         .While SENSOR_3, SENVAL, LT, VAR, 1
                         .EndWhile
                         .Wait CON, 180 ' 1.8 seconds
                         .Off OUTPUT_A
                       .EndIf
                     .EndOfSub

                     .BeginOfTask 0
                     .PlaySystemSound 6
                     .SetSensorType SENSOR_1, LIGHT_TYPE
                     .SetSensorType SENSOR_2, LIGHT_TYPE
                     .SetSensorType SENSOR_3, LIGHT_TYPE

                     .SetVar 0, CON, 1  ' Current floor
                     .SetVar 1, CON, 40 ' Light sensor value of yellow brick

                     .StartTask 1
                     .StartTask 2

                     .Loop CON, 0
                       .While SENSOR_1, SENVAL, LT, CON, 99
                       .EndWhile

                       .GoSub 1

                       .SetVar 0, CON, 1 ' The elevator is now on the 1st floor
                     .EndLoop
                     .EndOfTask

                       .BeginOfTask 1
                       .PlaySystemSound 6
                     .Loop CON, 0
                       .While SENSOR_2, SENVAL, LT, CON, 99
                       .EndWhile
                       .Wait CON, 10
                       .If SENSOR_3, SENVAL, GT, CON, 99 ' If touch sensor #3 is
                                                         '  also pressed
                         .GoSub 4                        ' Go to the 4th floor
                         .SetVar 0, CON, 4
                       .Else                             ' or Else,
                         .GoSub 2                        ' Go to the 2nd floor
                         .SetVar 0, CON, 2 ' The elevator is now on the 2nd floor
                       .EndIf
                     .EndLoop
                   .EndOfTask

                 .BeginOfTask 2
                 .Loop CON, 0
                   .While SENSOR_3, SENVAL, LT, CON, 99

                   .EndWhile
                   .Wait CON, 10
```

```
      .If SENSOR_2, SENVAL, GT, CON, 99 ' If touch sensor #2 is
                                       '   also pressed
       .GoSub 4                        ' Go to the 4th floor
       .SetVar 0, CON, 4
      .Else                            ' or Else,
       .GoSub 3                        ' Go to the 3rd floor
       .SetVar 0, CON, 3 ' The elevator is now on the 3rd floor
      .EndIf
     .EndLoop
     .EndOfTask

  End With
End Sub
```

NQC

The following is the program for the Elevator in NQC:

```
// Elevator

#define LIGHT 48  // The light sensor value of the yellow
                  //   brick
int floor=1;      // The current floor

void go_1()       // Go to first floor routine
{
 if (floor != 1)  // As long as the current floor is not 1
 {
  PlaySound(0);
  until(SENSOR_1 < 100); // Wait until the touch sensor is
                         //   released
  OnRev(OUT_A);
  until(SENSOR_1 > LIGHT);
  Off(OUT_A);
 }
}

void go_2() // Go to second floor routine
{
 if (floor !=2)  // As long as the current floor is not 2
 {
  if (floor > 2) // If the elevator is on the 3rd or 4th floor
  {
   PlaySound(0);
   until(SENSOR_2 < 100);
   OnRev(OUT_A);
   until(SENSOR_2 > LIGHT);
   Off(OUT_A);
  }

  if (floor < 2) // If the elevator is on the 1st floor
  {
```

```
      PlaySound(0);
      until(SENSOR_2 < 100);
      OnFwd(OUT_A);
      until(SENSOR_2 > LIGHT);
      Off(OUT_A);
     }
   }
 }

void go_3() // Go to third floor routine
{
 if (floor !=3)  // As long as the current floor is not 3
 {
  if (floor > 3) // If the elevator is on the fourth floor
  {
   PlaySound(0);
   until(SENSOR_3 < 100);
   OnRev(OUT_A);
   until(SENSOR_3 > LIGHT);
   Off(OUT_A);
  }

  if (floor < 3) // If the elevator is on the 1st or 2nd floor
  {
   PlaySound(0);
   until(SENSOR_3 < 100);
   OnFwd(OUT_A);
   until(SENSOR_3 > LIGHT);
   Off(OUT_A);
  }
 }
}

void go_4() // Go to fourth floor routine
{
 if (floor !=4) // As long as the current floor is not 4
 {
  PlaySound(0);
  until(SENSOR_2 < 100);
  until(SENSOR_3 < 100);
  OnFwd(OUT_A);
  until(SENSOR_3 > LIGHT);
  Wait(180); // 1.8 seconds
  Off(OUT_A);
 }
}

task main()
{
 SetSensor(SENSOR_1, SENSOR_LIGHT);
 SetSensor(SENSOR_2, SENSOR_LIGHT);
```

```
SetSensor(SENSOR_3, SENSOR_LIGHT);

start second_floor; // Check other touch sensors at the
                    //  same time
start third_floor;

while(true) // Check first floor touch sensor
{
 until(SENSOR_1 > 99);
 go_1();  // Go to first floor
 floor=1; // The elevator is now on the first floor
}
}

task second_floor()
{
 while(true)
 {
  until(SENSOR_2 > 99);
  Wait(10);
  if (SENSOR_3 > 99)
  {
   go_4();
   floor=4; // The elevator is now on the fourth floor
  }
  else
  {
   go_2();
   floor=2; // The elevator is now on the second floor
  }
 }
}

task third_floor()
{
 while(true)
 {
  until (SENSOR_3 > 99);
  Wait(10);
  if (SENSOR_2 > 99)
  {
   go_4();
   floor=4; // The elevator is now on the fourth floor
  }
  else
  {
   go_3();
   floor=3; // The elevator is now on the third floor
  }
 }
}
```

Further Work

A number of improvements can be made to the program for the Elevator. For example:

- When the Elevator is on the way to the third floor from the first floor and touch sensor #2 is pressed, the Elevator should stop at the second floor.
- A pointer and a paper dial could be added to the top of the Elevator to represent which floor the Elevator is on.
- LEGO lamps on ports B and C could light up when the Elevator is at the first or second floor.
- A LEGO lamp could flash when the Elevator is in motion.
- The second motor could be used for a sliding door.

20
Data Logging

When using Visual Basic, ROBOLAB, or NQC, the RCX can be programmed to collect data with its sensors. Once the data is collected, these programs can then be used to upload the data back into the computer to be graphed and analyzed. This chapter features four data logging projects that are discussed in four sections in this chapter: "Refrigerator," "Doorway," "Motor Speed," and "Motor Power Level."

Introduction

In addition to storing variables, the RCX has the ability to collect and store large amounts of data. Data collected by the RCX can then can be uploaded via infrared communication back to your computer to be stored and displayed. Data logging is useful for the following:

- Science experiments, such as an RCX weather station outside your window
- Finding out things about places that you can't go (like the inside of the refrigerator)

- Collecting information about a place when you are not there (such as whether or not your family members have been sneaking into your room)

Data logging is a feature of the RCX that is not accessible with RCX Code. The code examples in this chapter use Visual Basic, ROBOLAB, and NQC.

Refrigerator

Designing and Building

Taking data from inside the refrigerator can tell you a lot of information. For example, you can figure out the following:

- How much the temperature rises when the door is left open
- Whether the light really does go off when you close the door
- The time of day when someone in your family took the leftover birthday cake that you have been saving

These three ideas require an RCX, a temperature sensor, and a light sensor (see Figure 20.1).

Figure 20.1

The light sensor and the temperature sensor can be mounted on the RCX and placed inside the refrigerator.

Programming and Testing

Visual Basic

In Visual Basic, taking data involves two new commands: **SetDatalog** and **DatalogNext**. The **SetDatalog** command tells the RCX how many data points you expect to take. The **DatalogNext** command actually takes the data. The following is a Visual Basic program for taking light, temperature, and timer data while in the refrigerator:

```
' Datalogging example - Refrigerator

Option Explicit

Public Const SENSOR_1 = 0
Public Const SENSOR_3 = 2
Public Const LIGHT_TYPE = 3
Public Const TEMP_TYPE = 2
Public Const CON = 2
```

```
Public Const SENVAL = 9
Public Const TIMER = 1

Sub datalog()
 With UserForm1.Spirit1
   .InitComm
   .BeginOfTask 0
   .SetSensorType SENSOR_1, LIGHT_TYPE
   .SetSensorType SENSOR_3, TEMP_TYPE
   .SetDatalog 600          ' Take 600 points of data
   .ClearTimer 0            ' Reset the timer
   .Loop CON, 0
    .DatalogNext TIMER , 0 ' Take timer data
    .DatalogNext SENVAL, 0 ' Take light data
    .DatalogNext SENVAL, 2 ' Take temperature data
    .Wait CON, 500          ' Wait for 500 hundredths of a
                            '  second

   .EndLoop
   .EndOfTask
 End With
End Sub
```

In this Visual Basic program, 600 points of the light sensor, temperature sensor, and timer have all been logged every 5 seconds.

To retrieve the data, a separate Visual Basic code window is needed. The new command for uploading data is **UploadDatalog**. The Software Developer's Kit includes an example program for uploading data and placing it in a list box on the Visual Basic Form window. Before this code can be used, two text boxes and a list box must be placed on the form (see Figure 20.2) along with Spirit1, represented by the LEGO logo.

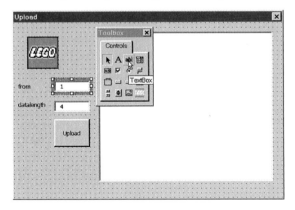

Figure 20.2
To upload data, a list box and two text boxes must be added to the form.

Then, instead of creating a new module window from the menu bar, double-click on the Upload button while still in Edit mode. This brings up a window that already has the two lines of code:

```
Private Sub Command1_Click()
End Sub
```

The code that specifies what should happen when the Upload button is clicked goes between those two lines of code. The following code taken from page 93 of the Software Developer's Kit can be used to display the data:

```
Private Sub Command1_Click()
 Dim arr As Variant
 Dim I As Integer
 Dim from As Integer
 Dim datalength As Integer

 from = Val(Text1.Text)
 datalength = Val(Text2.Text)
 Arr = PBrickCtrl.UploadDatalog(from, datalength)
 If IsArray(arr) Then
  For I = Lbound(arr, 2) To Ubound(arr, 2)
  List1.AddItem "Type: " + Str(arr(0, I)) + "  No. " +
  Str(arr(1, I)) + "  Value: " + Str(arr(2, I))
  Next I
 Else
  MsgBox "Upload NOT a valid array"
 End If

End Sub
```

Figure 20.3

Five Areas that make up an Investigator project

This code assumes that you have not changed the names of the text boxes or list box from Text1, Text2, and List1, respectively. If you have changed their names, then you need to modify this code accordingly.

ROBOLAB

Taking data with ROBOLAB involves using ROBOLAB Investigator, available in ROBOLAB 2.0. After clicking on Investigator from the main screen of ROBOLAB, click on New Project to start an Investigator project. In the upper-left corner of the screen is a circle depicting the five Areas of an Investigator Project (see Figure 20.3).

The first area is the Programming Area. The Programming area is available from the traffic light icon, which is highlighted by default. The programming window appears to the right. Multiple pages can be stored within each Area. To add more programs to an Area, click on the add or subtract page buttons (see Figure 20.4). In addition to multiple pages, multiple levels of functionality and difficulty also exist for each Area. To write a program that takes light and temperature sensor data in the re-frigerator, only Programming Level 2 out of 5 is required (see Figure 20.5). Unlike Visual Basic, ROBOLAB automatically records the time that the data is taken without having to take timer data.

Figure 20.4
Add or subtract pages from an Area with the add and subtract buttons.

Figure 20.5
ROBOLAB Investigator Level 2 program to capture 500 points of light and tem-perature data in the refrigerator every 5 seconds

The next Area clockwise from the Programming Area is the Upload Area. Here you can upload multiple sets of data from different programs. In the Upload Area, you also assign each set of data to a color and give each set a name, so that it can be distinguished on a graph. I have chosen to set the light data to blue and the temperature data to orange, to roughly match the color of the sensors themselves (see Figure 20.6).

After the data has been uploaded, it can be viewed in the View and Compare Area, and manipulated in the Compute Area. The last Area, in the center of the circle, is the Journal Area. Here, notes can be taken about your Investigator project, JPG images that you have taken of your project (or JPG images that you find on the Internet) can be imported, and pages from other Areas can be imported and written about.

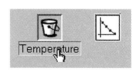

Figure 20.6
The color, name, and plotting style of each graph can be chosen in the Upload Area.

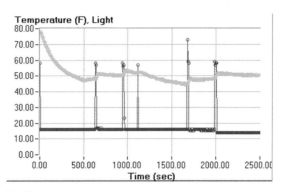

Figure 20.7

The graph of temperature and light data from inside the refrigerator in the View and Compare Area

In the View and Compare Area, the Compare Level allows you to choose two different sets of data that you would like to see side by side. Figure 20.7 shows the orange and the blue data that were chosen so that a direct comparison of temperature and light can be made. As can be seen from the graph, the temperature sensor took about 500 seconds, or 8.3 minutes, to cool down from room temperature. This does not mean that the temperature inside of the refrigerator really started out at 78 degrees Fahrenheit. It means that the temperature sensor takes a long time to react to big changes in temperature, something you should keep in mind when using the temperature sensor. The temperature sensor available from DCP is more accurate than the standard LEGO temperature sensor. By zooming in on the graph, you also can see that the temperature rose between 0.5 and 3 degrees after the refrigerator door was opened, depending on how long the door was open (see Figure 20.8).

At around 1,700 seconds (28.3 minutes), the light from the refrigerator door opening went up further than usual. This is when I lifted the RCX to check if the little person was still running on the display, meaning that the program was still taking data. This caused the light sensor to face the refrigerator light more directly. The drop-off in light sensor reading at 2,000 seconds (33.3 minutes) was due to the fact that I removed a water bottle that had been in front of the light sensor from the refrigerator to drink from it.

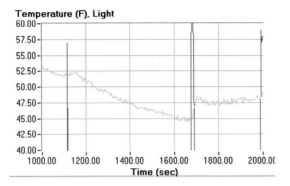

Figure 20.8
Zooming in on a graph allows you to see more details.

NQC

Writing an NQC program for taking data is similar to doing so in Visual Basic. There are also two new commands to learn: **CreateDatalog** and **AddToDatalog**. The following is an NQC program for taking light and temperature data inside the refrigerator:

```
// Datalogging - Refrigerator

task main()
{
 SetSensor(SENSOR_1, SENSOR_LIGHT);
 SetSensor(SENSOR_3, SENSOR_FAHRENHEIT);

 CreateDatalog(0);   // Clear the datalog
 CreateDatalog(600); // Create a new datalog with 600 points
                     //  available

 ClearTimer(0);

 while(true)
 {
  AddToDatalog(Timer(0)); // Add a new value to the datalog
  AddToDatalog(SENSOR_1);
  AddToDatalog(SENSOR_3);
  Wait(500);
 }
}
```

Uploading data with NQC is much easier than with Visual Basic. A one-step NQC command outputs the data to the screen or a text file. The command **nqc -datalog** at a command prompt uploads the data log from the RCX and displays it in the prompt window. Using `nqc -datalog_full` presents all of the information about the data on the screen, such as which sensor and which port the data came from. If there is so much data that it scrolls off of the screen, use `nqc -datalog_full |` `more`. Better yet, using `nqc -datalog >data.txt` outputs the data to a text file called data.txt, where it can be graphed and further manipulated using a program like Microsoft Excel. An example text file looks like the following:

```
Uploading Datalog..
Timer 0: 0
Sensor 1: 32
Sensor 3: 811
Timer 0: 50
Sensor 1: 32
Sensor 3: 811
Timer 0: 100
Sensor 1: 32
Sensor 3: 815
Timer 0: 150
Sensor 1: 32
Sensor 3: 811
Timer 0: 200
Sensor 1: 32
Sensor 3: 811
```

■ ■

Programming Aside: Using Microsoft Excel to Graph RCX Data

To graph data from a file that was created with Visual Basic or NQC, you can use a program such as Microsoft Excel. The following instructions explain how:

1. Create a full text file of the data, complete with the name(s) of the sensor(s).

2. Copy and paste the text file into Microsoft Excel, starting from cell A1.

3. If not already selected, select the entire A column by clicking on the letter A heading above the column.

4. Go to Data | Text to Columns to separate the headings of your data from the data itself. Excel will first make a guess

as to how the data columns are divided. It should guess that the data is divided by fixed-width white space. If it has done so, click the Next button.

5. The next screen makes a guess as to how many divisions you want in your data. Excel guesses that you want two divisions in the data, first between the name of the sensor and the sensor port, and then between the port and the data itself. Because you do not care about dividing the sensor from its port, double-click on this division to get rid of it and click the Next and then Finish buttons.

6. If you have data from multiple sources, such as a timer and a sensor or two, choose Data | Sort and sort by column A ascending. Then cut and paste to divide your data into different columns.

7. Choose Insert | Chart and pick an XY scatter plot with points and straight lines. You must tell Excel that you want the timer data to be the x-axis and the sensor data to be the y-axis. You can also choose custom labels and colors for your graph (see Figure 20.9).

■■■■■■■■■■■■■■■■■■■■■■■■■■■■■■■■

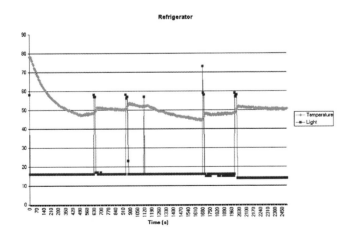

Figure 20.9
The refrigerator data in Microsoft Excel

Doorway

Designing and Building

A light sensor in the doorway of your room (see Figure 20.10) can turn into several different types of projects:

- An alarm system: the RCX beeps when somebody enters.
- A booby trap: a motor is triggered to drop something on the intruder's head.
- A passive detection system: taking data of how many times the door has been opened and when.

The two long wires can be connected to the light sensor to maintain a long distance between the light sensor and the RCX.

Programming and Testing

Visual Basic

The following is a Visual Basic program to take data from a light sensor mounted above a doorway:

Figure 20.10

A light sensor can be taped above a doorway and used for a variety of projects.

```
' Datalogging example - Doorway

Option Explicit

Public Const SENSOR_1 = 0
Public Const LIGHT_TYPE = 3
Public Const CON = 2
Public Const SENVAL = 9
Public Const TIMER = 1

Sub datalog()
 With UserForm1.Spirit1
  .InitComm
  .BeginOfTask 0
  .SetSensorType SENSOR_1, LIGHT_TYPE
  .SetDatalog 500
  .ClearTimer 0
  .Loop CON, 0
   .DatalogNext TIMER , 0 ' Take timer data
   .DatalogNext SENVAL, 0 ' Take light data
   .Wait CON, 50          ' Wait for 50 hundredths of a
                          '  second
  .EndLoop
  .EndOfTask
 End With
End Sub
```

ROBOLAB

To take data with only one sensor, only Investigator Programming Level 1 is required (see Figure 20.11).

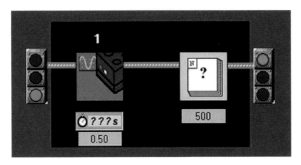

Figure 20.11

An Investigator Programming Level 1 program to take 500 points of data with the light sensor every 0.5 seconds

Whenever the door to the room is opened, a double-spike appears on the graph (see Figure 20.12). The first spike represents the door opening, and the second spike represents it closing. The two spikes that are about a minute apart from each other are from when my neighbor knocked on my door to talk to me. I stood in the doorway for a minute and talked to him before closing the door again.

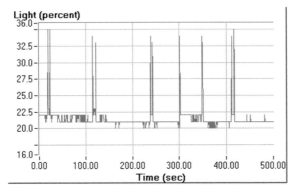

Figure 20.12

The data from the light sensor in the doorway

NQC

The following is an NQC program for taking data from a light sensor mounted above a doorway:

```
// Datalogging - Doorway

task main()
{
 SetSensor(SENSOR_1, SENSOR_LIGHT);

 CreateDatalog(0);
 CreateDatalog(500);

 ClearTimer(0);

 while(true)
 {
  AddToDatalog(Timer(0));
  AddToDatalog(SENSOR_1);
  Wait(50);
 }
}
```

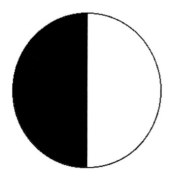

Figure 20.13

The black-and-white wheel can be used with a light sensor in determining the speed of the motor.

Motor Speed

The documented speed of the LEGO motor without a load (free spinning) is approximately 350 RPM. One idea for a data logging project is to verify this with LEGO sensors. By gearing down the motor, such as with Machine with Minifig in Chapter 11, the speed of the motor can be verified by eye. However, when connected to a gear train, the motor is under a load and therefore spins slower than its maximum rate. Figuring out the maximum speed of the motor this way is not accurate. A better way of determining speed is to place an angle sensor directly onto the shaft of the motor, or by placing the black-and-white spinning disk onto the motor shaft (see Figures 20.13 and 20.14).

Figure 20.14
The speed of the LEGO motor can be determined with a light sensor.

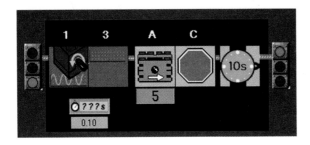

Figure 20.15

*An Investigator Level 2 program for finding out the speed of the motor with an
angle sensor*

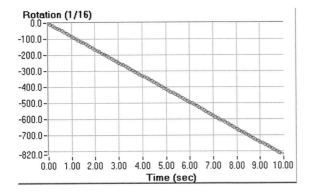

Figure 20.16

The data that comes back from the angle sensor is in 1/16ths of a rotation.

The motor speed can then be verified by data logging
the angle or light sensor values (see Figure 20.15). Doing so
demonstrates some of the additional features of ROBOLAB
Investigator.

When taking data with the angle sensor, the direction
that the motor spins affects the sign of the angle sensor values
(see Figure 20.16). The data that comes back from the angle
sensor is in 1/16ths of a rotation and can be positive or negative depending on the direction of rotation. To change the angle sensor data to full, positive rotations, it is necessary to use
the Compute Area and divide the data in the graph by –16 (see
Figure 20.17). From this graph, it can be determined that the
motor went approximately 5 rotations per second, or 300 revolutions per minute.

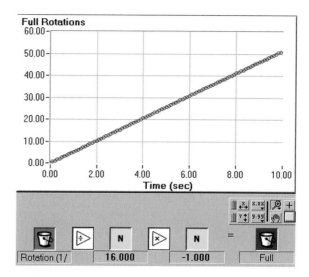

Figure 20.17
Dividing by 16 and multiplying by –1 turns negative 1/16ths of a rotation into positive full rotations of the motor.

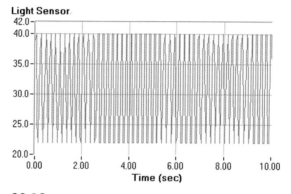

Figure 20.18
The light sensor data from a spinning black-and-white wheel attached to the motor

With the light sensor attached to the motor, the graph looks very different (see Figure 20.18). The light sensor alternates between light and dark very quickly. By counting spikes, it can also be determined that the motor was spinning at approximately 300 RPM. Alternatively, Compute Level 5 could be used to calculate the speed of the motor with advanced mathematical functions (see Figure 20.19). The Compute Level 5 program cal-

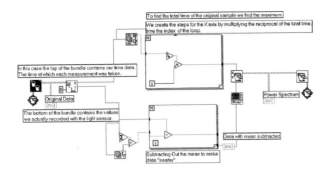

Figure 20.19
The Compute Level 5 program for calculating the speed of the motor from a wave of light sensor data

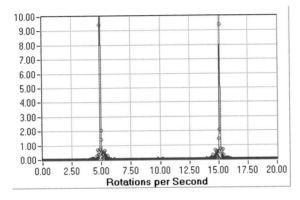

Figure 20.20
The results of the Compute Level 5 program

culates the motor speed as two possible values: 5 rotations per second (300 RPM) or 15 rotations per second (900 RPM). We know that the motor could not possibly turn 900 RPM, so the answer must be 300 RPM (see Figure 20.20).

Motor Power Level

As was mentioned in Chapter 11, the speed of the LEGO motors does not change much with the **set power** command when little load is on the motor. With data logging, we have the opportunity to prove it. The first step is to write a data logging program that will turn on the motors at successively higher power levels. In ROBOLAB, this requires Program Level 4 or 5 (see Figure 20.21).

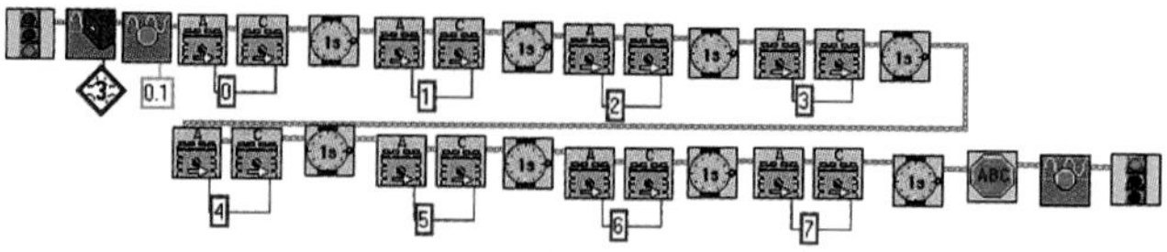

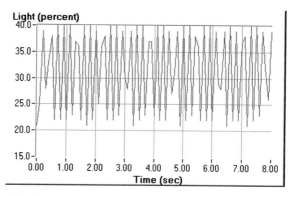

Figure 20.21

The Program Level 4 program for taking speed data while the speed of the motor is successively increased

The program in Figure 20.21 gathers light sensor data every 0.1 seconds for eight seconds. Every second, the speeds of the motors are increased by 1.

Note: In ROBOLAB, speeds 1 through 5 really correspond to RCX speeds 1,2,4,6,and 8. You must use raw numbers if accurate RCX speeds are desired, such as in this example.

Figure 20.22

The results of the program shown in Figure 20.21 and a free-spinning motor with constantly increasing power level

First, this program was run with a free-spinning motor (see Figure 20.22). The graph in Figure 20.22 shows that the speed of the free-spinnng motor did not perceptibly change when the power levels were successively increased.

Next, the program for increasing speed little by little was run with a motor under a load. A motor is under a load when, for example, it is trying to drive a robot across the floor. The Acrobot was used to perform this experiment (see Figure 20.23). When the program that increases speed little by little was run on the Acrobot, different results were ob-

Figure 20.23

A light sensor and a black-and-white wheel are added to the Acrobot to determine changes in speed with changes in power level when the motor is under a load.

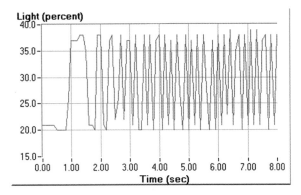

Figure 20.24

The speed of the Acrobot, as measured by the light sensor and a spinning wheel

tained than when the motor was free-spinning (see Figure 20.24).

The graph in Figure 20.24 shows that when the motor has a load, such as when it has to get a heavy Acrobot to drive along the floor, the power level of the motors do indeed have an effect. Furthermore, the effect is most pronounced at the lower power levels. After power level 5, the speed of the Acrobot remains intact at 4.5 revolutions per second of the front wheel.

■ ■

Scientific Aside: Momentum and Inertia

After power level 5, the Acrobot and the inside of the motors have both picked up so much *momentum* that changes in the power level have a barely noticeable effect on the speed of the Acrobot. The momentum of something is the force of its movement. The higher the speed or the mass of the object, the higher its momentum.

Momentum = Speed × Mass

In the beginning, when the Acrobot has no momentum, the power of the motors have to overcome the *inertia* of the Acrobot sitting still. At this point, changes in power level have a big effect on the speed of the robot. Inertia is the property by which things stay at rest (or in straight-line motion at a constant speed) until acted upon by an outside force.

■■■■■■■■■■■■■■■■■■■■■■■■■■■■■■■■

By using an angle sensor (see Figure 20.25), we can easily calculate the speed of the Acrobot more readily using Compute Tools 3 (see Figures 20.26 and 20.27). The free-spinning motor remained at a constant speed regardless of power-level, while

Figure 20.25

An angle sensor can be attached to the Acrobot to determine speed and acceleration.

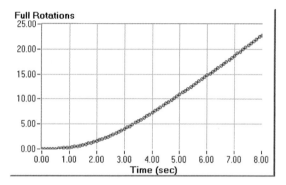

Figure 20.26

The number of rotations of the angle sensor versus time for the Acrobot

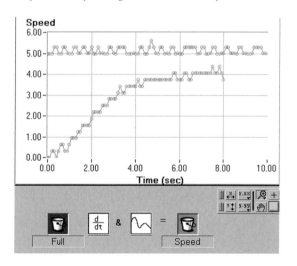

Figure 20.27

The speed of the motor in revolutions per second for the free-spinning motor (top) and when attached to the Acrobot (bottom curve)

the Acrobot gradually picked up speed before reaching its top speed. The top speed of the Acrobot was less than the top speed of the free-spinning motor.

What about the actual land speed of the Acrobot? We know angle sensor rotations per second; what about feet per second or meters per second along the floor? Knowing the circumference of the wheel of the Acrobot, this speed can be calculated. LEGO makes this easy by always printing the diameter and width of its wheels on their sides. On the large Acrobot wheels is printed "81.6," which stands for 81.6 millimeters, or 8.16 centimeters in diameter. Because the circumference of the wheel is π × diameter, the circumference must be around 25.6 centimeters. If we multiply the rotations of the angle sensor by 25.6, the result will be centimeters per second (see Figure 20.28).

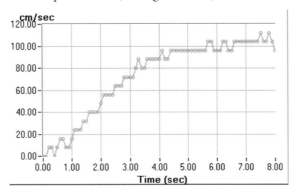

Figure 20.28
The speed of the Acrobot in centimeters per second, when the power level is successively increased from 1 to 8 over eight seconds (0–100 cm/sec in 6 seconds!).

Further Work

Some other ideas for data collection:

- A voting machine with three touch sensors can monitor the opinions of your friends.
- Log the number of times that the Keep On Moving robot has bumped into something while you were out of the room.
- Log light sensor data from Smart Acrobot to determine which method is better: a spinning black-and-white wheel or a box of yellow bricks.

21
Advanced Communication

In RCX Code, you can only send numbers *from one robot to another. With Visual Basic, ROBOLAB, and NQC, robots can send other information, such as the value of their sensors. This ability enabled the creation of the first two robots in this chapter, the Copycat and the Infrared Fax Machine. Taking the topic of advanced communication even further, this chapter explores ROBOLAB's built-in ability for robots to communicate over the Internet with the Internet Copycat.*

Copycat

Inspiration

Once during a visit to the MIT Media Lab in the early 1990s, I saw a demonstration of a project experimenting with the sense of touch over the Internet. Two rollers were connected to two different computers over the Internet. When one person moved one roller, the other roller moved in unison. It amazes me that two people with RCXs and a copy of ROBOLAB can now do this on their own.

Designing and Building

By using angle sensors, Copycat robots can be made that can imitate each other's movements. The Copycat robots use the basic chassis of the Flashlight Follower, with larger wheels and an angle sensor attached to one axle. I placed axle extenders on each motor to extend the axle of rotation out further from the body of the vehicle.

■■■■■■■■■■■■■■■■■■■■■■■■■■■■■■

LEGO Aside:
The Inside of the Angle Sensor

The RCX determines the value of the angle sensor when four gray plastic blades pass through two different sensors (see Figure 21.1). The four blades are attached to the shaft that turns when an axle is inserted into the angle sensor. As the shaft rotates, the individual blades are inside or outside the slots of the two sensors. For every quarter of a rotation, there are four possible states that the angle sensor can be in, resulting in four different values sent to the RCX. For a full turn, a total of 16 values are sent to the RCX: the same four values repeated four times. Because the four values are all different from each other, the angle sensor also can determine the direction that the angle sensor has been turned and register negative and positive values accordingly.

Figure 21.1
The inside of the angle sensor

■■■■■■■■■■■■■■■■■■■■■■■■■■■■■■

Programming and Testing

Although the programming for such robots is pretty straight-forward, it requires going beyond the capabilities of RCX Code. The logic of the program is as follows:

- Sending robot: Continually send the value of the angle sensor through infrared.

- Receiving robot: Continually compare the value received from the sending robot to the current value of the local angle sensor. If they are the same, stop the motors. If the message value is greater, move forward; if less, move backward.

ROBOLAB

Figure 21.2 shows the program for the sending robot in ROBOLAB.

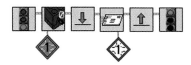

Figure 21.2
One robot continually sends the value of its angle sensor to the other one.

Figure 21.3 shows the program for the receiving robot.

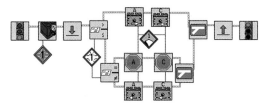

Figure 21.3
The Copycat robot takes the value received, compares it to its own angle sensor, and acts accordingly whether the values are identical or different.

■ ■

Programming Aside:
Encoding and Decoding

These programs work well with one exception. When the angle sensor reports negative values, nothing happens. This is because a negative value cannot be sent as an infrared message. To solve this problem, negative angle sensor values have to be treated differently. They can be *encoded* when they are sent to the Copycat RCX, and then the Copycat RCX can *decode* them. Figure 21.4 shows an example:

In the example shown in Figure 21.4, negative values are first turned into positive values by taking their absolute value.[1] After the negative value is turned into a positive value, 100 is added to these numbers. The Copycat robot can then decode these on the other end (see Figure 21.5):

In this example, the Copycat robot turns the high message values back into their original negative values by subtracting 100 and multiplying by –1. Once this is done, the Copycat robot can deal with the negative numbers as variables.

---

1. Commands such as absolute value are available in ROBOLAB after the Extras are installed by going to Project | Install (Remove) Extras and following the instructions.

■ ■

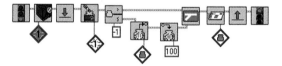

Figure 21.4
When the angle sensor value is negative, the absolute value is taken, and then a value of 100 is added.

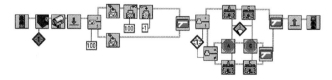

Figure 21.5
The Copycat robot can decode the negative angle sensor values.

Visual Basic

The program for the sending robot in Visual Basic is as follows:

```
' Sending Copycat Robot
Public Const VAR = 0
Public Const CON = 2
Public Const LT = 1
Public Const SENVAL = 9
Public Const SENSOR_1 = 0
Public Const ANGLE_TYPE = 4


Sub CopyCatSend()
 With UserForm1.Spirit1
  .InitComm
  .BeginOfTask 0
  .SetSensorType SENSOR_1, ANGLE_TYPE ' An angle sensor
  .ClearSensorValue SENSOR_1
  .ClearPBMessage              ' Clear the message
  .Loop CON, 0
   .SetVar 0, SENVAL, SENSOR_1
   .If VAR, 0, LT, CON, 0
    .AbsVar 0, VAR, 0          ' Take the absolute value of
                              '  the variable
    .SumVar 0, CON, 100       '  and add 100
   .EndIf
   .SendPBMessage VAR, 0      ' Send the variable as the
                              '  message
  .EndLoop
  .EndOfTask
 End With
End Sub
```

And for the receiving robot:

```
' Receiving Copycat Robot
Public Const VAR = 0
Public Const CON = 2
Public Const PBMESS = 15 ' Programmable Brick Message
Public Const GT = 0
Public Const LT = 1
Public Const EQ = 2
Public Const NE = 3
Public Const SENVAL = 9
Public Const SENSOR_1 = 0
Public Const ANGLE_TYPE = 4
Public Const OUTPUT_A = 0
Public Const OUTPUT_C = 2
```

```
Sub CopyCatReceive()
 With UserForm1.Spirit1
  .InitComm
  .BeginOfTask 0
  .SetSensorType SENSOR_1, ANGLE_TYPE
  .ClearSensorValue SENSOR_1
  .SetPower OUTPUT_A, CON, 0
  .SetPower OUTPUT_C, CON, 0
  .Loop CON, 0
   .If PBMESS, 0, GT, CON, 100 ' If the message > 100
    .SetVar 0, PBMESS, 0       ' Set variable = message
    .SubVar 0, CON, 100        ' Subtract 100
    .MulVar 0, CON, -1         ' Multiply by -1
   .Else
    .SetVar 0, PBMESS, 0
   .EndIf
   .If VAR, 0, EQ, SENVAL, SENSOR_1  ' If variable = angle
    .Off OUTPUT_A                    ' Stop
    .Off OUTPUT_C
   .Else
    .If VAR, 0, GT, SENVAL, SENSOR_1 ' If variable > angle
     .SetFwd OUTPUT_A                ' Go forward
     .SetFwd OUTPUT_C
     .On OUTPUT_A
     .On OUTPUT_C
    .Else
     .If VAR, 0, LT, SENVAL, SENSOR_1 ' If variable < angle
      .SetRwd OUTPUT_A                ' Go backward
      .SetRwd OUTPUT_C
      .On OUTPUT_A
      .On OUTPUT_C
     .EndIf
    .EndIf
   .EndIf
  .EndLoop
  .EndOfTask
 End With
End Sub
```

NQC

The NQC program for the sending robot:

```
// Copy Cat Send

task main()
{
 int rotation;

 SetSensor(SENSOR_1, SENSOR_ROTATION);
```

```
while(true)
{
 rotation = SENSOR_1;

 if (rotation < 0)
 {
  rotation = abs(rotation); // absolute value
  rotation += 100;
 }
 SendMessage(rotation);
}
}
```

And for the receiving robot:

```
// Copy Cat Receive

task main()
{
 int mail;

 SetSensor(SENSOR_1, SENSOR_ROTATION);
 ClearMessage();

 SetPower(OUT_A + OUT_C, 0);

 while(true)
 {
  mail = Message();

  if (mail > 100)
  {
   mail -= 100;
   mail *= -1;
  }

  if (mail == SENSOR_1)
  {
   Off(OUT_A + OUT_C);    // Stop
  }
  if (mail < SENSOR_1)
  {
   OnRev(OUT_A + OUT_C); // Go Backward
  }
  if (mail > SENSOR_1)
  {
   OnFwd(OUT_A + OUT_C); // Go Forward
  }
 }
}
```

Further Work

By adding a second angle sensor to each robot, the movements of the sending robot can be mimicked more precisely. See www. ceeo.tufts.edu/Me94 for an example of how this can be done.

Infrared Fax Machine

Figure 21.6
Infrared Fax Machines

The Infrared Fax Machine (see Figure 21.6) was designed and programmed by Dan Hooks and Sam Oberter, who are under-graduate students at Tufts University. The Infrared Fax Machine was created from two Technic 8094 kits. They added two angle sensors to each kit to keep track of the position on the paper. On the sending machine, a light sensor looks for light and dark values. On the receiving machine, a fine-point black marker rises up and down depending on the values received from the sending machine.

Programming and Testing

The somewhat simplified logic for the sending fax machine is as follows:

1. Start scanning.

2. If the light sensor encounters a dark value and the pen is up, send the value of the angle sensor via infrared to the receiving fax machine. If the light sensor encounters a light value and the pen is down, do the same.

3. If the end of the range of the angle sensor has been reached, send an "end of line" signal via infrared and advance forward by one line.

And for the receiving fax machine:

1. Wait for a message to be received. If the message is an angle sensor value, 1–160, move the pen until reaching the same angle sensor value and then move the pen up or down depending on which action is necessary.

2. If the message is an angle sensor value larger than 160, signaling an "end of line" message, move until the angle sensor detects the edge of the scan and then advance forward by one line.

Figures 21.7 and 21.8 show the sending and receiving fax machines in action. The ROBOLAB programs for the machines are shown in Figure 21.9 and 21.10.

Figure 21.7
The sending fax machine halfway through scanning the name "Ben"

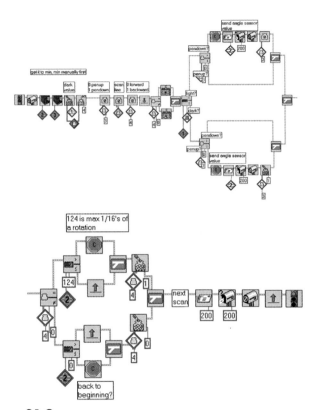

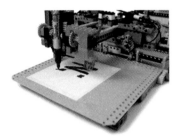

Figure 21.8
The receiving fax machine is halfway through drawing the name "Ben." Instructions of where to put the pen down are received from the scanning machine.

Figure 21.9
The ROBOLAB program for the sending IR Fax Machine

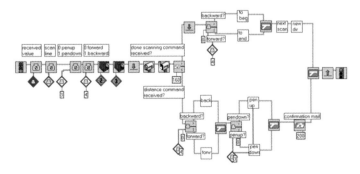

Figure 21.10
The ROBOLAB program for the receiving IR Fax Machine

NQC

The following is the sending program for the IR Fax Machine in NQC:

```
// IR Fax Receiver

// sensors
#define HPOS SENSOR_2
#define VPOS SENSOR_3

// motors
#define VMOVE   OUT_A
#define PENMOVE OUT_B
#define HMOVE   OUT_C

// useful constants
#define MAX_HPOS      124
#define LINE_HIEGHT   12
#define PEN_DOWN_TIME 51 // 0.51 seconds
#define PEN_UP_TIME   53 // 0.53 seconds

// some messages
#define REPLY_MSG     200
#define END_MSG       200

int msg;         // received message
int scanline=0; // current vertical position
int pendown=0;  // 0=up, 1=down
int backward=0; // 0=forward, 1=backward

task main()
{
 SetSensor(HPOS, SENSOR_ROTATION);
 SetSensor(VPOS, SENSOR_ROTATION);

 while(true)
 {
  read_msg();

  if (msg == END_MSG)
  {
   move_to_end();
   next_scan();
   backward = 1 - backward;
  }
  else
  {
   move_to_msg();
   move_pen();
  }
```

```
     SendMessage(REPLY_MSG);
  }
}

void move_pen()
{
 if (pendown)
 {
  //  lift pen up
  Rev(PENMOVE);
  OnFor(PENMOVE, PEN_UP_TIME);
  pendown = 0;
 }
 else
 {
  // drop pen
  Fwd(PENMOVE);
  OnFor(PENMOVE, PEN_DOWN_TIME);
  pendown = 1;
 }
}

void move_to_msg()
{
 if (backward)
 {
  OnRev(HMOVE);
  until(HPOS <= msg);
  Off(HMOVE);
 }
 else
 {
  OnFwd(HMOVE);
  until(HPOS > msg);
  Off(HMOVE);
 }
}

void move_to_end()
{
 if (backward)
 {
  OnRev(HMOVE);
  until(HPOS <= 0);
  Off(HMOVE);
 }
 else
 {
  OnFwd(HMOVE);
  until(HPOS > MAX_HPOS);
  Off(HMOVE);
 }
}
```

```
void read_msg()
{
 ClearMessage();
 do
 {
  msg = Message();
 }
 while(!msg);
}

void next_scan()
{
 scanline += LINE_HIEGHT;
 On(VMOVE);
 until(VPOS > scanline);
 Off(VMOVE);
}
```

The following is the program for the receiving IR Fax Machine in NQC:

```
// IR Fax Sender

// sensors
#define EYE  SENSOR_1
#define HPOS SENSOR_2
#define VPOS SENSOR_3

// motors
#define HMOVE OUT_C
#define VMOVE OUT_A

int dark;        // value considered "dark"
int scanline=0; // current vertical position
int pendown=0;   // 0=up, 1=down
int backward=0; // 0=forward, 1=backward

task main()
{
 SetSensor(EYE, SENSOR_LIGHT);
 SetSensor(HPOS, SENSOR_ROTATION);
 SetSensor(VPOS, SENSOR_ROTATION);
 dark = EYE - 4;

 while(true)
 {
  // begin a line
  if (backward)
   Rev(HMOVE);
  else
   Fwd(HMOVE);
```

```
  On(HMOVE);

  // read the line
  readline();
  Off(HMOVE);

  // go to next line,
  backward = 1 - backward; // reverse direction
  nextscan();
  send(200);
 }
}

void readline()
{
 int newpen;

 while(true)
 {
  // look at paper
  if (EYE > dark)
   newpen = 0;
  else
   newpen = 1;

  // should pen change states?
  if (newpen != pendown)
  {
   Off(HMOVE);
   send(HPOS);
   pendown = newpen;
   On(HMOVE);
  }

  // check for end of line
  if (backward)
  {
   if (HPOS <= 0) return;
  }
  else
  {
   if (HPOS > 124) return;
  }
 }
}

void nextscan()
{
 scanline += 12;
 On(VMOVE);
 until(VPOS > scanline);
 Off(VMOVE);
}
```

```
void send(const int &m)
{
 // send message and wait for reply
 ClearMessage();
 SendMessage(m);
 until(Message() == 200);
}
```

Internet Communication

Controlling robots over the Internet is a part of a rapidly growing field called *telerobotics*. Researchers and individuals around the country are setting up Web sites where you can control a robot from a Web browser. A number of such Web sites use the RCX.

The level of telerobotic interactivity varies from site to site. With most telerobotics sites, the communication is one way. You can send messages to the remote robot but cannot get any information from the robot, such as the value of its sensors. The only feedback often is a video image. One such site is 8ball.federated.com/, where a toy eight-ball is shaken by a Mindstorms apparatus. Another site, fastolfe.net/cam/telecam.php, enables you to control the movements of a Web cam mounted inside of a Mindstorms contraption. By downloading Web-Remote software at webremote.co.uk/, the movements of a remote RCX can be controlled over the Internet and Microsoft NetMeeting. A NetMeeting window shows you the live video of the other RCX.

In addition to these Web sites and others, there are more advanced ways of communicating with LEGO robots over the Internet. One such interface is Red Rover software, made by LEGO Dacta in cooperation with Visionary Products and the Planetary Society, and distributed by www.pitsco-legodacta.com/ in the United States. Only LEGO robots that are also running a copy of the Red Rover software can communicate with each other, however. The Planetary Society in California always has a Red Rover set up on a Mars-like terrain.

Another interesting Web site is SENSORS, which stands for the "Science and Engineering NASA Site of Remote Sensing," at www.ceeo.tufts.edu/sensors/. This site enables you to compose and send simple programs from your Web browser to a remote LEGO robot without downloading or buying any special software. Sensor data from the robots are sent back as graphs, so that you can figure out what the robot was doing. This is very similar to the way that NASA engineers operate the rovers on Mars. If you have a copy of ROBOLAB, you can send your complete ROBOLAB programs to the robots through the SENSORS site and have the remote robots perform more sophisticated tasks.

ROBOLAB

A high level of robot interactivity can easily be achieved between two people that both have a copy of ROBOLAB 2.0. ROBOLAB 2.0 has built-in commands for communication over the Internet. For example, you can program your LEGO bubble machine in California to turn on when the LEGO temperature sensor connected to an RCX in Australia reaches 35 degrees Celsius. The possibilities are endless. ROBOLAB is the only software written for the RCX that has these capabilities built into the software. Therefore, only ROBOLAB will be discussed with regard to Internet communication.

The first thing that is necessary to do within ROBOLAB is to install the Extras folder. The Extras folder contains commands that are installed when you install ROBOLAB. However, these commands are normally hidden from your icon palette. Go to Project | Install (Remove) Extras. Read through the entire description of the Extras and then select Install Extras. After the Extras are installed, ROBOLAB must be restarted. The Extras commands show up in Programmer Inventor Level 4 and Investigator Level 5. Once the Extras have been installed, an Internet communication program can be written.

For Internet communication to take place, one computer has to run the ROBOLAB Server, while the other computer must run ROBOLAB 2.0. To start the ROBOLAB Server, quit ROBOLAB and start the ROBOLAB\Extras\Server\ROBOLAB Server.exe program. ROBOLAB cannot be running on the computer that is running the ROBOLAB Server. That does not mean, however, that the RCX within sight of the Infrared Transmitter connected to the server cannot be running a program. A simple example where a ROBOLAB program is written on only one computer will be explained first.

From the computer that is not running the ROBOLAB Server, four different types of communication programs can be written. The first type is the standard program that downloads into your local RCX. For this program to run, the green Run button must be pressed on the RCX (see Figure 21.11).

Figure 21.11
A standard ROBOLAB program for the RCX

The second type of program, also for your local RCX, is a direct mode program. The direct mode folder was installed when you installed Extras. A direct mode program runs in real time to the RCX. For these programs, the Run button need not be pressed (see Figure 21.12). Now that the Extras have been added, you will also notice that more commands have been added to the RCX-to-RCX Communication menu, such as the ability to run different programs or even shut off the RCX.

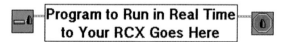

Figure 21.12
A real-time program for your local RCX

The third and fourth types of programs are for communicating with a remote RCX that is near a computer running the ROBOLAB Server. These programs are similar to the first two, in that they can either download an entire program to the remote RCX or communicate with it in real time (see Figures 21.13 and 21.14).

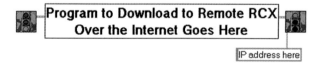

Figure 21.13
A program that will be downloaded into another RCX over the Internet

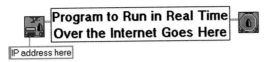

Figure 21.14
A program that will communicate with an RCX over the Internet directly

For these last two types of programs, you need to know the IP address of the computer you are trying to communicate with.

Multiple communication programs can be run at the same time. For example, two direct mode programs, one for a local RCX and another for a remote RCX, can be run simultaneously from one ROBOLAB window, and they can pass information to each other.

The first example in Figure 21.15 is a program that turns on the motor of your local RCX when the touch sensor of the remote RCX has been pressed, and turns it off when it has been pressed again.

These ROBOLAB programs were created with the Internet **direct mode** commands and local **direct mode** commands within Investigator Programming Level 5. First, a LabVIEW

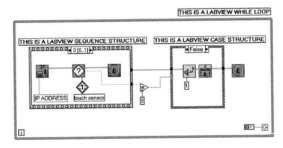

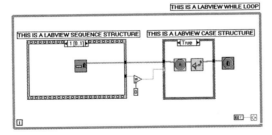

Figure 21.15
A ROBOLAB program for reading and responding to a touch sensor value on an RCX elsewhere in the world

while loop is placed on the diagram window and a "true" wired into it. This causes the program to loop indefinitely, similar to the `while(true)` in NQC. Next, a sequence structure is placed on the left side of the window so that Internet communication is established before communication with the local RCX is attempted. The value of the sensor on port 1 is requested from the distant RCX where the ROBOLAB Server is running. This value is then sent into a decision maker, called a "Case Structure." The Case Structure is like an If statement in Visual Basic or NQC. If the touch sensor is equal to 0, or not pressed, then motor A turns off, and a beep sound plays. If the touch sensor is not equal to 1, or pressed in, then motor A turns on, and a click sound plays.

Internet Copycat

The Copycat example from the beginning of the chapter can become an Internet Copycat with modified programs. Although it could, the sending robot does not need to be running a ROBOLAB program at all, because its angle sensor values will be taken from the remote robots' Internet direct mode program. The sending robot needs to be aware only that an angle sensor is on port 1. To do this, the simplest program involving an angle sensor can be downloaded and run on the sending RCX (see Figure 21.16).

Figure 21.16

The sending RCX does not need to be running a ROBOLAB program at all; yet it needs to know that it has an angle sensor attached.

The receiving RCX can run a simple program that checks the value of a variable and responds accordingly (see Figure 21.17).

The receiving robot no longer needs to be concerned about negative angle sensor values, because negative values can be placed into variables without a problem. Negative values are

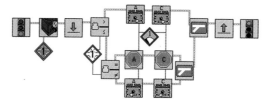

Figure 21.17

The program for the receiving robot

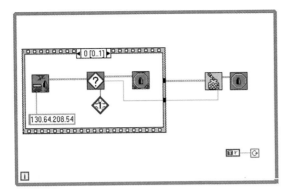

Figure 21.18
The program running on the receiving robot's computer

a problem only with infrared communication. Figure 21.18 shows the program that needs to run on the computer near the receiving robot. The local direct mode starting command is in number 1 of the two-part sequence that is hidden.

This program takes the value of the remote RCX's angle sensor and places it into a variable on the local RCX. The local RCX is already running a program that is responding to the changes in its variable. Any manual movements of the remote RCX are mimicked by the receiving RCX somewhere else in the world.

Further Work
Make the Infrared Fax machine into an Internet Fax Machine!

PART VI

Appendixes

- Appendix A, "Further Work," presents even more ideas for RCX projects for more fun.

- Appendix B provides a table of frequencies and their corresponding musical notes.

- Appendix C, "Where to Buy," lists where LEGO Mindstorms and LEGO Mindstorms for Schools products can be purchased.

- Appendix D is a directory of related Internet sites.

- Appendix E lists some of the ROBOLAB commands that are used in the book and the Help menu text for the commands.

- Appendix F, "Resources and Suggested Readings," lists books and other media for learning, exploration, and inspiration.

Appendix A
Further Work

The following examples are robots that did not receive their own chapter for one reason or another. These ideas were too short to be a full chapter (Train), were taken apart before complete photographs could be taken (Intelligent House), or were a little too risky for people to build themselves (Submarine).

Train

The RCX is compatible with the LEGO nine-volt electric trains. By connecting one of the output ports of the RCX to the train motor, the speed and direction of the Train can be programmed (see Figure A.1). By attaching sensors such as a light sensor, the Train can become a "smart" Train as well. Figure A.2 shows the Train with a light sensor; the Train is programmed to slow down and stop when the light sensor encounters the black signal.

Besides placing the RCX on the Train, the RCX can be used to control the train tracks, too (see Figure A.3). A sensor on this stationary RCX can detect the Train going by and can change the power level to the train tracks accordingly.

Intelligent House

At the Engineer's Club at the Paraclete Center in South Boston, some fifth-grade through eighth-grade students designed an Intelligent House with the RCX as their final project. This

Figure A.1
The RCX connected to a train motor

Figure A.2
The RCX on the Train with a light sensor

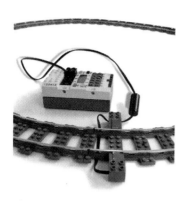

Figure A.3
The train tracks can be controlled by the RCX as well.

Intelligent House was one of the first creations to use the RCX, because these students were using beta-RCXs and a beta copy of ROBOLAB. After making bumper cars and Line-Followers, an Intelligent House was decided upon as a group project that everyone could become involved with. The house had many features, including interior lights, a television set, a rotating satellite dish, a small greenhouse, a kitchen, an elevator, a doorbell, and a porch light. The program for the Intelligent House looked something like Figure A.4:

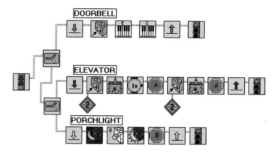

Figure A.4
The Intelligent House program

Pictures of the house can be found at ldaps.arc.nasa.gov/ Curriculum/systems.html.

Submarine

Inspiration

After reading the book *Build Your Own Underwater Robot and Other Wet Projects*, by Harry Bohm and Vickie Jensen, I was inspired to make a LEGO submarine. One of the Models of the Month at mindstorms.lego.com/ had been a submarine but not the kind of submarine that I wanted to make. That submarine could only rise up and down. I wanted a submarine like the ones that I saw in the book that could drive around!

If you want to make a LEGO submarine, be very careful. Precautions have to be taken to make sure that the motors do not get water inside of them. A motor can be ruined if these precautions are not taken. Make a submarine only at your own risk!

Designing and Building

To make the container of air, I bought a piece of 1 1/2" Schedule 40 (referring to the thickness) PVC pipe and two end caps. I found that it wasn't necessary to seal the PVC. Once the end caps were on, the tube didn't let in any water. The pipe was cut so that the length of pipe in the middle after the end caps are on is equal to the length of a 1x16 beam. Approximately 75 pennies were used as ballast weight underneath the PVC. Forty-tooth gears meshed with eight-tooth gears were connected to the impellor axle. I tested the vessel in my large bathroom sink. I attached wires to the RCX from the motors but held the RCX in my hand, above the water. I used two touch sensors to control the direction of rotation of the motors. I used both adhesive/sealant and petroleum jelly on the motors to make sure that water could not get inside of them. See the instructions on the CD-ROM for details. My Submarine is shown in Figure A.5.

Figure A.5
The Submarine

Programming and Testing

The program for the Submarine used two touch sensors to control the direction of rotation of the motors. If a third touch sensor were added, it could be used as a Stop button (see Figure A.6).

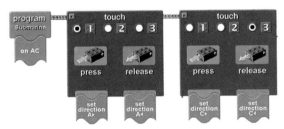

Figure A.6
The program for the Submarine

By creating an airtight enclosure, several LEGO Mindstorms members have made underwater vehicles where even the RCX can go underwater. Go to mindstorms.lego.com/ and ask for "sub".

Appendix B
Musical Notes

The table in this appendix can be used to figure out which frequencies correspond to which notes on a piano (A, B, C#, and so on).

Pitch	1	2	3	4	5	6	7	8
G#(A♭)	52	104	208	415	831	1661	3322	
G	49	98	196	392	784	1568	3136	
F#(G♭)	46	92	185	370	740	1480	2960	
F	44	87	175	349	698	1397	2794	
E	41	82	165	330	659	1319	2637	
D#(E♭)	39	78	156	311	622	1245	2489	
D	37	73	147	294	587	1175	2349	
C#(D♭)	35	69	139	277	554	1109	2217	
C	33	65	131	262	523	1047	2093	4186
B	31	62	123	247	494	988	1976	3951
A#(B♭)	29	58	117	233	466	932	1865	3729
A	28	55	110	220	440	880	1760	3520

Frequencies in the chart are in Hertz (Hz).

Appendix C
Where to Buy

At the beginning of 2000, PITSCO-LEGO Dacta (www.pldstore.com) and LEGO Shop at Home (shop.lego.com) started charging the same prices for LEGO Mindstorms peripherals. Although it is always a good idea to shop around, the prices for various components should not vary by much. Sometimes the best bet is to search an auction site like www.ebay.com/ for someone parting with a Mindstorms set for cheap, or the LEGO-specific auction site www.auczilla.com/.

The following is a list of places to purchase LEGO products. It is not a comprehensive list. LEGO Mindstorms products can be found in retail toy stores such as Kay Bee Toys and Toys "R" Us (click on "Where to Buy" at mindstorms.lego.com/ for a complete list of stores), and some LEGO Dacta products can be found at specialty hobby and teacher stores. PITSCO-LEGO Dacta sells products only to U.S. customers. See www.lego.com/dacta/addresses/wheretobuy.asp for information on LEGO Dacta products in other countries.

- **LEGO World Shop**
  shop.lego.com

- **Mondo-tronics, Inc.**
  www.RobotStore.com
  1-800-374-5764

- **PITSCO-LEGO Dacta**
  www.pitsco-legodacta-store.com/ or www.pldstore.com/
  1-800-362-4308

- **LEGO Shop at Home**
  shop.lego.com
  1-800-453-4652

- **Robot Books**
  www.robotbooks.com/

Although all of the previously listed places sell Mindstorms peripherals such as the remote control, extra sensors, and extra motors, PITSCO-LEGO Dacta offers some items that cannot be found anywhere else for individual sale. For example, PITSCO-LEGO Dacta sells the 1x2 lamp brick (in packs of two), the Macintosh Infrared Transmitter cable, the RCX AC adapter, and the RCX that has the AC adapter port. PITSCO-LEGO Dacta also sells thematic RCX kits such as the Amusement Park, Starter Set, and Cities and Transportation, which all come with colorful building instructions, and also sells specialty software packages that use the RCX such as Red Rover. They are also the sole retailer of all ROBOLAB components, such as the ROBOLAB software, curricula, *Teacher's Guides*, and DCP sensors such as humidity, air pressure, sound, pH, and voltage that are calibrated for use with the RCX when ROBOLAB is used. PITSCO-LEGO Dacta also differs from LEGO Shop at Home in the kinds of "spare parts" packages they sell. Check both sources when looking for a specific element.

Appendix D

Related Internet Sites

This appendix lists a number of Web sites that can inspire and help you build LEGO creations.

LEGO Curricula and Ideas

- **www.build-it-yourself.com/**
  Build-It-Yourself is a site run by John Galinato. It's full of creative project ideas.

- **mindstorms.lego.com/fll/**
  The FIRST LEGO League (FLL) Web site. FLL is a robotics contest for students ages 9 through 14.

- **robotics.arc.nasa.gov/**
  NASA's main Web site for robotics in the curriculum.

- **ldaps.arc.nasa.gov/**
  The LEGO Design and Programming System Web site hosts various curriculum ideas, workshop ideas, and Microsoft PowerPoint presentations about using LEGO in the curriculum.

- **www.weirdrichard.com/**
  Richard Wright posts plentiful curricula ideas about using LEGO as a learning tool.

- **news.lugnet.com/edu/**
  news.lugnet.com/dacta/

news.lugnet.com/robotics/edu/
news.lugnet.com/robotics/rcx/robolab/
The LEGO User Group Network is the most important
Web site for LEGO enthusiasts to ask questions, exchange
information, and discuss all sorts of LEGO-related topics.

- www.occdsb.on.ca/~proj4632/
  Janis and Jenni's Robotics in the Classroom site.

- www.media.mit.edu/
  The Epistemology and Learning Group at the MIT Media
  Laboratory is involved in a number of educational LEGO
  projects.

ROBOLAB

- www.lego.com/dacta/
  The official LEGO Dacta home page can be found here.
  Also see www.lego.com/dacta/robolab/

- www.ni.com/robolab/
  National Instruments is the company that makes
  LabVIEW, the programming environment that was
  used to create ROBOLAB.

- www.ceeo.tufts.edu/
  The Center for Engineering Educational Outreach at
  Tufts University was involved in creating the ROBOLAB
  programming environment.

- www.pitsco-legodacta.com/
  PITSCO is the retail site for ROBOLAB software,
  curriculum, and components in the United States.

NQC

- www.enteract.com/~dbaum/lego/nqc/
  Dave Baum's NQC site. NQC stands for "Not Quite C." It
  is a C-like programming environment for the RCX and
  can be downloaded for free. A Macintosh version is also

available. Like ROBOLAB, NQC allows full access to the capabilities of the RCX. NQC examples of the programs in this book can be found on the accompanying CD-ROM.

Software Developer's Kit

- mindstorms.lego.com/sdk/
  The Software Developer's Kit is a document that describes how you can access Spirit.ocx from software such as Visual Basic.

Appendix E
ROBOLAB Commands

Program Begin and End

	Begin	Beginning of program, required as the first command in every Inventor program.
	End	End of program, required as the last command of each task in an Inventor program.
	Stop A	Stop power to RCX port A.
	Stop All Outputs	Stop power to RCX ports A, B, C.
	Stop	Stop power to specified RCX ports; default: ports A, B, C.

Simple Outputs

	Motor A, Forward	Turn RCX port A on in forward direction at full power.
	Motor A, Reverse	Turn RCX port A on in reverse direction at full power.

	Lamp A	Turn RCX port A on full power.
	Play Sound #4	Play a rising sweep on the RCX.

General Outputs

	Lamp	Turn lamp on; default: all ports, power level 5.
	Motor Forward	Turn motor on; default: all ports, power level 5.
	Motor Reverse	Turn motor on in reverse direction; default: all ports, power level 5.
	Flip Direction	Flip direction of power to specified RCX ports; default: all ports.
	Play Sound	Play a sound on the RCX. The sounds available are: 1—Key Click 4—Rising Sweep 2—BeepBeep 5—Buzz 3—Descending Sweep 6—Fast Rising Sweep

Wait For?

	Wait for 1 Second	Wait 1 second before continuing.
	Wait for Time	Wait for specified amount of time; default: 1 second.
	Wait Random Time	Wait for a random amount of time; default: between 0 and 5 seconds.
	Wait for Push	Wait until touch sensor is pushed in; default: input port 1.
	Wait for Release	Wait until touch sensor is released; default: input port 1.

	Wait for Light	Wait until light sensor reads a value that is brighter than the number specified; default: 55, input port 1.
	Wait for Dark	Wait until light sensor reads a value that is darker than the number specified; default: 55, input port 1.
	Brighter	Wait for light sensor to read a value that is greater than current value; default: input port 1, value difference of 5.
	Darker	Wait for light sensor to read a value that is less than current value; default: input port 1, value difference of 5.

Modifiers

	Input 1	String this modifier to a command to select input port 1.
	Output A	String this modifier to a command to select output port A.
	Power Level 4	String this modifier into a motor or lamp to set the power level to 4.
	Numeric Constant	String this modifier into a sensor or timer to set a constant value.
	Value of Red Container	The value of the red container.
	Red Container	String this to a container command to select **red container**.
	Random Number	A random number between 0 and 8.
	Value of Port 1	The value of port 1.
	Red Timer	String this to a timer command to select **red timer**.

	Value of Red Timer	The value of **red timer**.
	Mail Value	The value of the mail.

Music

	Music Note	Play musical note on the RCX; default: quarter note in the standard scale.
	Musical Note Rest	Insert a pause in the music.
	Musical Duration	Specify the length of time for a note to play.
	Up an Octave	String to a music command to raise the pitch by an octave or more (if more than one is strung together).

Structures

	Touch Sensor Fork	Have the program choose between one of two paths depending on the state of touch sensor; default: input port 1.
	Fork Merge	Merge the two strings of a fork back together. It must be used with a fork.
	Task Split	Start a new task with this command to run multiple tasks simultaneously.
	Start loop	Start a loop structure; default: loop one time.
	End of Loop	Jump back to start of loop a specified number of times.
	Jump	Make the program jump to a specific place in the string.

| | Land | This command is where the program will jump to when you use the **red jump** command. |

Container

	Add to Container	Add a number to container; default: add 1 to red container.
	Remove from	Subtract a number from container; default: subtract 1 from red container
	Fill Container	Set container to a certain value; default; set red container to 1.
	Touch Container	Set container to the value of touch sensor; default; set red container to the value of touch sensor connected to port 1.
	Timer Value Container	Set container to the value of the timer; default: set red container to value of red timer.

RCX to RCX

| | RCX Send Mail | Send mail to another RCX; default: send the number 1. |

Reset

	Empty Container	Reset container value to 0; default: set red container to 0.
	Zero Timer	Reset the timer value to 0; default: set red timer to 0.
	Zero Angle Sensor	Reset the angle sensor to 0; default: input port 1.
	Empty Mailbox	Reset RCX mailbox value to 0. This empties mailbox so that mail can be received from another RCX.

Advanced Wait For?

	Wait for Increase C	Wait until the temperature is greater than the number specified; default: 30° Celsius on input port 1.
	Wait for Rotation	Wait until the angle sensor value is greater than the number of rotations specified; default: 16 (one rotation) on input port 1.
	Wait for Angle	Wait until the angle sensor value is greater than the angle specified (in either direction); default: 180° on input motor 1.
	Wait for Container	Wait until the container is equal to the number specified; default: red container equal to 1.
	Wait for Timer	Wait until the timer reaches a specified value; default: red timer equal to 1 second. YOU MUST ZERO TIMER FIRST!
	Wait for Mail	Wait until mail received from another RCX is equal to the specified number; default: any one number.

Appendix F

Resources and Suggested Readings

This appendix lists books and papers that I read in preparation for writing this book, or ones that I read in the past that helped to form my philosophy about designing and learning with LEGO. A few of them (preceded with an asterisk) served as direct inspiration for projects in this book, and the others are more for general reference.

For Teachers

Those sources that provided direct inspiration for robots are preceded with an asterisk.

Activities Integrating Mathematics and Science (AIMS). *Brick Layers: Creative Engineering with LEGO Constructions.* Fresno, Cal.: AIMS Education Foundation, 1996.

Activities Integrating Mathematics and Science (AIMS). *Brick Layers II: Creative Engineering with LEGO Constructions.* Fresno, Cal.: AIMS Education Foundation, 2000.

*Clayfield, Helen, and Robyn Hyatt. *Designing Everyday Things: Integrated Projects for the Elementary Classroom.* Portsmouth, N.H.: Heinemann, 1994.

Dewey, John. *Experience and Education.* New York: Kappa Delta Pi, 1938.

Dunn, Susan, and Rob Larson. *Design Technology: Children's Engineering.* New York: Falmer Press, 1990.

Papert, Seymour. *Mindstorms: Children, Computers, and Powerful Ideas.* New York: Basic Books, 1980.

Papert, Seymour. *The Children's Machine: Rethinking School in the Age of the Computer.* New York: Basic Books, 1993.

Papert, Seymour. *The Connected Family: Bridging the Digital Generation Gap.* Atlanta: Longstreet Press, 1996.

Resnick, Mitchel, and Yasmin Kafai, eds. *Constructionism in Practice: Designing, Thinking, and Learning in a Digital World.* Mahwah, N.J.: Lawrence Erlbaum Associates, 1996.

Inspirational/All Ages

Those sources that provided inspiration for robots are preceded with an asterisk.

*Bohm, Harry, and Vickie Jensen. *Build Your Own Underwater Robot and Other Wet Projects.* Vancouver, B.C.: Westcoast Words, 1997.

Pickering, David, Nick Turpin, and Caryn Jenner, eds. *The Ultimate LEGO Book.* New York: DK Publishing, 1999.

Elementary School/For Kids

Fowler, Allan. *It Could Still Be a Robot.* New York: Children's Press, 1997.

Potter, Tony, and Ivor Guild. *Robotics.* Tulsa: Usborne Publishing, 1993.

Reeve, Tim, and Gavin MacLeod. *Action Robots: A Pop-Up Book Showing How They Work*. New York: Dial Books for Young Readers, 1995.

Vogt, Gregory L. *Space Robots*. Mankato, Minn.: Capstone Press, 1999.

Middle School/Young Adults

Jefferis, David. *Artificial Intelligence: Robotics and Machine Evolution*. New York: Crabtree Publishing Company, 1999.

Skurzynski, Gloria. *Robots: Your High-Tech World*. New York: Bradbury Press, 1990.

Thro, Ellen. *Robotics: The Marriage of Computers and Machines*. New York: Facts On File, 1993.

Wickelgren, Ingrid. *Ramblin' Robots: Building a Breed of Mechanical Beasts*. New York: Franklin Watts, 1996.

High School/College/Adult Hobbyists

Baum, Dave. *Dave Baum's Definitive Guide to LEGO Mindstorms*. New York: Apress, 1999.

Baum, Dave, Michael Gasperi, Ralph Hempel, and Luis Villa. *Extreme Mindstorms: An Advanced Guide to LEGO Mindstorms*. New York: Apress, 2000.

Davies, Bill. *Practical Robotics*. Richmond Hill, Ontario: WERD Technology, 1997.

Iovine, John. *Robots, Androids, and Animatrons: 12 Incredible Projects You Can Build!* New York: McGraw-Hill, 1998.

Jones, Joseph L., Bruce A. Seiger, and Anita Flynn. *Mobile Robots*. Natick, Mass.: A.K. Peters, 1999.

Knudsen, Jonathan. *The Unofficial Guide to LEGO Mindstorms Robots*. Sebastopol, Cal.: O'Reilly & Associates, 1999.

McComb, Gordon. *Robot Builder's Bonanza: 99 Inexpensive Robotics Projects*. New York: TAB Books, 1987.

McComb, Gordon. *Gordon McComb's Gadgeteer's Goldmine! 55 Space-Age Projects*. New York: TAB Books, 1990.

Raucci, Richard. *Personal Robotics: Real Robots to Construct, Program, and Explore the World*. Natick, Mass.: A.K. Peters, 1999.

Psychology

Braitenberg, Valentino. *Vehicles: Experiments in Synthetic Psychology*. Cambridge, Mass.: MIT Press, 1996.

Minsky, Marvin. *The Society of Mind*. New York: Simon & Schuster, 1986.

Wiener, Norbert. *Cybernetics or Control and Communication in the Animal and the Machine*. Cambridge, Mass.: MIT Press, 1999.

Videos

*"Extreme Machines: Incredible Robots" at shopping.discovery.com/product/1116-1489-724377.html

*"Robots Rising" at shopping.discovery.com/product/1116-1489-712570.html

Magazine Articles

Ditlea, Steve. "LEGO Mania." *Popular Mechanics*. 176 (1999): 99.

Papers

This section lists sources of programmable brick-related research.

Bourgoin, Mario. "Using LEGO Robots to Explore Dynamics." Master's thesis, MIT Media Laboratory, 1990.

Describes the new programming language specifically developed to help kids think about dynamics when working with small LEGO robots.

Granott, Nira. "Microdevelopment of Co-Construction of Knowledge During Problem Solving: Puzzled Minds, Weird Creatures, and Wuggles." Ph.D. diss. MIT Media Laboratory, 1993.

Analysis of the thinking processes of adults trying to understand the behaviors of small LEGO robots.

Hogg, David, Fred Martin, and Mitchel Resnick. "Braitenberg Creatures." Epistemology and Learning Memo #13. Cambridge, Mass.: MIT Media Laboratory, 1991.

Available at lcs.www.media.mit.edu/people/fredm/ papers/vehicles/

Martin, Fred. "Children, Cybernetics and Programmable Turtles." Master's thesis, MIT, 1988.

Describes work with fifth-grade children using an early version of the programmable brick technology.

Martin, Fred. "Building Robots to Learn Design and Engineering." ed. Lawrence P. Grayson. In *Proceedings of the 1992 Frontiers in Education Conference*, Nashville, Tenn.: Vanderbilt University, 1992.

Describes the MIT LEGO Robot Design Competition project.

Martin, Fred. "Circuits to Control: Learning Engineering by Designing LEGO Robots." Ph.D. diss. MIT Media Laboratory, 1994.

Genesis and analysis of the MIT LEGO Robot Design Competition, an intensive month-long robot design course for MIT undergraduates based on bricklike technology.

Martin, Fred. "Ideal and Real Systems: A Study of Notions of Control in Undergraduates Who Design Robots." In *Constructionism in Practice: Designing, Thinking, and Learning in a Digital World*, edited by Y. Kafai and M. Resnick.

Adaptation of one chapter from Martin's 1994 dissertation "Circuits to Control."

Martin, Fred, and Mitchel Resnick. "LEGO/Logo and Electronic Bricks: Creating a Scienceland for Children." ed. David L. Ferguson. In *Advanced Educational Technologies for Mathematics and Science*. Berlin: Springer-Verlag, 1993.

> Describes LEGO/Logo work circa 1990.

*Papert, Seymour, and Cynthia Solomon. "Twenty Things to Do with a Computer." 1971.

> Short, visionary memo suggesting 20 different project activities kids could do on computers were they ubiquitous. This was written in the teletype days but describes projects that are yet to be fully exploited. Many of the projects are prescient of LEGO/Logo and the programmable brick.

Resnick, Mitchel. "LEGO, Logo, and Life." In *Artificial Life*, edited by C. Langton. Reading, Mass.: Addison-Wesley, 1988.

Resnick, Mitchel. "Xylophones, Hamsters, and Fireworks: The Role of Diversity in Constructionist Activities." In *Constructionism*, edited by I. Harel and S. Papert. Ablex Publishing, 1991.

> Available at el.www.media.mit.edu/groups/el/Papers/mres/Xylo/XH.html

Resnick, Mitchel. "Behavior Construction Kits." *Communications of the ACM* 36, (July 1993).

> Available at el.www.media.mit.edu/groups/el/Papers/mres/BCK/BCK.html

Resnick, Mitchel, Fred Martin, Randy Sargent, and Brian Silverman. "Programmable Bricks: Toys to Think With." *IBM Systems Journal* 35. (1996): 443-452.

> Available at www.research.ibm.com/journal/sj/mit/sectionc/martin.html

Sargent, Randy. "The Programmable LEGO Brick: Ubiquitous Computing for Kids." Master's thesis. MIT Media Laboratory, 1995.

> Discusses hardware and software design goals of the Programmable Brick project and a number of different activities using the brick with kids.

Sargent, Randy, Mitchel Resnick, Fred Martin, and Brian Silverman. "Building and Learning with Programmable Bricks."
Logo Update 3 (1995).

Good overall introduction to the Programmable Brick
project. Discusses features of the pocket programmable
brick. Available from the Logo Foundation, 250 West 57th
Street, New York, NY 10107-2228; 1-212-765-4918.

Sargent, Randy, Mitchel Resnick, Fred Martin, and Brian Silver-
man. "Building and Learning with Programmable Bricks."
In *Constructionism in Practice: Designing, Thinking, and
Learning in a Digital World*, edited by Y. Kafai and M.
Resnick.

Based on Sargent's 1995 thesis.

Glossary

algorithm A series of rules for how to solve a problem. Oftentimes finding the right commands to program a LEGO robot involves finding the right algorithm.

ambient light The average light level in the room surrounding your robot.

Dave Baum The creator of Not Quite C (NQC), a C-like programming environment for the RCX.

bottom-up design Involves taking inventory of the available materials and resources and figuring out how you can use them to your best advantage. For example, bottom-up design is when you look at all of the LEGO elements in your kit and think "what can I make with these?" While top-down design enables you to think about the overall function of your robot, bottom-up design focuses you on the actual physical limitations that you have to work with.

command A programming unit that instructs the RCX.

comments Words in a program written by the programmer that help people understand what the program does.

COM port The communications port on your computer with which you have set up communication between your programming software and the Infrared Transmitter.

compound gear train Involves situations where multiple gears are on the same axle. This kind of configuration results in a multiplying effect for the gear ratio.

constants Numbers in a program that never change value.

constructionism   A phrase coined by Seymour Papert, constructionism is an educational philosophy that extends the ideas in constructivism. Constructionism states, for example, that construction of objects outside of the head facilitates construction of understanding of concepts inside of the head.

constructivism   The educational philosophy of constructivism states, among other things, that knowledge is constructed inside of the learner's head and cannot be forced into his or her head.

Constructopedia   A book of building instructions that comes with the Robotics Invention System kits and LEGO Dacta Team Challenge kits. The Mindstorms and Dacta *Constructopedia*s differ considerably.

cricket   The "third-generation" computerized LEGO device. The cricket has similar functionality to the RCX but runs on a nine-volt battery instead of six AA batteries and is a lot smaller than the RCX.

Droid Developer Kit   Part of the LEGO Mindstorms Star Wars product line, the Droid Developer Kit enables you to build a model of R2D2 with the microscout. The microscout is a small white programmable brick with one built-in motor and a built-in light sensor.

expansion sets   Sets designed to work with the Robotics Invention System set in the LEGO Mindstorms product line to increase the flexibility in the kinds of robots that are possible to build.

Exploration Mars   One of the LEGO Mindstorms expansion sets.

Extreme Creatures   One of the LEGO Mindstorms expansion sets.

feedback   When a robot gathers information from its environment that can help control its own operation, such as using a light sensor to detect when the edge of a table has been reached.

firmware   The microprogram that enables the RCX to interpret programs that are downloaded into it. Without the firmware, the RCX can run only its built-in programs.

FIRST   Stands for "For Inspiration and Recognition of Science and Technology."

FIRST LEGO League (FLL)   A competition for middle-school age students ages 9 through 14 that takes place around September through December.

form follows function   The phrase that refers to the design philosophy that the function of a design should be considered before its form. In other words, the behavior of a robot should be thought about before its physical design. Following this philosophy prevents you from getting stuck in one kind of thinking.

frequency   Used when measuring how fast something vibrates or moves back and forth. In music, this is called the "tone." In RCX Code, frequencies are entered into the commands to play tones.

friction   When different surfaces rub against each other. It is always a factor when designing robots and is the cause of many different problems. Sometimes there is a problem in not having enough friction, such as when a robot gets dust on its wheels, or the surface it is driving on is too slippery. Other times there is a problem in having too much friction, such as when bushings or gears are rubbing too much on the edges of beams as they turn.

Anthony Fudd   A LEGO Mindstorms master builder. Some of his models include the ATM Machine, Copy Machine, Refrigerator Fred, Card Dealer, and a machine that can pick up LEGO bricks off the floor.

gearing down   Driving a large gear with a smaller one is called "gearing down." Gearing down increases strength but decreases speed. Gearing down is useful in situations where you need strength, such as climbing up a hill, grabbing something, or lifting something.

gearing up   Driving a small gear with a larger one is called "gearing up." Gearing up increases speed but decreases strength. Gearing up is useful when you need speed.

gear ratio   Expressed as number of turns of the driver : number of turns of the follower, where the driver is the first gear in the gear train, and the follower is the last. For example, a 40-tooth gear turning an 8-tooth gear has a gear ratio of 1:5. One turn of the 40-tooth gear results in five turns of the 8-tooth gear.

idler   A gear that transmits force and motion from a driver to a follower without actually changing the amount of force or speed of the follower. Only the direction of rotation is changed when an idler is put between a driver and a follower. With a driver, idler, and follower, all of the teeth mesh together in a row, and no two gears are on the same axle.

inertia   The property by which things stay at rest (or in straight-line motion at a constant speed) until acted upon by an outside force. A robot rolling across the floor has inertia.

Infrared Transmitter (IR Transmitter)   Connects to a serial or USB port on your computer and transfers the program instructions to the RCX.

lamp   The LEGO lamp is the other output that can be used with the RCX besides the motors. The lamp comes in the LEGO Mindstorms Ultimate Accessory Set and various LEGO Dacta sets.

LEGO   The word "LEGO" is a combination of the two words "play well," which in Danish is "leg godt."

LEGO Dacta   The educational division of the LEGO Group.

LEGO Engineer   The graphical software for the serial interface box developed by Chris Rogers and others at Tufts University in Medford, Massachusetts. Based on National Instruments LabVIEW software, LEGO Engineer is in some ways a precursor to ROBOLAB software for the RCX.

LEGO Mindstorms   The robotic division of the LEGO Group.

loop   Causes a certain set of commands to repeat for a certain amount of times in a program.

LUGNET   The LEGO User Group Network, a series of Web pages full of resources, information, and newsgroup discussions online.

MIT   The Massachusetts Institute of Technology in Cambridge, Massachusetts.

momentum   The speed and mass associated with a robot's movement. A force causes a change in momentum.

motor   The primary output device for the RCX. The motor's function is to spin, providing force and motion, or actuation, to the robot. There are three main types of nine-volt motors. They are the micromotor, regular nine-volt motor, and the gear motor. The gear motor comes with the Robotics Invention System (RIS) kit.

multitasking   The RCX can do multitasking, that is, perform multiple actions at once.

NQC   Stands for "Not Quite C." It is a C-like programming environment for the RCX written by Dave Baum.

Seymour Papert   Seymour Papert wrote a book called *Mindstorms* in 1980 with the subtitle "Children, Computers, and Powerful Ideas." He is a professor at the MIT Media Laboratory and is a creator of the LOGO language.

PITSCO-LEGO Dacta   The distributor of LEGO Dacta products in the United States. Its Web site is www.pldstore.com/.

Plastruct   A liquid compound that fuses two pieces of plastic for good. Plastruct can be used to keep a LEGO structure together when transporting it or to make it waterproof. The directions for Plastruct should be followed carefully.

program   An RCX program is the instructions that are given to the RCX for how to behave. The program for a certain task can be written in any programming environment on the computer, but what gets sent to the RCX for a given task is always the same.

pulse width modulation (PWM)   A way of controlling the speed of a motor by turning it on and off quickly. The rate at which the motor is turned on and off is changed to change the speed.

RCX   A microprocessor inside of a plastic LEGO casing. The RCX is the "brain" of the LEGO robot, processing program commands and sending and receiving information to and from motors and sensors.

RCX Code   The graphical programming environment that comes with the Robotics Invention System software.

remote control   Enables you to control your robot by sending it direct output commands, messages, and program execution commands. The remote control does not work until the firmware has been downloaded into the RCX.

ROBOLAB   The graphical software sold as a part of the Mindstorms for Schools product line by LEGO Dacta distribution partners. ROBOLAB was a joint development between the Tufts University College of Engineering, LEGO Dacta, and National Instruments of Austin, Texas.

Robosports   One of the LEGO Mindstorms expansion sets.

robot   The modern term "robot" comes from the Czech word "robota," which means worker. The term "robot" came from the play *Rossum's Universal Robots*, written by Karl Capek in 1920. A robot, according to the definition, is a machine or device that operates automatically.

Robotics Discovery Set   Part of the LEGO Mindstorms product line. It contains a different and less sophisticated programmable brick than the RCX called the "Scout." The Scout can be programmed by pressing the buttons near its display and does not require a computer to use.

Robotics Invention System (RIS) The flagship kit of the LEGO Mindstorms product line, the RIS and RIS software form the core components of high-level LEGO robotics building and programming.

rotation sensor Also called the "angle sensor," the rotation sensor senses 1/16ths of a rotation of a LEGO axle. The rotation sensor can be used for measuring distances or angles.

Scout Looking like a blue RCX, the Scout is a programmable brick that can be programmed by pressing buttons and does not require a computer.

sensor Receives information from the robot's environment and communicates it back to the RCX. The four types of sensors made by LEGO are the touch sensor, light sensor, temperature sensor, and angle sensor.

serial interface box The precursor to the RCX technology, the serial interface box was a set of eight outputs and eight inputs that must be connected to a computer with a cable to operate. LEGO models were attached to the serial interface box with wires and therefore could not be autonomous like RCX models.

Software Developer's Kit (SDK) A set of commands, example code, and an OCX file that enables you to develop Windows-based software using the "Spirit control."

Team Challenge Kit Similar to the Robotics Invention System 1.0 kit, except that it has a green plastic storage tub and smaller sorting trays than the RIS.

temperature sensor One of four LEGO sensors that can be used with the RCX. Technically the temperature sensor is a thermistor.

top-down design Deciding on a goal and then designing something that meets that goal is called "top-down design."

torque The ability of a force to cause something to turn.

touch sensor   One of four LEGO sensors that can be used with the RCX. Technically the touch sensor is a momentary switch.

trade-offs   When you must make a decision between two choices, and both choices have a good side and a bad side. For example, going up the ramp in the FIRST LEGO League contest (Chapter 6) was quick but risky. The alternative, line-following, was slow but reliable.

Ultimate Accessory Set   Includes a rotation sensor, remote control, lamp, extra touch sensor, and other building elements.

USB port   Some newer computers, particularly Macintosh iBook, iMac, and G4 computers, only have Universal Serial Bus (USB) ports, and no longer have regular serial ports.

variable   A piece of the RCX's memory that can record and store values for later use. In ROBOLAB, variables are called "containers."

View button   Pressing the View button causes a little arrow to appear on the RCX display that points to the sensor and motor ports. When the View button is pressed multiple times, the arrow on the display moves between these input and output ports. The current value of the sensor or speed of the motor shows up in the RCX display window. It is useful, for example, to always use the View button and a light sensor to check the light level in the room before finalizing any light sensor program.

Visual Basic   A Windows-based programming environment written by Microsoft. Visual Basic is one of the programming environments that can be used with the Spirit control to create custom programming interfaces to the RCX. Visual Basic is used as the example programming environment in the Software Developers Kit (SDK).

Index

A

Absolute values, 246n
AC adapter, 17
Acrobot, 21–25
    motor power, 238–241
    See also Smart Acrobot
Add to counter command, 201
AddToDatalog command, 229
Advanced Set Up Options, 14
Algorithm, 77
Allen, Matthew, 95
Ambient light
    Line-Follower robot, 81–82
    Smart Acrobot, 31–33,
    167–168
Angle sensors, 201, 244
    bumper car, 139–140
    infrared communication,
    250
    internet communication,
    260–261
    motor speed, 234–235
Animal Feeder, 95–103
Ariel, 26
Artificial life, 7n
Axles
    extenders, 201, 244
    vibration, 130

B

Batteries
    installation, 14
    IR Tag, 155
    life, 16–18
    troubleshooting, 15
Baum, Dave, 20, 189, 274
Beams, 48–52
    height and width, 49–50
    and plates, 50
BeginOfTask command, 166
Belt and pulley wheels, 140–141
Bohm, Harry, 266
BotCode, 180
Bottom-up design, 38–39
Bricks, LEGO, 4–5, 49–50
Bubble Copter Toy, 126–127
Bubble Machine, 121–134
Bug, 63–66
Build Your Own Underwater Robot,
    266
Bump sensors, 89–90
Bumper car, 71–73, 140

C

Camera mechanism, 96–97, 101
Case Structure, 260

Category, element, 8–10
CD-ROM contents, 6
Check and choose command, 133,
    154
Clock display, 14
Clutch gears, 141–142
Codemaster, 105–111
COM port, 14
Comments, programming, 165,
    190
Compound gear train, 124–126
Conditionals, 29
Connector pegs, 49–50
Constants, 169–170
Constructopedia, 21–22
Containers, 185
Copycat, 243–250
    Internet Copycat, 260–261
    NQC, 248–249
    ROBOLAB, 245–246
    Visual Basic, 247–248
Counters, 200–203
CreateDatalog command, 229

D

Dacta Team Challenge kit, 4n
Darr, Amy, 95

Data logging, 223–241
  doorway, 232–234
  graphing data, 230–231
  motor speed and power, 234–241
  refrigerator, 224–231
DatalogNext command, 224
DCP adapter, 182n
Decoding, 245–246
define command, 197
Design process, 10–11
  breaking down problems, 40
  form and function, 123
  top-down/bottom-up, 38–39
Designing Everyday Things, 121–122
Direct Mode commands, 259
Dog, 59–62
Doorway, 232–234
Downloading firmware, 14
Driver, 65
Dynamic values, 33
Dynamically stable mechanism, 63–64

E

Element, LEGO, 8–10
Elevator, 209–222
  NQC, 219–221
  Visual Basic, 216–219
Elmo. *See* Tickle Me LEGO robot
Encoding, 245–246
EndOfTask command, 166
Excel, Microsoft, 230–231
Expansion sets, 5

F

Fan, 124, 130–131
Fax Machine, Infrared, 250–256
Feedback, 26–27
Figure eight pattern, 117
Firmware, 14
FIRST LEGO League (FLL), 69–82
  bumper car, 71–73
  competition, 80–81

Line-Follower robot, 73–80
  playing field, 70
Flashlight Follower, 145–150
  NQC, 196–198
  ROBOLAB, 187–188
  Visual Basic, 176–178
For loop, 24
Fork, 186
Form, 123
Frequency, 91–93, 269
Friction, 56, 126–127
Fudd, Anthony, 8, 129
Fulcrum, 98–99
Function, 123

G

G Code, 183
Galinato, John, 95, 273
Ganson, Arthur, 136
Gears, 42–47
  clutch, 141–142
  compound gearing, 124–126
  gear ratios, 65, 136–137
  gearbox, 44, 47
  gearing down, 46
  gearing up, 47
  idlers, 65–66
  LEGO motor, 86–88, 124
  pinion, 122
  worm, 47, 135
Getstart.zip file, 169, 179
Getting Started, 14
Giraffe, 37–57
  beams, 48–52
  gears, 42–47
  walking mechanism, 41–43, 52–55
Going the Distance, 199–208
  NQC, 206–208
  ROBOLAB, 205–206
  Visual Basic, 203–205
Graphical user interface (GUI), 189
Graphing data, 230–231

Greek key pattern, 118
Guided mode, 18

H

Half-steps, 93
Hertz, Heinrich, 92
Himmelstein, Kayty, 95
Home page, personal, 8, 19
Hooks, Dan, 250

I

Idler gears, 65–66
If statements, 29, 148, 186
Inertia, 128–129, 239–240
Infinite loop, 24, 148
Infrared communication
  Copycat, 243–250
  Infrared Fax Machine, 250–256
  IR Transmitter, 14–16, 18
Infrared Fax Machine, 250–256
  NQC, 252–256
  ROBOLAB, 251
Intelligent house, 265–266
Interfaces, 179–180, 189
Internet communication, 256–261
  Internet CopyCat, 260–261
  ROBOLAB, 257–260
  Web sites, 256–257
IP address, 257, 259
IR Tag, 151–155

J

Jensen, Vickie, 266
Joystick wheel, 155–156

K

Keep On Moving robot, 139–144
Kellner, Tom and Brendon, 113
Kinetic sculptures, 121–138
  Bubble Machine, 121–134
  linkage system, 134–135

Machine with Minifig, 136
Twisting and Turning, 135
Kramer, Paul and Julian, 105

L

LabVIEW, 182
Laser Tag, 151
LEGO Mindstorms. *See* Mindstorms
LEGO Shop at Home, 272
LEGO User Group Network, 20
LEGO World Shop, 20, 271
Light sensors, 19, 105–106
  ambient light, 31–33, 81–82, 167–168
  Bubble Machine, 132–134
  Codemaster, 106–108
  Elevator, 213–214
  Flashlight Follower, 146
  infrared communication, 250
  Keep On Moving robot, 143–144
  Line-Follower robot, 74–82, 171–172, 193
  Remote Control, 155–156
  Smart Acrobot, 31–33, 167–168, 185
  Tickle Me LEGO robot, 94
  View button, 29–30
  walking mechanisms, 67
  See also Data logging
Line-Follower robot, 73–80
  NQC, 192–194
  ROBOLAB, 186
  Visual Basic, 171–174
Linkage system, 134–135
Locking programs, 14
Looping, 24
  Flashlight Follower, 148
  Line-Follower robot, 77
  repeat loops, 77, 148, 184
  spirals, 175, 187, 195
  while loops, 148, 192, 260
LUGNET, 20

M

Machine with Minifig, 136
Macintosh, 16, 182, 189
Martin, Fred, 130
Micromotor, 115–116
Miller, Matthew, 139
Mindstorms
  products and outlets, 4–5, 271–272
  Software Developer's Kit, 5n
  Ultimate Accessory Set, 5
  Web sites, 19–20, 41–42, 273–275
MIT Media Laboratory, 37
Modifiers, 185
Momentum, 239–240
Mondo-tronics, Inc., 272
Motor, LEGO, 86–88, 121
  Acrobot, 22–23
  compound gearing, 124
  micromotor, 115–116
  speed and power, 80, 234–241
Multitasking, 75, 177, 197
Music, 91–93, 269
My Commands, 117

N

Newton-centimeter, 141
Not Quite C (NQC), 5, 6, 189–198
  comments, 165
  counters, 206–208
  data logging, 229–230, 233–234
  Elevator, 219–221
  Flashlight Follower, 195–197
  GUIs, 190
  infrared communication, 248–249, 252–256
  Line-Follower robot, 192–194
  sensors, 167
  spirals, 194–195
  Spirit.ocx file, 190

syntax, 197
  variables, 197–198
  Web sites, 20, 198, 274–275
nqc -datalog command, 229–230

O

Oberter, Sam, 250
Octave, 92–93
On for command, 200
Online community, 8, 19

P

Painter, 113–118
  See also Spirals
Pbrick.zip file, 179
Pinion, 122
Pitch, 91–93, 269
PITSCO-LEGO Dacta, 4n, 20
  products and outlets, 271–272
Planetary Society, 256
Plastruct, 129
Plates, 50
Power down time, 14
Programmable bricks, 4–5
Propeller, 121, 124, 130–131
Pulse width modulation (PWM), 128

Q

QuarkXPress, 110

R

Rack and pinion, 122
RCX. *See* Robotic Command Explorer (RCX)
RCXdata.bas file, 169
Rechargeable batteries, 17
Red Rover software, 256
Refrigerator, 224–231
Remote control, 14, 155–159

Repeat loops, 24
   repeat forever, 77, 184
   repeat while, 148
ROBOLAB, 5, 6, 181–188
   commands, 277–282
   comments, 165
   containers/modifiers, 185
   counters, 205–206
   data logging, 226–228, 233, 237–238
   Extras, 257
   Flashlight Follower, 187–188
   fork, 186
   infrared communication, 245–246, 251
   internet communication, 257–260
   Line-Follower robot, 186
   Pilot/Inventor, 182–184
   Programmer/Investigator, 182, 226
   spirals, 186–187
   SubVIs, 211–212
   variables, 185
   Web sites, 20, 274
Robot Books, 272
Robotic Command Explorer (RCX), 4
   battery installation, 14
   battery life, 16–17
   IR Tag, 151–155
   IR Transmitter, 15–16
   low power, 18
   Remote Control, 155–159
   touch sensors, 210
Robotic Zoological Park, 37
Robotics Invention System (RIS) kit, 4
Robots, 6–8
Rotation sensor, 14

S

Saving state, 33
Seesaw, 44–46, 96–100

Sensor adapter, 4n
Sensor watcher, 28–29, 62
   Flashlight Follower, 147–149
   Line-Follower robot, 79
   multitasking, 75
Sensors, 7, 72
   bump, 89–90
   NQC, 167
   temperature/rotation, 14, 132, 228
   View button, 19, 29–30
   Visual Basic, 167
   See also Angle sensors; Light sensors; Touch sensors
SENSORS (Science and Engineering NASA Site of Remote Sensing), 256–257
Set direction command, 188
Set power command, 71, 128–129
Set Up Options, 14
SetDatalog command, 224
SetSensorType command, 167
Shaking mechanism, 86–88
Sinha, Natasha, 95
Six-legged walker, 63–64, 124
Smart Acrobot, 25–33
   NQC, 191–192
   ROBOLAB, 184–186
   Visual Basic, 166–170
   See also Acrobot
Sound meter, 184
Speed, land, 241
Spinning wheel
   Going the Distance, 199–202
   Keep On Moving, 142–143
   motor speed, 234
   Smart Acrobot, 27–28
Spirals, 117–118
   NQC, 194–195
   ROBOLAB, 186–187
   Visual Basic, 174–176
Spirit Control, 164
Spirit.ocx file, 163–164, 190

Start command, 197
StartTask command, 177
Static values, 33
Statically stable mechanism, 63–64
Stop button, 158
Submarine, 266–267
Subroutines, 117, 186–187, 195
SubVIs, ROBOLAB, 211–212
Swivel wheel, 79

T

Task Split command, 188
Telerobotics, 256
Temperature sensor, 14, 132, 228
"The Art of LEGO Design," 130
Tickle Me robot, 85–94
Time, system, 14
Time, wait, 71–72
Tones, musical, 91–92, 269
Top-down design, 38–39
Torbot, 140
Torque, 141–142
Touch sensor
   Bubble Machine, 131–132
   Codemaster, 109
   Elevator, 209–210, 213–214
   internet communication, 259–260
   IR Tag, 152–153
   Line-Follower robot, 82, 173, 193–194
   Remote Control, 158
   seesaw, 96–100
   Smart Acrobot, 185–186
   Tickle Me robot, 89–90
   walking mechanisms, 61–62, 67
Tour video, 14
Tracks, 140
Trade-offs, 73
Train, 265
Training Center, 18
Troubleshooting, 15–16
Twisting and Turning, 135

U

Unlocking programs, 14
UploadDatalog command, 225
User Group Network, LEGO
    (LUGNET), 20
Usernames, 13

V

Variables, 33, 150
    ambient light, 81–82
    NQC, 197–198
    ROBOLAB, 185
    Visual Basic, 175–178
View button, 19, 29–30, 156
Visual Basic, 5, 6, 163–180
    comments, 165
    constants, 169–170

counters, 203–205
data logging, 224–226, 232
Elevator, 216–217
infrared communication,
    247–248
Line-Follower robot, 171–174
sensors, 167
spirals, 174–176
Spirit.ocx file, 163
variables, 175–178
VBA, 164–166

W

Wait commands, 71–72, 184–185
Walking mechanisms, 59–67
    bug, 63–66
    dog, 59–62

giraffe, 41–43, 52–55
puppy, 62–63
Wands, bubble, 127–128
Web sites, 8, 19–20
    Build-It-Yourself, 95
    Mindstorms, 41–42, 273–275
    NQC, 20, 198, 274–275
    ROBOLAB, 20, 274
    telerobotics, 256–257
Weight, 141n
While loops, 24, 148, 192, 260
With command, 166
World Shop, LEGO, 20
Worm gears, 47, 135
Wright, Richard, 273

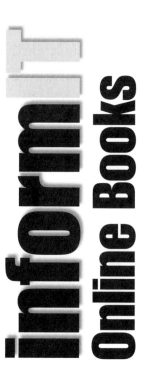

Register
Your Book

at www.awprofessional.com/register

You may be eligible to receive:

- Advance notice of forthcoming editions of the book
- Related book recommendations
- Chapter excerpts and supplements of forthcoming titles
- Information about special contests and promotions throughout the year
- Notices and reminders about author appearances, tradeshows, and online chats with special guests

Contact us

If you are interested in writing a book or reviewing manuscripts prior to publication, please write to us at:

Editorial Department
Addison-Wesley Professional
75 Arlington Street, Suite 300
Boston, MA 02116 USA
Email: AWPro@aw.com

Addison-Wesley

Visit us on the Web: http://www.awprofessional.com

CD-ROM Warranty and User Information

Addison-Wesley Professional warrants the enclosed disc to be free of defects in materials and faulty workmanship under normal use for a period of ninety days after purchase. If a defect is discovered in the disc during this warranty period, a replacement disc can be obtained at no charge by sending the defective disc, postage prepaid, with proof of purchase to:

Editorial Department
Addison-Wesley Professional
Pearson Technology Group
75 Arlington Street, Suite 300
Boston, MA 02116
e-mail: AWPro@awl.com

After the 90-day period, a replacement will be sent upon receipt of the defective disc and a check or money order for $10.00, payable to Addison-Wesley Professional.

Addison-Wesley Professional and Benjamin Erwin make no warranty or representation, either expressed or implied, with respect to this software, its quality, performance, merchantability, or fitness for a particular purpose. In no event will the author, Addison-Wesley Professional, its distributors, or dealers be liable for direct, indirect, special, incidental, or consequential damages arising out of the use or inability to use the software. The exclusion of implied royalties is not permitted in some states. Therefore, the above exclusion may not apply to you. This warranty provides you with specific legal rights. There may be other rights that you may have that vary from state to state. The contents of this CD-ROM are intended for non-commercial use only. More information and updates are available at:

http://www.awl.com/cseng/titles/0-201-70895-7

General Instructions

Insert the CD-ROM and open start_here.html in a Web browser.

System Requirements

Minimum Requirements

Windows 95/98/NT/ME/2000, Macintosh (except for RCX Code and RcxCC)

Additional Requirements

- **Instructions**—Netscape Navigator, Internet Explorer, or other Web browser
- **Programs**—Visual Basic: a Microsoft application with Visual Basic for Applications such as Word or Visual Basic; ROBOLAB: ROBOLAB 1.0, 1.5, or 2.0 must be installed (2.0 required for some programs); RCX Code (Windows only): Mindstorms Robotics Invention System 1.0 or 1.5 Software installed; NQC: NQC installed (included on CD)
- **Software**—ROBOLAB 2.0 Demo: 33Mhz processor, 16Mb RAM, 50Mb hard drive space to install, 1 free serial port (COM1 or COM2 [PC], serial or printer [Mac]); NQC: 1 free serial port (COM1 or COM2 [PC], serial or printer [Mac]); RcxCC (Windows only): 1 free serial port
- **Movies**—Animated GIFs: Web Browser; QuickTime: QuickTime Player; Real: RealPlayer 7 or later; AVI: AVI-compatible player; MPG: MPG-compatible player